Fresh Eggs and Dog Beds

Book Two

Still Living the Dream in Rural Ireland

By Nick Albert

Copyright © Nick Albert, 2018
Cover Art Copyright © Nick Albert, 2018

Published by Ant Press, 2018
First Edition

The author asserts the moral right under the Copyright, Designs and Patents Act 1988 to be identified as the author of this work.

All rights reserved. No part of this publication may be reproduced, stored in a retrieval system, or transmitted, in any form or by any means without the prior written consent of the author, nor be otherwise circulated in any form of binding or cover other than that in which it is published and without a similar condition being imposed on the subsequent purchaser.

For Violet.

Table of Contents

1. You're most welcome!......7
2. Swords and storytellers......19
3. All's well that ends well......27
4. Trench warfare......39
5. Living the wild life......49
6. Stovepipe blues......59
7. Playing Chicken......69
8. New friends......79
9. Best laid plans......89
10. Delays and distractions......101
11. Breaking ground......109
12. Amber's addiction......119
13. Car wars......129
14. Stormy weather......139
15. A bad first impression......147
16. The bomb in the kitchen......155
17. A matter of death and life......165
18. The pillar palaver......175
19. It's a dog's life......185
20. The magic potion......195
21. Lucky me......205
22. Bums and bombs......215

23. Luv a duck... 225

24. Oil and water.. 233

25. Mouldy melamine... 243

26. Doggy Ball Games 253

27. A close call.. 263

28. A new beginning.. 273

29. Epilogue.. 283

Acknowledgments... 285

About the Author 285

Contact the Author 285

Ant Press Books 286

1. You're most welcome!

"How long you here for?" the big guy asked in a heavy County Clare accent.

As he spoke, his foot kicked idly at the stones on my driveway, causing Amber, our tiny Pomeranian Terrier-cross puppy, to pounce on his boot like an overexcited kitten. Romany, our Lhasa Apso, balanced on her bum nearby, hoping forlornly to attract some attention through her acrobatics.

The man fired the words at me like bullets from a machine gun, but his lips hardly moved. It took a moment to process the sounds into a coherent sentence, but his meaning remained stubbornly illusive.

Whilst Ireland is a truly beautiful country, populated by some of the friendliest people you could imagine, it can be a challenge for a visitor to understand the nuances of the Irish accent, particularly in the more rural areas.

"How long you here for?" he asked again.

I gave Diarmuid my best smile and shrugged noncommittally. He had pronounced his name *Deer-mid* and explained at some length that it came (almost directly) from one of the legendary early Kings of Ireland. Diarmuid was a contractor, here to quote for drilling a deep bored well. Recently, I had developed a useful hearing difficulty, a non-existent malaise that excused my constant requests for repetition when confronted with such an indecipherable accent. I was about to raise my hand to my ear, when the question was repeated, this time a little slower.

"How long *are* you here for?"

"I don't know." I shrugged noncommittally. "We've only just moved here. We're not planning to leave anytime soon."

Despite his regal moniker, Diarmuid huffed and rolled his eyes dramatically.

"No! How long *were* you here for?" he tutted and pointed at the ground. "Here in Ireland."

"Oh!" I nodded, finally understanding the question. "We moved here in April, so we've only been here for a few weeks."

"You with them *New Age* travellers, so?" he asked, eyeing me suspiciously.

I shook my head and smiled; I knew the answer to this question. The old farmhouse we had bought was unchanged from the decorating quirks of the previous owner, still adorned with yin and yang signs and wind chimes, and with walls painted in colours normally associated with dreadlocks and strange smelling tobacco. Diarmuid wasn't the first person to question my social standing.

"Don't worry, I have a job," I replied. "I coach golf."

He nodded, apparently happy to accept my assertion at face value. "You're an English blow-in then," he observed.

Since moving to Ireland on a whim at the beginning of the year, my wife, Lesley, and I had encountered this description several times. At first, we were mildly concerned by the xenophobic undertone, but we soon realised that the good people of County Clare used 'blow-in' as a term of endearment, to describe anyone born outside of the local parish. We were indeed blow-ins, and likely to remain so for 40 or 50 years.

"I'm afraid so," I conceded.

"That's okay then," he mumbled to himself.

"Glad to hear it."

"What made you choose Ireland?" he asked.

"It's hard to say." I shrugged again. "Before we bought Glenmadrie, we'd never even visited Ireland. But we came over on a scouting trip and just fell in love with the place – and the people."

"Well, you're most welcome!" Diarmuid gave me a mighty pat on my back, almost winding me in the process. He smiled widely, showing all six of his teeth.

"Thank you," I wheezed, doing my utmost to draw a breath.

People say 'You're most welcome' a lot In Ireland, but it isn't the throwaway banality of 'Mind how you go' or 'Have a nice day'. When an Irish person says 'You're most welcome', I think they really mean it.

"Why'd you move?" he asked. "You got family here?"

"None," I admitted. "My wife and I were keen to start a new life. England seems so overcrowded and stressful these days. It's all flash cars and credit cards. We had a hankering for simple living, somewhere quiet with a bit of land, where we could grow our own vegetables and mind our own business."

Diarmuid slowly cast his eyes west, towards the hundreds of

acres of pine forest that lay behind our house. Then he looked to the east, where the summer palette of green, gold, purple and brown brought the moorland to life, a spectacular river of flowers and heather flowing softly into the distance.

"Well, you certainly picked a beautiful spot. Nobody's going to trouble you up here."

"Thank you. We like it," I replied. "After living in a busy town centre and then on a noisy main road, the peace and solitude up here is just delightful."

He nodded silently while I continued.

"On the other hand, we're a long way from civilisation, shops, hospitals and our neighbours, so it is easy to let the days drift idly by without seeing a soul. Privacy is valuable, but without regular contact with the outside world, it is all too easy to become accidental hermits."

"There be no buses up here!" he remarked, gesturing towards my car, still shamefully adorned with British number plates.

"That's a fact," I admitted. "We hoped to save a little money, but it's clear we'll need two cars just to stay in touch."

"Yea didn't have a crash yet?" he joked.

"Close, but not quite," I admitted. After years of driving on well-maintained British roads, the cavernous potholes on Irish roads, combined with unexpected encounters with farm machinery and suicidally-aggressive dogs, require a stout heart, a steady nerve and lightning-fast reactions.

"Some folks here's about like to drive with a certain death-defying flamboyance," he confessed, "and frequently on the wrong side of the road."

"I've seen that," I agreed, "and it wasn't funny."

"So – you settling in good?" Diarmuid asked. His concern seemed genuine.

I huffed and chewed on my thumbnail for a moment while I formulated a reply that was honest and diplomatic, but didn't sound like a whine. Apart from our difficulty with the local dialect, since moving to Ireland Lesley and I had encountered several unanticipated challenges to the idyllic life we had planned. Living up a mountain in the west of Ireland, exposed to the fresh Atlantic air, the weather can be gloriously sunny, depressingly overcast, drearily wet, or terrifyingly windy – and sometimes all four together.

"The weather can be rather a challenge," I said.

"Well, it's fierce mild today!" Diarmuid said, smiling optimistically. "The good thing about Ireland is, if you don't like the weather, just wait a bit and something different will soon come along."

"That's true," I admitted. "Yesterday morning, I got soaked through twice and then sunburned."

"There be no such thing as bad weather, just the wrong clothes."

"Good advice," I laughed.

Diarmuid nodded politely as he graciously accepted my compliment. "So, you planning to fix this old place up?"

I puffed loudly, blowing out my cheeks.

"That was my expectation, but we've recently discovered there's a shortage of builders willing to undertake a renovation."

The big guy nodded. "All too busy building them new estates, like."

"So we hear," I said.

Diarmuid nodded towards our house. "Much to do?" he asked.

I ran my fingers through my hair – it didn't take long.

"Rather more than we had first thought," I admitted. "The roof and walls are fundamentally sound, but pretty much everything else has to go. As such, we're going to gut the place and build a new house inside the shell."

"It'd be easier to knock it down and build a new house, like," Diarmuid said.

"True," I admitted, "but we like the character of this old place. That's why we didn't buy a new-build house."

"Aye, it's a fine place," he nodded. "Are yea handy?"

I frowned in confusion.

"Are yea good with your hands?" he translated. "You English are always at the DIY. Are yea handy?"

"Not really, but we're going to be," I confessed. "We've got a very comprehensive DIY manual and a lot of incentive to learn – and save some money."

Diarmuid gave an ironic laugh. "Good luck!"

"Thank you. I suspect we'll need it."

"You wants a well drilled – so?" Diarmuid asked, dragging the conversation around to business, with all the subtlety of a drunk driver changing lanes. Finishing a sentence with a hanging '*so*' is quite common in County Clare.

"Yes, we d–" I stopped myself, before making an unintentional commitment. "What I mean is, we're hoping to get some quotes first."

Diarmuid suddenly looked as if he was sucking a lemon, but put on a brave face. Keen to convince me his was the best well-drilling operation in the west of Ireland, he pulled up his sagging trousers and took a deep breath before launching into his sales pitch.

"You'll not find better than us…"

There was a long silence while I waited for some brochures, or a few personal recommendations guaranteeing the quality of his work, but that was it. I couldn't help but like the man.

He looked around, briefly assessing the lay of the land. "Where do you want it then?"

"I was hoping you would tell me," I pleaded. "The planning notice says it has to be a hundred feet above the septic tank."

"That's essential," he agreed, "otherwise your water can get polluted." He nodded vaguely towards our meadow. "I reckon we could drill on that flat area just up the hill. The water would be safe and the well would comply with the planning notice."

I smiled. "We had a quote yesterday. It was a contractor from Limerick. The guy said not to worry about the planning as he could get a certificate of compliance wherever the well was drilled."

"That's fine until your water is poisoned," Diarmuid snorted in derision. "Where did he say to drill the well?"

"Just there." I pointed to a spot at the end of our driveway. "He used a couple of bits of bent wire as divining rods and that's where he got the strongest signal."

"It's more likely he chose this spot because it gives him the best access for his drilling rig." Diarmuid hawked loudly and spat something onto my driveway. Amber wisely decided not to investigate. "Did he give you a quote, like?"

I nodded evasively.

Diarmuid raised his eyebrows quizzically.

Bending like a chocolate bar on a hot day, I resisted his steady gaze for almost five seconds.

"He said ten thousand," I mumbled my confession.

"Feck's sake!" he exclaimed, loudly enough to scare both dogs. "What a snake!"

I reached down to stroke Amber with a calming hand. Romany ignored me, preferring to hide behind my car until the coast was clear of angry, shouting men.

"You need to cop on and stop acting the maggot!" Diarmuid exclaimed.

I frowned in confusion. "Excuse me?"

"Wake up – don't be a fool!" he translated, waving his arms for emphasis.

After a moment's consideration, Diarmuid gave a sigh and put a fatherly hand on my shoulder. "You're still learning how things are done here, aren't you?"

"Well, yes," I admitted, "and I probably will be for some time to come."

Diarmuid shook his head. "Ten thousand!" he whispered.

"Is that a lot?" I asked.

"I'll say. If I charged that much, I'd only have to work weekends and I'd be able to spend the weekdays in Spain." He shook his head and walked a short angry circle.

"Look, there's no way of knowing how deep we have to drill, or if we'll ever hit water," Diarmuid explained, when his temper had cooled a little. "But a respectable company will only ever charge by the foot for the drilling and the liner. If we haven't hit water by the time you've spent €1,500, I'd give up."

Right then I decided the big guy with the indecipherable County Clare accent was someone I could trust.

"Come in and have a cup of tea," I suggested.

Diarmuid nodded and rubbed his rough hands together so enthusiastically I feared he would start a fire. "Savage!" he said, perhaps sensing the deal was done.

I couldn't help smiling. "When do you think you can start drilling?"

***

Through the kitchen window, I saw Lesley's white Citroën estate pull into the driveway. By the time she had parked the car, fussed and then shouted at our recalcitrant dogs, I was ready to swap her shopping bag for a cup of coffee.

"Did the guy come to see about drilling the well?" she asked, slipping off her shoes and carefully sipping at her hot drink.

"Yep. He left about half an hour ago."

"How'd it go?"

"Very well." I nodded enthusiastically. "*Deer-mid* seems to be the real deal, certainly better than that other lot. I've asked him to start work as soon as possible."

Lesley smiled, but her face fell.

"Oh no!"

For a change, I knew what she was thinking. In a few days, our daughter, Joanne, was due to visit our new home for the second time. Having a drilling crew working on our land would be interesting, but rather an inconvenience for our planned sightseeing trips.

"Don't worry, they're pretty busy just now, so they won't start drilling until after Joanne flies back to England."

Lesley nodded and smiled. "That's good."

"There's more," I added. "*Deer-mid* will only drill the well and fit the liner, but he recommended a guy who will install the pump and arrange a water test so we can get the grant."

"*A grant?*" Her eyes lit up.

"Apparently, because we don't already have a suitable source of drinking water, what with the well being full of frogs and too close to the septic tank, we qualify for a home improvement grant. I understand it's quite substantial."

"That's very generous. We've only just bought the house."

I shrugged. "I presume the government figures helping us to get a permanent source of clean water is far cheaper than paying for hospital trips and funerals."

Lesley waved her coffee mug at me. "This water isn't so bad, although it does taste a bit like something from a duck pond."

"I guess it's an improvement on the bleach used to purify the water back in England."

"Will it take long to get the well drilled?" Lesley asked.

I grimaced and wobbled my hand to show my uncertainty.

"The drilling won't take very long, but it will be a while before the water is connected up."

"How so?"

"*Deer-mid*, bless him, said the drilling could take several days, assuming they even find water. Before the other guy can install the pump, I'll need to dig a hundred feet of trenches for the pipes and electrics. That'll take a while, even if I hire a digger. After that, I'll get on with building the pump house. Assuming I'm not too busy at work, I'll be lucky to finish within a month."

Lesley was rinsing her cup in the sink. She paused for a moment and stared out of the window.

"I suppose this is our life now, all DIY and renovations. It's odd to think that just a short while ago we were worrying about work and paying the bills."

"Are you having regrets?" I asked, quietly dreading her answer.

"No," Lesley replied, not sounding particularly convincing. "It's just – well, I've been thinking…"

My earlier sense of dread became a sudden chill, like a blast of Arctic air running down my spine. Allow me to explain. My wife is a very intelligent woman, she is my best friend and I love her to bits. As well as being my walking dictionary, she is my go-to source for any questions on history, geology, music, dance, and above all, gardening. But the phrase 'I've been thinking' gives me an overwhelming urge to run and hide, because it is usually followed by a request to drain the oceans, move the planet a bit to the left, or rearrange the furniture several times until it's back in the same place it started from. My traditional response to such a comment is to say something like, "Now, dear, I thought we agreed you would stop thinking for a while," to which she will usually give me a loving thump, worthy of a nightclub bouncer. On this occasion, my reaction was involuntary.

"Oh *nooo!*" I squealed, "We've only just arrived here, you can't want to move already."

"Don't be silly, it's not like that," she chided, laughing and shaking her head. "I was just thinking about all the work we're taking on. Are we doing the wrong thing, trying to do it all ourselves?"

I took a deep breath and stretched back with my fingers

interlocked behind my head. The kitchen stool I was sitting on creaked precariously, but I bravely ignored it. Lesley had a good point. Our dream of moving to Ireland and begin a new life was in danger of being derailed by the sheer enormity of the DIY task we were facing. We hadn't really made any firm plans, beyond living debt-free and stress-free, somewhere with a few acres of land and beautiful views. I hadn't even thought about finding a job. I'd been wonderfully lucky to land a position as a golf coach, a career that had been pushed to the back burner twenty years before by the need to earn a decent living. Our sudden decision to quit work, sell our house and migrate to a country we had never visited was totally out of character for me – even if it was precipitated by a health scare. Whereas Lesley likes her life to be casual and unscripted, I am a stickler for careful planning, to-do lists, and having all my ducks lined up before I step forward into the well-known.

    The one plan we had both agreed on was to hire a competent builder to undertake the urgently needed renovations to the house. But with the Irish economy booming, we were horrified to discover even the most inept construction workers were all committed to well-paying new-build projects for the foreseeable future, leaving us with no other option than to do it ourselves. Although Lesley and I had previously undertaken a little 'British DIY', decorating, tiling, fitting a kitchen, some minor plumbing, and moving the odd electrical socket, we were woefully inexperienced for such a massive job.

    Glenmadrie was once a small thatched cottage, but over a period of 150 years, multiple enthusiastic-yet-underfunded owners had quadrupled the footprint of the original structure, as well as adding a second story and several outbuildings. On first inspection, Lesley had nicknamed it Higgledy-Piggledy House, an inspired title aptly describing the confused layout and illogical floorplan. We had fallen in love with the location, and then the house – turning myopic eyes to the obvious flaws in the plumbing, electrical wiring, and sagging, woodworm-ridden floors. Whilst maintaining the delightful character and stone walls, we needed to gut, rebuild and insulate the draughty old place, and turn the outbuildings into useful storage rooms and a guest apartment. At least that was the plan. Now it had become a DIY project.

"Well?" Lesley raised an eyebrow, interrupting my musing.

"Huh?"

"Are we doing the wrong thing here," she repeated, somewhat testily, "trying to do it all ourselves?"

I shrugged. "I guess it's rather a moot point, given we have no other option. Nobody else will do the work, and I don't think we can leave the house how it is." I rolled my pleading eyes towards my beautiful wife. *Last chance,* I thought.

Her tightly crossed arms and sour frown confirmed my fear – there was no getting out of it, the renovations must be done. There would be no relaxing retirement, no golfing holidays, and no free time to write that thriller I had planned – at least not for a good while.

I frowned in defeat. "In that case, I don't think we're doing the wrong thing. It's exactly the right thing to do, irrespective of our lack of choice. We're going to save a bundle of cash and turn this old place into an attractive and warm family home."

"Do you think we can cope?" Lesley asked. "It's a bit beyond hanging wallpaper or building some kitchen units."

"I know it's a challenge, but we'll just have to learn as we go. I'm sure we'll be able to handle it."

"Sort of 'on the job training' via a DIY manual," Lesley joked.

"Pretty much," I agreed. "The pump house is just a glorified concrete garden shed. I'll build that first. If everything goes okay, I'll move on to turning the cowshed into an apartment. It's going to be a pretty big building, almost a midsized bungalow. To make it habitable I'll need to add plumbing, electrics, some walls and a roof, so by the time I'm finished in there I'll be an experienced builder." I mimed polishing my nails on my lapel. "You'll be able to rent me out!"

She smiled, but remained silent.

"Now what?" I pleaded.

"It's just..." Lesley let out a big sigh. "Well, it's not how I pictured things would be."

"No sitting with your feet up on the veranda, sipping Pimm's and reading a good book?" I joked.

"Hardly! I suppose we were so fixated on getting here I hadn't really considered how our lives would be. I'd expected something different, not renovating another house."

"And this time doing all of the work ourselves?" I added.

"Precisely!"

"We had plenty of chances to buy one of those jelly-mould newly-built houses on some faceless estate, but we decided we wanted a home with character and some land "

"And dust and cobwebs and woodworm…" Lesley added.

"There you go. We're guilty as charged, so we'd better get on with it." I waved towards the bare rafters, the bright purple paintwork and the sagging floorboards. "This is our life now, and likely to remain so for several years."

Lesley nodded. "With the building work and what I have planned for the garden, these renovations are certainly going to dominate and define our lives."

"Nah!" I snorted in gentle discord. "We're chicken farmers now."

"But we only have three chickens. That hardly makes us farmers."

"But we're living the dream," I joked. "We *really are* living the dream!"

2. Swords and storytellers

Despite our best intentions, the renovations were put on hold for a short time. We were expecting visitors and I was suddenly very busy at work. The weather had turned unexpectedly fine, with dry days and some warming, early spring sunshine. They were great conditions for golf, and as the players dusted off their clubs and ventured out onto the course, many for the first time since the previous autumn, I was inundated with urgent requests for lessons and club repairs. Nice for the wallet, but inconvenient for wannabe builders.

The first of our guests was the elder of my two sisters, Natasha. Even though I am a married man, heading towards fifty and planning an early retirement, I will always be the youngest child of the family and therefore the subject of well-intentioned scrutiny. It was thoughtful of my sister to visit so soon after we had moved to Ireland. Naturally, she was curious to see our new home and check up on her little brother, but her presence was also a tremendous statement of support, and validation for our decision to begin a new life. It was something for which I was truly grateful.

One unforeseen aspect of living in such a delightful and interesting land, was the requirement to become tour guides for each of our guests. It was a responsibility we took very seriously, even though our enthusiasm for the task quickly dwindled through repetition. At least in the early days we had the luxury of visiting new and interesting places, along with the recurring favourites like Bunratty Castle, the Burren, and the breath-taking Cliffs of Moher. Natasha's visit was only for a few days, so the schedule was hectic, with a lot of driving to and fro, but we still managed to achieve a couple of memorable highlights.

In Limerick city, we spent a pleasant afternoon exploring King John's Castle. This is a magnificently impressive structure overlooking the mighty river Shannon. Once we had bought our tickets and guide books, we slowly navigated a serpentine route through the gift shop. Just like every tourist shop in Ireland, it was bursting at the seams with knitted scarves from the Aran Islands, black Guinness t-shirts, emerald-green 'I love Ireland' hats, bookmarks with Irish names, handmade chocolates, toffees and fudge, tins of Irish coffee and boxes of Barry's tea, CDs of gigs and reels for your listening pleasure, tin whistles for children and the torture of parents, and the inevitable plastic Leprechauns. Such irresistible delights took a toll on our wallets and purses, so it was a while before we emerged from the shop, laden with bags and blinking at the daylight.

My sister walked on ahead, but Lesley paused for a moment to read a few extracts from the guide book.

"King John's Castle dates from the 13th century and is built on King's Island, next to the river Shannon."

"A 13th century castle? It's old but not that old," I observed. "Norwich Castle was started around 1066. That's about the same time as the Tower of London."

Lesley gave me a look that sat somewhere between annoyance and surprise.

"What?" I asked, defensively. "I remember from when Joanne was little. We used to take her there."

"Anyway…" Lesley continued. "Although the site dates back to 922 when the Vikings lived here, the castle was built on the orders of King John in 1200."

"Vikings! Here in Ireland?" I exclaimed.

"Apparently." My wife waved my interruption away with the guide book. "They got to Greenland and America, so why wouldn't they stop off in Ireland?"

The question was clearly rhetorical, so I remained quiet.

"Oh look, it says the remains of a Viking settlement were discovered on the island in 1900, during an archaeological dig." She looked at me over her glasses, like a school teacher addressing a disruptive pupil. "Happy now?"

I nodded reluctantly. Satisfied with my capitulation, Lesley continued reading.

"King John was the brother of Richard the Lionheart. Apparently, he's associated with Robin Hood and the Knights of the Round Table–" She saw my sceptically-raised eyebrow. "Or, if you prefer, the legend of Robin Hood."

I shrugged and delivered my best smile.

"Anyway, although he was not as popular as Richard the Lionheart, John was known to be a formidable force in battle. He earned his place in the history books when he set about claiming territory in Ireland, and he certainly made his mark here in Limerick."

I looked up at the high towers and the massively thick castle walls. "Well, it's definitely an impressive fortification."

"Ah! Not so fast..." Lesley held up a finger and then pointed at the guide book. "This site wasn't only used for defensive purposes. King John was also made 'Lord of Ireland', a title that allowed him to mint his own coins. The royal moneyer would have struck the coins right here in the castle mint. And it seems the castle may have attracted quite a bit of unwanted attention. Apparently Limerick was besieged several times during the 17th century: in 1642 after the Irish Confederates took the castle from the English garrison, then again in 1651 – that was Cromwell's army." She paused and shook her head in disbelief. "Good grief! More than 5,000 people died during that siege, most from starvation and sickness."

As we walked towards my sister, I looked around at the pristine courtyard, with its recreated blacksmith's shed, stable, and market stalls. Several groups of happy tourists were wandering around, and there were dozens of laughing children, brandishing plastic shields and swords and running to and fro, excited to see the next exhibit. It was hard to imagine that so many people had died on this spot. I shivered, but not from the cold.

Following the signposts, we climbed a spiral staircase to the top of a high tower. From there we had a magnificent view of Limerick and the Shannon River. After taking some photographs of the City, river, and the distant mountains, we made our way across the ramparts to a second slightly higher tower. Ahead was a group of American tourists, listening to a local tour guide. Although she was a small woman, the tour guide delivered a very animated presentation, theatrically waving her arms and wailing loudly. Feeling rather like naughty children, we stealthily sidled closer, to where we could hear what she was saying.

"...but as the English forces attacked, there was panic within the castle, and as a result the drawbridge was pulled up too early, trapping many hundreds of the defenders on the bridge."

With commendable enthusiasm, the tour guide described a frantic swordfight, swinging her arms with such fervour that she almost lost her balance. In mid-slash she abruptly stopped, dropped her arms and hung her head.

"Despite their hopeless position, the Jacobites fought bravely on, but the cruel English attacked without any mercy, massacring 850 brave Irishmen and turning the river red with their blood."

These final words were delivered in a ghostly whisper. We all looked down at the bridge and imagined the carnage, almost as if it had just occurred. I was horrified and, not for the first time, found myself feeling embarrassed to be English.

Nodding towards the staircase I whispered in my wife's ear, "We'd better go back down before someone realises where we're from."

Lesley pulled a grimace and joked, "If they do, we're likely to be lynched or thrown into the river!"

***

After the depressing tales of death and famine during our visit to King John's Castle, our trip to the town of Ennis was a mixture of light relief and unbridled joy. As we walked through the narrow streets, my sister was delighted to see so many small and quirky shops – something Lesley and I had already begun to take for granted. Feeling rather like parents attempting to corral an inquisitive toddler, we chased after Natasha, occasionally backtracking as she oohed and aahed her way through the town.

"It's like we've stepped through a window in time, and we're back in the 1960s!" Natasha exclaimed as she peered through the window of a sweet shop. "Look, all the sweets are in big jars – just like when I was a child. Let's go in."

When Natasha left the shop her pockets were stuffed with small brown paper bags, filled with sherbet dips, flying saucers, and a dozen other sticky vintage classics. My big sister seemed so excited, I thought she would begin skipping, but perhaps it was just a sugar rush. Further along the street we passed a greengrocer, selling loose vegetables dusted in real mud and weighed out on scales that looked like an ancient 'guess your weight' machine. Here you could purchase almost any fruit or vegetable your heart desired, from a single carrot to a crate of cooking apples. They were all locally grown, and there wasn't a plastic bag in sight.

The shops in these narrow side streets were fascinating, but we soon realised that even the busy high street had a surprising variety of retailers. There were book shops, shoe shops, clothes stores, camping supply shops, a toy shop next to a butcher, alongside a jeweller and a newsagent. Every one of them was privately owned. The girls would easily have whiled away the day drifting aimlessly from shop to shop, had it not been for the Irish dancers.

Rounding a corner at the end of a narrow alleyway, we came across a crowd watching a troupe of immaculately dressed young girls dancing an Irish jig on a low plywood stage. To one side, a small band of musicians with a fiddle, a flute, a drum and a concertina, were playing with commendable energy and alacrity. In the tradition of Irish dance, the girls, all wearing identical short, dark green dresses highlighted with gold braid, stood stiffly erect with their arms fixed to their sides. As they danced, their legs, clad in black tights, flicked and flew with incredible speed, precision and dexterity. Their shoes thundered a magnificent cacophony of rhythmic thunder on the plywood stage, like a hundred drummers beating the charge.

"It's mesmerising!" I shouted in Lesley's ear. "Like tap-dancing. They must have special shoes."

"They're called hard shoes," an unfamiliar voice interjected. I turned to find an elderly man standing at my side. He had unruly white hair and wore a crumpled black three-piece suit and brown leather shoes. His thin, sloping shoulders were lightly dusted with dandruff. With his top button missing, only the knitted red tie around his neck held the frayed collar of his check shirt in place. We exchanged smiles.

"They're very good," I commented.

He nodded in agreement, or so I thought – but he may just have been keeping time with the music.

"Are they busking?" I asked. I couldn't see a hat or fiddle case ready to receive my contribution.

He shook his head. "This is part of the Ennis Street Fair. It's held every year on this week."

"Oh splendid!" I replied, rather louder than was necessary. The music had unexpectedly stopped just as I shouted my appreciation, causing several heads to turn in my direction. I grimaced in embarrassment and began clapping for the dancers. Everyone joined in.

"Shall we stay a while and watch?" Natasha asked.

Lesley and I agreed.

Just then the dancers took a bow, turned and with formal aplomb, marched off stage like a small but perfectly drilled army. As soon as they cleared the crowd these disciplined performers instantly relaxed, once again becoming an ordinary group of schoolgirls, joking and giggling as they collected their bags and chatted amongst friends. A moment later a member of the band stood to announce the next act.

"And now, ladies and gentlemen, boys and girls, our famous storyteller will entice us with his description of the instruments used in Irish music."

With a dramatic flourish he waved his arm and beckoned the next performer to come forwards. Because of the wild applause, I missed hearing his name, but I instantly recognised the face. It was the elderly gent I had been talking with a few moments earlier. Someone lent a steadying hand as this old man shuffled up onto the stage, but as he began his act something magical happened. Perhaps it was part of the performance, some planned illusion, or simply the positive effects of adrenalin, but before our very eyes, he was transformed into a younger man. His back straightened, his shoulders squared, the pain disappeared from his arthritic joints, and the years fell away.

After giving a cheeky smile he began telling us about the musical instruments used in traditional Irish music. But this was no formal lecture. With his arms waving and his excitable blue eyes sparkling mischievously under his bushy eyebrows, he delivered an extraordinary oratory full of mimic and mime.

"These musical instruments do not make happy bedfellows," he explained. "In normal circumstances, they shouldn't be allowed in the same room together. Yet somehow they combine to make a magical sound."

Skipping around the stage like an excitable teenager, he painted a glorious image of each instrument living as an animal or a person, content with its own sound, but either combative or subversive in the presence of others. First there was the bodhrán, an Irish drum (pronounced bow-rawn):

"The bodhrán is the heartbeat of traditional Irish music for good reason. This large drum is covered with stretched animal skin and struck with a stick or double-ended knucklebone. The bodhrán provides our music with a pulsating beat that turns listeners into dancers."

The drummer began to play a rhythmic beat.

"But beware!" the old man shouted and held up a finger. The drummer stopped. "The bodhrán always wants to be the centre of attention–"

He was interrupted by a short burst of energetic drumming.

We all laughed at this, and even more when the storyteller's scowl caused the drummer to stop and hang his head in mock shame.

"Worse still, the bodhráns will not only drown out the other instruments, but they will compete with each other, like squawking geese, creating such a racket that everyone will leave the pub." His blue eyes became wide, causing his shaggy eyebrows to rise up his forehead like white caterpillars. His voice fell to a stage whisper as he conveyed the horror of the situation. "Sometimes the racket is so horrific that the poor people in the pub are unable to even finish their drinks!" He raised his forearm across his brow.

There where shouts of "No!" and "Shame!" from the crowd.

"And that is why…" he continued, "the best establishments will have a sign that says: 'Only one bodhrán!'"

There was a cheer and someone in the crowd shouted, "Praise be. The beer is saved!" We all laughed.

This wonderful verbal portrait continued for fully half an hour. Our storyteller described the uilleann pipes (meaning "pipes of the elbow" because of their pump-operated bellows) and likened the sound of poorly played pipes, to the braying of a stubborn donkey. Next came the flute and the penny whistle, *tiddly-dee, tiddly-dee!* Then the Celtic harp, "A gentle tinkling cascade, like deer walking through frozen grass on a crisp autumn morning." And finally, the fiddle, which he likened to trout, "Darting and dashing between the stones of a babbling brook."

His verbal depictions were enthusiastic, funny and fascinating, and with the help of the musicians, pulling them all together at the end to create a harmonious tune that had everyone tapping their feet. As the storyteller left the stage, we all clapped so long and loud that our palms were red and tingling. That show, and the hearty meal we had at a nearby pub, was a perfect ending to

Natasha's visit to Ireland. I was grateful she had taken the time to make the trip and pleased she would be able to make a positive report to my mother and sister back in England.

3. All's well that ends well

A few days later, our daughter, Joanne, visited for a long weekend. This was her second trip in as many months. Yet again we did the usual round of visitor attractions: The Cliffs of Moher, the Burren, and of course the wonderful Bunratty Castle and folk park, which we had recently renamed 'Bloody Bunratty Castle'. This was a genuine term of endearment. It's a fantastic day out, which I highly recommend, but four visits in as many months was a bit much for anyone.

It was lovely to see our daughter again. We had a great time chatting, walking the dogs, eating too much, and hearing her news from England.

"My new job's going really well," she said. "Working for a large American firm is rather a culture shock, but very exciting. They really seem to appreciate success."

"How so?" I asked.

"Well, I had a couple of early wins with my new clients. At my old firm, if I was lucky, they would have given me a small nod of appreciation."

"But the new firm is different?" I added.

"I'll say," she replied, beaming a huge smile. "As a reward, they gave me a new account to manage."

"Oh, that's great!" I said, genuinely pleased for her. "I guess that's the benefit of being head-hunted."

"But there's more."

"Go on." I could see my daughter was fit to burst with excitement.

"Guess who the client is?"

I knew Joanne's new job was based in London, working as an account manager for a big marketing firm. I did my best to keep up, but most of what she did was still just technical mumbo-jumbo to me.

"I haven't a clue." I shrugged and smiled. "Chances are, I haven't heard of them."

"You've heard of this company," and she mentioned the name.

"Well, everyone's heard of them!" I exclaimed.

Joanne was grinning as if she had just won the lottery. I was genuinely delighted for her, and as proud as a dad could be.

On Sunday, we took a drive to Mountshannon with the intention of taking a walk alongside Lough Derg, the huge lake that sits astride the river Shannon in the east of County Clare. It was mid-June and unusually hot for Ireland. What had begun as an overcast and rather chilly day improved dramatically. The wind dropped and the heavy grey cloud transformed into balls of white cotton wool on a sky of warm azure. I parked our car in the village and we walked together through a small park and down the hill towards the harbour and yacht club.

"My goodness!" Joanne exclaimed. "This is like Monaco. I've never seen so many yachts."

"They're not quite as ostentatious as Monaco, but you're right," I nodded, "there's certainly some value here."

"There must be a hundred boats," Lesley remarked. She turned and looked back up the hill towards the village. Much of Mountshannon was situated along a single road on the hillside, providing panoramic views of Lough Derg and the mountains along the opposite bank. "I bet the houses here are expensive."

"Pricey enough to keep riffraff like us out," I joked.

Turning left we walked along a tarmac path towards a distant dock, where we could see a car park and a collection of smaller boats bobbing in the water. Once we had passed the yacht club moorings, we had an unobstructed view of the Lough.

We stopped and stared at the view. There was barely a breath of wind. The water stretched out before us like a sheet of glass.

"That's some view," Joanne sighed. "I'm amazed nobody is water-skiing or racing up and down on a jet ski."

"The lakes here are mercifully quiet," Lesley observed. "I think there's a good bit of fishing, and of course the yachts, but otherwise people prefer to stand and look."

"I can see why," Joanne responded. Her voice was a gentle whisper, as if she were in church. "How big is this lake?"

Lesley shrugged, and I was quick to step in with an answer.

"It's 24 miles long and eight miles wide," I said. "If you drove around the outside you'd cover about 120 miles."

"Pretty big then," she agreed.

I nodded. "It's the biggest lake in Ireland."

"Anyway, how do you even know that?"

"I was curious, so I looked it up," I explained.

"Uh-huh," Joanne grunted.

We began walking towards the dock. Clearly my daughter was unimpressed with my encyclopaedic knowledge. Fishing for compliments, I threw some more bait.

"There is another Lough Derg up north in Donegal, but it's much smaller than this one." I waited patiently, but I didn't get a bite.

Up ahead we saw a sign, propped against the wheel of an old and very rusty tractor. It was a whitewashed square of rough plywood, hand painted with uneven red letters. *Bowt's 4 Rent.*

The red gloss paint had run in several places, but we could still decipher the meaning.

"Shall we get a boat?" Lesley asked, pointing at the sign.

Joanne and I shared a nod of agreement.

"So you wants to rent a boat?" a soft voice whispered in my ear.

I jumped and gave a short squeal of surprise. As if by some sleight of hand, a weather-beaten old man wearing an equally weather-beaten full length waxed coat, had appeared at my side. It was a moment before I could calm myself and formulate a reply.

"How…how much is it?" I asked.

He looked us up and down, perhaps assessing our worth.

"Twenty euros," he nodded, almost to himself.

"For how long?"

"All day." He walked towards the dock and pointed. "You can take this one."

It was an untidy, but functional, 14 foot fiberglass rowboat, with a small outboard motor at the rear. Just as I was thinking that twenty euros was an incredibly reasonable price for a day's rental, the old man – perhaps mistaking my silence for doubt – sweetened the deal.

"I'll chuck in some lifejackets and a tank of fuel."

Who was I to argue? He smiled broadly as I handed over the cash. Ten minutes later we were slicing a gentle furrow through the glassy smooth water towards Holy Island.

"Why is it called Holy Island?" I had asked our boat guy.

"Every lake in Ireland has a lump of land with a derelict monastery or convent. They're all called Holy Island. I reckon the church sent all the troublemakers to the island."

"Or perhaps the good folk went to the island and the troublemakers stayed behind?" I suggested.

He nodded thoughtfully and then smiled. "I hadn't thought of that."

The island was quite small, only twenty acres in size. We circled it once. I eased off the throttle until the outboard motor was bubbling quietly, doing little to disturb the abundant wildlife we could see in and around the tall rushes. As the boat slowed, we excitedly waved at each other and silently pointed to each bird we spotted. There were great crested grebes, some ducks, several cormorants, the blue flash of a kingfisher, and as a finale we were treated to a magnificent flypast from a group of pure white swans, glistening in the sunshine. Once I'd gently nudged the boat into the wooden dock and tied it securely, we set off to explore the island, one of the most significant monastic sites in Ireland.

We saw the ruins of six churches, a well-preserved round tower, a holy well, a graveyard and a 'bargaining' stone, apparently a handy spot for brokering a marriage. Interesting as these historical sites were, we soon moved on, keen to enjoy a quiet stroll in the warm sunshine. In a long circle, we passed through a small wood, walked along the shoreline and entered a large meadow. Here the grass was tall and healthy, bursting with wild flowers and alive with butterflies and bees. On the way back to the boat, we encountered a small herd of cows.

"I wonder how they got onto the island," Joanne commented.

"Perhaps they rented a boat," I replied.

"Actually, they swim," Lesley interjected.

"No!" Joanne and I said together.

Lesley nodded. "I read about it. When the water is calm, they swim across from island to island, looking for the lush spring grass."

"Well now I've h-e-r-d everything!" I joked. I sidestepped quickly to avoid my wife's loving attempt to kick me.

The trip back to our house was uneventful, and after a late lunch, it was time for our daughter to head back to England. She was upstairs packing when we heard a squeal of surprise. Whilst getting changed, Joanne noticed she had unexpectedly caught the sun. Her shoulders were glowing a deep pink, with the exception of two very obvious white strap marks.

"Who would have thought I'd get sunburned in Ireland," she complained.

"It's not too bad," Lesley replied reassuringly. "Nobody will notice."

"But you don't understand," Joanne wailed. "I'm going to a wedding on Saturday, and I've just bought a strapless dress!"

***

Within days of Joanne returning to England, I was back at Shannon airport dropping Lesley off for the 'Red Eye' flight to Stansted and onward to see an osteopathic physician. We have both suffered with back pain for some time. My discomfort will usually ease after a few minutes on the golf practice range, or a brisk walk, but Lesley's back problem was much worse. She has several arthritic joints and a couple of slipped discs thrown in for a bit of variety. On this trip she would be receiving a course of steroid injections directly into the spine – a delightful prospect, as well as being extraordinarily expensive. Fortunately for our bank balance, this course of treatment was still covered by the group medical insurance from my old job, but not for long. Soon we would have to transfer her care to Ireland.

With the house to myself and the weather promised fine for a few days, I decided to do some outdoor chores. Although it appeared the previous owner had removed the piles of junk we had noticed when we first visited Glenmadrie, on closer inspection I found there was still a considerable amount of clearing away to do. Several huge sheets of one-centimetre-thick black plastic had once lined the floor of an old goat shed, but over time they had been repurposed to act as a weed suppressant. They now lay scattered around our land, half-buried by soil and camouflaged by the very weeds they were supposed to be suppressing. These sheets were the size of a single bed and constructed from recycled plastic, making them slippery, inflexible and extremely heavy. It's a good job we live a long way from the nearest neighbour, as there was much humping and swearing from me before the last sheet was neatly stacked, ready for disposal. With that job finished, I decided I'd try to cut the grass.

In England I had purchased, second-hand, a solid American-built petrol lawnmower, which had done sterling work keeping the grass of our garden under control. It had a powerful Briggs and Stratton motor, a 14 inch rotary cutting action, powered wheels, and a handy grass box. After giving this sturdy steel thoroughbred machine a good service and oil change, the engine was purring efficiently and the freshly-sharpened blade was whirring in eager anticipation. Confident everything was working as advertised, I began cutting the half acre of front lawn at Glenmadrie for the first time.

After just three paces, the engine stalled. Several hard pulls on the starter cord failed to restart it and, on further inspection, I discovered the blade was completely jammed by a large chunk of grass. I cleared the obstruction and began cutting again, with a similar result. Growling in frustration, I pulled the grass away by hand and re-started the mower. Three more steps and the engine stalled again. As I screamed in frustration, my self-assured smile was quickly replaced by a grim scowl.

This mower was obviously a well-designed machine, perfectly suitable for the neat cutting and collection of dry grass in the heat of California, or Texas, or even Essex. But it had no chance of coping with the lush and constantly dew-wet meadow grass growing in Ireland. Clearly, I needed to do some modifications. Or buy several goats.

To upgrade our mower for Irish conditions, I attacked it with a hammer, a saw and a recently acquired electrical gismo called a disc cutter. This evil-looking toy made a terrifying noise and vibrated like a live snake, but it produced a delightfully pretty spray of sparks as I chomped through the steel case of the mower. The end result of my modifications looked rather like a family car with the boot cut off. It would surely have reduced the manufacturer to tears, as well as breaching most European health and safety rules. Nevertheless, with all of the obvious impedances to the free movement of wet grass removed, I began a test run.

With its gaping backside on show for all to see, my American lawn mower bellowed into life. A few inches from my toes, the cutting blades spun into a blur and buzzed like a swarm of angry hornets. I made a mental note to take shorter steps, or I would soon have shorter legs. Aiming at a thick swathe of tough looking grass,

I pulled the lever to engage the drive wheels. As I pushed forward, there was barely a dip in the roar of the motor to signal the successful cutting of grass. There was no sign of tangling nor a suggestion that the motor would ever stall again. It was safe to say my modification was a triumphant success – with one minor exception. The moment I began to cut, a torrent of wet grass and other unidentifiable debris hit me full in the face.

Ever the practical fellow, and determined to make my modifications work, I closed my eyes to the merest slit and pressed on. Unfortunately, with the blizzard of grass adding to my already-restricted vision, I went slightly off line and collided with a tree. Plan B was to turn my head sideways, shut one eye and use my sizable proboscis to deflect most of the flying debris from entering the other eye. Although my nose did a splendid job protecting my eye, there was now nothing preventing the grass and grit from filling my exposed ear and threatening to deafen me. Plan C was to lower my height sufficiently to remain below the level of the flying debris. To do this I had to bend my knees and walk like an aged orangutan with a bad back. Whilst this method was partially successful, I quickly began to feel like an aged orangutan with a bad back. Pulling myself upright and trying to shake some life back into my wobbly legs, I reluctantly conceded the need for some robust protection and made a trip to our local hardware store.

So, two hours behind schedule, decked out in new thick leather gloves, ear protectors, goggles, and my trusty purple overalls, I began cutting the lawn again. Apart from the frequent need to wipe my goggles, and my bright purple overall slowly changing to chlorophyll green as I was sprayed with wet grass, my redesigned mower worked splendidly. Admittedly, the constant stream of fragments hitting my face was annoying, but after swallowing something that may once have been a slug, I soon learned to cut the grass with my mouth shut.

After an hour of hard walking and breathing through clenched teeth, my modified American mower had transformed a scruffy patch of grass into a neat front lawn. It wasn't perfect, but it was definitely an improvement. To finish the job, I did a final lap of the garden, just to tidy up the edges. As I mowed these last few yards, I cast my eye over my handiwork. "At least it looks like someone lives here," I thought, quietly proud of my resourcefulness.

Murphy's Law states that if something can go wrong, it will, but only at the most inopportune moment.

Just then the mower hit a patch of rough ground, perhaps a clod of earth pretending to be a clump of grass. I was instantly enveloped in a cloud of muddy dust and, as the mower groaned in anger, there was a sharp *ting* and a large pebble shot out. This rocky ballistic missile, travelling only slightly slower than the speed of light, would surely have broken a window, had it not hit me squarely in the groin. Cross-eyed and knock-kneed in agony, I let go of the lawnmower, grabbed my 'crown jewels' and collapsed like a man shot. Fortunately the mower stopped without hitting anything valuable, or running me over. I'm pleased to report that apart from a slightly dented blade, there was no permanent damage to the mower, but it was quite some time before I was able to uncross my eyes.

Early the following morning, Diarmuid and his team arrived to commence the well drilling operation. I knew he was coming soon, but I didn't know exactly when. When I had asked for a specific start date, all he could say was, "Sometime soon. Me pumps banjaxed. I'll call ye."

He hadn't called, but I didn't mind. Drilling the well was the first significant step towards making Glenmadrie into a home. This symbolic breaking of ground marked the beginning of our renovations. Furthermore, I was thrilled at the prospect of our house having water that didn't look like weak tea and smell of frogs. My excitement was short-lived.

Diarmuid arrived with two huge lorries, covered in exciting and interesting pipes, pumps, cranes and drills. To reach the agreed drilling site, these mammoth trucks drove halfway up my driveway then made a sharp right turn before ploughing a succession of muddy furrows across the entire length of my newly-cut lawn.

My face fell momentarily, but I shrugged stoically and whispered to myself, "Oh well, you can't make an omelette without breaking a few eggs."

I'm embarrassed to say, it had never occurred to me that the well drilling operation would do any damage to the garden, other than making a neat hole in the ground. How wrong could I be? Over the following three days, the machines thundered away almost non-stop, digging ever deeper into the bedrock until sunset brought a break and some welcome silence. As it spun downwards, the drill added to an ever-growing pile of light blue rock fragments and sprayed the grass with grey slime and water. Twice a day, the two lorries traversed my lawn, their huge tyres spinning and sliding through the track of mud that was once my tidy front garden. After 30 hours of drilling, Diarmuid banged on our front door and gave me a toothy smile.

"We've hit water." He pronounced it 'warther'.

"Oh wonderful! How deep have you drilled?" I asked.

"Just past three hundred feet," he replied. "We'll drill a small bit more, to make sure you've got a good bit of head, like."

I was delighted. By the end of the week, the well was finished. It was 355 feet deep, with the first 30 feet lined in plastic to avoid water runoff from the land entering the well.

A few days later, Sean, the well engineer, popped around to inspect the site and plan the layout of the water pipes and electrical wiring needed to run the pump. He was a small wiry fellow aged about 50. His sleepy eyes, grey hair and handlebar moustache were strangely at odds with his brisk nature, quick movements and fast-paced speech.

In a whirlwind quarter of an hour, he checked our fuse box, inspected the well head, took water samples for testing, told me where and how to build the pump house, and further desecrated the remains of our lawn with sprayed lines of yellow paint, indicating where I needed to dig trenches. Feeling like a harassed personal assistant to the sort of executive that would be too busy to buy his wife an anniversary gift, I followed Sean from place to place whilst taking copious notes. At a trot, nodding blankly, and doing my best to keep out of the way, I attempted to record his terse directives without tripping over my own feet.

As he climbed into his van, Sean delivered his final instruction. "Get all that done and then call me," he ordered. "But not before!" With a stiff nod, he slammed the door and drove away.

"Blimey!" I said, scratching my head and trying to decipher my hurried handwriting. I hoped that 'Lay warning tripe' would make sense later, or be forgotten without jeopardising the entire project.

***

I collected Lesley from the airport that evening. Even after a couple of days' bedrest to recover from the back injections, her face was wan and rigid with pain as I helped her into the passenger seat of our car.

"That's the last of the injections," she said.

"Good job too," I replied, "you look awful."

Lesley shifted in her seat and winced. Sensing I had stumbled into a minefield I added, "I meant you look like you're in a lot of pain…but you're as beautiful as ever."

Silence.

I drove slowly, taking care to miss the biggest potholes. There's always one you don't see. Lesley groaned in pain.

"Sorry!" I felt awful.

"It's alright, don't worry," she whispered through clenched teeth. "It's not your fault."

"Do you have to go back for a check-up?"

My wife shook her head.

Time to change the subject.

"Diarmuid hit water," I said, trying to lift her spirits. I failed.

"It's Ireland," she growled. "You can't throw a stone without hitting water."

I did my best not to be goaded into a confrontation. It's never a bad idea to give Lesley a wide berth when she is feeling such pain. I went to pat her knee, then thought better of it. "Sean came round and told me where to put the pump house and ditches."

Lesley grunted and turned her head to look out of the side window.

"I'm afraid the lawn looks like a battle ground," I continued. "It's a hell of a mess."

"Probably," she mumbled.

"On the upside," I made a final attempt to raise my wife's flagging spirits. "I've found someone to dig the ditches."

"Have you?" Lesley turned her head in my direction. A sparkle of interest glinted in her tired eyes. "Who?"

"His name's Paul. He lives down below on the main road. I was passing by and I saw him driving a big yellow digger in a field, so I stopped and had a chat. I wanted to know where he rented it from, but it turns out he owns it. He's only a young lad, but he's really friendly." I smiled proudly.

"And?"

"Oh!" I exclaimed, realising I'd forgotten to deliver the punchline. "He's coming up tomorrow morning to dig out all the ditches so I can lay the pipes and cable for the pump."

We shared a smile.

4. Trench warfare

An hour later than expected, Paul came chugging up our driveway in his digger. He was a typical County Clare lad. In his mid-twenties, he was polite, intelligent, and independent. With pale skin, dark brown hair, narrow hazel eyes, a prominent chin, and a slightly up-turned nose, his features were characteristically Irish.

"Sorry I'm late," he said, jumping down from the cab. "The old girl broke down and I had to walk back to my car to get a spare part."

"Oh dear," I exclaimed. "I appreciate you offering to do this, but I hope we're not putting you out."

Paul held up a calming hand. "Oh you're grand! It's not a problem."

"Well if you're sure..."

Paul waved his hand dismissively. Any further conversation was forestalled as Lesley came out to say hello, accompanied by two excitable dogs.

Romany trotted across the lawn like a portly but diminutive sheep, woofing with all the gusto of a dog twice her size. But like a typical Lhasa Apso, she soon lost focus and wandered off to sniff an interesting bush. By comparison, Amber charged across the lawn like an overexcited kamikaze hamster, prepared to sacrifice everything in defence of her territory. Yapping loudly, she ran in frantic circles, pausing only to growl at any suspicious twigs. Given that all this noise and aggression was coming from a fluffy beige terrier, no larger than a healthy red squirrel, Paul found her frenzied barking quite amusing. As soon as the little dog realised our visitor was not only unthreatening, but a dog lover as well, Amber instantly transformed from guard dog to annoying pest, hopping up and down and demanding a fuss.

The young lad lavished Amber with attention and even taught her a new trick. Slightly bending his knee Paul made a clicking sound and slapped his thigh like a pantomime pirate. Somehow Amber instantly understood this instruction. Without hesitation, she raced across the lawn, threw herself into the air, bounced off Paul's thigh and dived into his waiting arms. Resisting the little dog's attempts to lick him to death, with a swing of his arms Paul despatched her across the lawn, as if he were throwing a bowling ball. Like a man jumping from a slow moving bus, Amber landed on the run, turned a tight circle and raced back to repeat her acrobatic leap. All the while Amber was grinning like an idiot while Paul held a casual conversation with Lesley.

"Yes, I'm planning to build a house on the land where I met Nick," he said, catching Amber as she bounded into the air. "I'm going to do my own groundwork," he explained, throwing the little dog across the lawn, "that's why I bought this JCB."

"Will that save you money?" Lesley asked.

"I expect so," Paul replied, bowling Amber across the grass again. "Because I'm not renting, it doesn't matter how long the digging takes."

Lesley was looking at Amber with some concern. Although she was clearly becoming exhausted, she was too tenacious to stop while the game was still available and deftly dodged my wife's attempt to catch her.

"Perhaps I should buy my own digger," I suggested, somewhat hopefully.

"No!" Lesley snapped, rather loudly.

"W...Well it was only a suggestion," I said defensively. We had recently agreed on the need to buy a cement mixer, but a digger seemed to be a step too far.

I noticed Lesley's withering look.

"I was talking to Amber," she snarled, scooping the dog into her arms.

"Oh," I mumbled apologetically.

"I'll take these dogs indoors and leave you two to sort out the digging," my wife said, before shouting for Romany. Perhaps hoping for a biscuit, for a change she obediently trotted along behind Lesley and Amber as they headed for the front door.

"That's a neat trick you've taught Amber," I said.

"Me?" Paul replied, obviously confused. "I presumed it was something you'd taught her."

I laughed. "It seems she's taught us both something!"

My eyes were drawn to the hulking form of the JCB, sitting in my driveway. The first time I had seen it was late in the evening. Now that it was in full sunshine, I could see this machine was somewhat less pristine than I had thought. The signature JCB yellow was more of a grubby beige, streaked with rivulets of rust. One door was missing, the windscreen was held together with copious amounts of grey duct tape, and in several places the hydraulic pipes were attached to the digger arms with bright orange twine. The phrase 'ridden hard and put away wet' came to mind. I nodded politely towards the digger.

"It must be very expensive to buy one of those," I suggested.

"Ah, it's not too bad," Paul sighed. "They were going to scrap it, so I got a good price."

"Oh good. That's a result then. Will it be up to the job?" I asked.

"It'll be grand," he answered with typical Irish optimism. "Anyway, I've only had it for a couple of days. I haven't had a chance to do any digging yet. This'll be good practice for me, before I start on my place."

"Right!" I clapped my hands together. "Let's get to it then."

Paul and I had a quick walk around the site to confirm what needed to be done, then he hopped up into the cab. After several unsuccessful attempts, and the jiggling of some loose wires, the digger eventually roared into life. I stepped back and covered my mouth as I was swathed in a cloud of soot and diesel fumes. There was a good bit of coughing and wheezing, most of it from the JCB, but eventually the digger lumbered across the lawn and took up station ready to begin digging.

Through the moss-stained windows, I could see Paul experimentally pulling the levers as he tried to fathom the controls. He must have figured it out because, with an asthmatic wheeze, the digger arm arched gracefully out and down. As the teeth of the bucket dug into the moist earth and began to scoop, I couldn't help but clap my hands and smile. This really was a 'breaking new ground' moment, and I was rightly excited.

Unfortunately, my elation was premature. As the first scoop of soil began to lift from the ground, there was a loud *pop* and the digger arm flopped down and began squirting red fluid like a ruptured artery. Once the engine had stopped, Paul hopped down. He stood scratching his head and surveying the damage.

I walked over. "Something broke," I suggested helpfully.

"It's busted a hydraulic line. I thought this might happen," he said. "Not to worry. I'll get another. Can you give me a lift?"

Two hours later, the pipe was repaired and the fluid topped up. The JCB roared back into life, only for the same thing to happen again, this time after 20 minutes of digging. So we jumped into my car once more and made for a local village where there was a hardware shop with a large stock of parts. Despite my protestations, Paul refused my determined offers to pay.

It was after lunch before the mighty digger was back at work, and for a while everything seemed to be progressing splendidly. The motor roared, the arm dipped and scooped, and the first trench gradually became a little longer. In fact everything would have worked out just fine, had it not been for the wheels.

Most people will be familiar with the standard JCB with wheels. They are sold all over the world. In the UK and India, JCB is often used colloquially as a generic description for mechanical diggers and excavators, and it even appears in the Oxford English Dictionary. So it's a safe bet that wherever you live in the world, you've been held up in traffic by a jolly yellow vehicle that looks rather like a tractor with a backhoe on the rear. If so, you may have noticed that, like a tractor, it had wheels. These are fine for trundling along the road and holding up the traffic, but they don't work very well in wet Irish soil.

We'd had a good bit of rain that week, making the ground even more wet and heavy than usual. The mud was slippery as ice to walk on and stuck to our boots like toffee, and was as difficult to remove as barnacles on the hull of an old barge. The huge tyres on the JCB slid and slipped and spun, churning at the mud, until the machine was embedded up to its axels. With some impressively clever manipulations at the controls, Paul used the digger arms to make the JCB pull itself out of the quagmire. It was fascinating to see, rather like watching a creature escape from the black lagoon. But after the digger became stuck for the third time, we had to admit defeat.

"It was a gallant effort," I said, trying to sooth Paul's obvious disappointment.

"Wrong tool for the job," he replied stoically. "You'll need a digger with a caterpillar track for this."

"I'll get on the phone and rent one as soon as you've gone," I replied.

Again I offered to pay Paul for his time, and again this nice young man refused to accept the proffered cash. Perhaps he felt he'd let me down, or maybe he had plans to sell the small lorry load of my soil he still had clinging to his JCB. In any event, I was grateful for his efforts.

A few days later, I managed to rent a three-ton digger with caterpillar tracks, at a surprisingly expensive weekend rate. Almost half the cost was the delivery charge, which made me realise that life in our remote location had hidden expenses. Such a large spend was a bit of a kick in the wallet, but with almost a hundred yards of trenches to dig, we had no other option. The digger was delivered by a local hire firm on a huge lorry. In a frantic ten minutes, the driver drove it onto my lawn, gave me a quick training session, wished me well, and shot off to his next job.

At some point every young boy dreams of driving a digger – and so do some older men. During the renovation work at our house in England, we hired a man with a digger to remove the old concrete driveway. Watching the operator working the controls, chain-smoking cigarettes and chugging on a can of XXXX lager, whilst effortlessly loading chunks of cement into a skip, I recall thinking, "*I could do that!*" Well, I now know that it's harder than it looks.

To begin with, I couldn't get the flipping thing started. In my excitement, I'd forgotten there was a safety switch to prevent accidental starting. Once the engine was running, I drove the machine across the lawn and positioned it ready to begin digging my first trench. My plan was to use the hydraulic arm to scoop a bucket full of soil, lift it out and drop it two yards to the right. Once I'd dug down 150 centimetres, I would move the digger back a couple of metres and dig some more. That way I was always moving away from the trench, and unlikely to fall in.

Staring down at the confusing array of knobs and joysticks, I tried to remember which one did what. I couldn't. The only instruction I recalled from the hasty training session with any certainty was, "If all else fails, let go of the controls and it will stop." My only option was trial and error. I chose one joystick and gave it a twist. Before I could react, the digger arm swung violently to the right and with a mighty clang, collided with a tree. I let go of the controls and sat very still for a bit. As I had been told, the beast appeared to have returned to its sleeping state.

Rather more cautiously, I twisted the joystick in the opposite direction and obligingly the arm swung back to its original position. After some careful experimenting for a couple of minutes, the tree was looking rather battered, but I felt confident enough to begin excavating.

Making only small movements on the controls, I dug into the ground and lifted my first load. I had intended to move the arm sideways and deposit the earth on the right, but I chose the wrong control input and dumped it back into the trench. I tried again, and did the same thing. I closed my eyes and growled in frustration. Over an hour had passed since the digger arrived, and apart from adding to the track marks on the lawn, I'd made zero progress. To make matters worse, when I opened my eyes, Lesley was standing there with her arms folded. Her face did not suggest joy or amusement. She was shouting something. When I opened the cab door and removed my ear defenders, I still couldn't hear, so I switched off the motor. Blessed silence.

"Yes, dear?" I asked, frustrated at the interruption.

"You're not doing very well," she observed.

"It's a bit tricky," I admitted, trying to calm my growing anger. "But I'll get the hang of it." I gave her my best smile.

She was unimpressed. "Do you want me to do it?"

Diplomatically, I restarted the motor so my dear wife wouldn't hear my reply.

With practice I got better at working the controls and by the end of day one, I'd successfully dug our trenches. Then it was a simple matter of laying the pipes and refilling the trench. By close of play on Sunday night, the job was complete. I'd even had enough time to wash the mud off the digger with a hosepipe before it was collected. All I had to do now was build the pump house.

***

Just like starting a new job, when you move to a new country, there is an adjustment period while you learn how things are done. Already we were becoming familiar with the slower pace of life, the relaxed attitude to rural driving whilst under the influence, cars blocking the road as the occupants lean out of the windows for a chat, outdoors dogs left free to roam, and even complete strangers coming into your house uninvited and helping themselves to a cup of tea. This last point is an indication of the trust people have for their fellow man in the rural communities, something that was once commonplace in Britain, but has largely gone. That trust came as a pleasant surprise when we ordered our first load of building materials.

Given we were about to begin a major renovation project, whilst working with a limited budget, I thought it would be prudent to find a good supplier. I did some research, but came up empty handed. Aside from a few firms in Dublin, the internet claimed there were no builders' merchants in Counties Clare, Galway, or Limerick. The Golden Pages business directory listed most firms by name, rather than by business type and the familiar British retail chains had not reached the west of Ireland. If you didn't know the business name, you were stuffed. I had spotted a lorry delivering to a new-build development, but when I asked the driver how I could go about ordering my building supplies, he told me their business was strictly trade only.

Our saviour lay behind the door of a nondescript shop in a local village. It was the same place where Paul had bought a hydraulic pipe. As well as selling pots, pans, batteries, clocks, shoes, sports equipment, and wheelbarrows, they were also a builder's merchant and tractor repair shop. Even though I was not a 'proper builder', the nice young girl behind the work-wearied counter was happy to take my order and even promised me free delivery for the duration of the renovations. It felt good to put some money into the local area. However, when the first lorry load of building materials arrived, the driver had not been given an invoice and refused to take a cash payment.

"I'm sorry," he shrugged. "I don't have anything to do with invoices."

"But this lot's worth several hundred euro!" I exclaimed. "You haven't even got a delivery note."

"No, I've got a delivery note," he replied, showing me some writing on the palm of his hand, "but you'll have to see the shop about payment."

"Right!" I replied. "I'll get my car."

"I shouldn't bother," he said, putting a calming hand on my shoulder. "They're shut for the day. Anyway, I'm sure there's no rush. Just pop in next time you're passing."

And he was right.

Even though we had never before met, it transpired the girl in the hardware store had automatically opened an account and extended us a substantial line of credit. Although Lesley and I were gradually learning the Irish ways, we had brought one unbreakable rule into our new lives – no credit, ever again. The young girl in the hardware store seemed a little baffled when I settled our invoice with cash and then insisted on paying for all of our future purchases before delivery, but she accepted anyway. Perhaps she was getting used to our strange British ways.

A few days later, a similar thing happened. Lesley arrived home from a shopping trip to Ennis and immediately crossed the lawn to where I was laying concrete blocks for the pump house walls. Earlier I had given up trying to master the bricklayer's trowel in favour of wearing bright yellow washing-up gloves and applying the mortar by hand.

Lesley watched me for a while, before she spoke. "Interesting technique." She smiled encouragingly.

"It works," I replied. "Perhaps I should patent it."

Unimpressed, she humphed quietly and then changed the subject.

"I've been thinking," my wife said brightly.

A cold shiver went down my spine, ran across the floor and hid in the corner quivering. I sensed she wanted to tell me something and I could see no obvious means of escape.

"Go on then, what have you been thinking?"

"Rugs!" she said triumphantly.

"Oh jolly well done!" I teased. "What are we having for dinner?"

She ignored my caustic wit. "I think we need rugs, for the sitting room floor."

"We do?" I asked, picturing the constant snow of woodworm dust and dead spiders that coated the floor daily. "Won't they just get dirty?"

She rolled her eyes and sighed dramatically, "Not for now! For afterwards – when the work is finished."

Sensing at least a temporary reprieve, I relaxed. "Oh. You mean for later. Well that's alright then."

She spoke quietly, whilst carefully inspecting a fingernail. "Only we need them now – because they were on sale."

I eyed her suspiciously. "Were on sale? What did you buy?"

"I didn't buy anything, yet. I was at a shop in Ennis and they had these Persian rugs. They're beautiful and they were practically giving them away."

"Okay, fine," I conceded. "The next time we're in Ennis, we can go and have a look."

"No need!" she said jubilantly. "They're in the car. All six of them."

"SIX?" I squealed.

Lesley nodded and smiled.

"But you said you didn't buy them," I whined.

"I didn't."

"I suppose they just gave them to you?" I suggested mockingly. "Without asking you for a deposit or anything?"

"Actually they did," she said with a big smile. "Come and see."

It was true. Lesley had arrived home with several thousand euros' worth of fine Persian rugs in the back of her car. The staff in the shop were so keen for her to buy, they had insisted she take them home – just to try them for size.

"It's incredible," she exclaimed. "They didn't ask for any deposit, or credit card details or identification. They didn't even bother to take a note of my name."

"Good grief!" I exclaimed. "The level of trust here is just wonderful."

"I think it's nice," Lesley sighed.

I agreed. It was nice, and further evidence of how delightfully innocent and crime-free County Clare was. Overall, it seemed that our lessons in 'Learning to be Irish' were going rather well.

5. Living the wild life

"Aaaaghh!" Lesley's scream echoed through the house, long and loud.

My slippers slapped on the polished wood like wet fish, as I charged down the stairs and ran through the sitting room. With my dressing gown flowing behind me like Superman's cape, I deftly dodged around one dog and hurdled the other. Ahead in the kitchen, my wife was standing with a hand over her mouth and eyes as wide as pudding basins.

"What?" I gasped, stumbling down the stairs.

Like the Grim Reaper – if it dressed in light blue flannel pyjamas and fluffy slippers – Lesley slowly lifted an arm and her shaking finger pointed towards the purple bulk of the pantry.

"*Whhaaat?*" I asked a little louder.

"R-a-t!" she hissed.

"Where?"

"In there. I saw a rat. It was in there." Still pointing, she backed away a couple of steps.

The kitchen, along with the rest of the house, was untouched since we had moved in. Our only progress towards renovating our dilapidated farm house and converting it into a dream home was to treat a woodworm infestation and knock out an internal chimney and fireplace. In most of the house, the walls were of bare stone, much of it lacking mortar, with holes where the wind blew through, disturbing the dust and cobwebs. The kitchen had a low ceiling with exposed beams, three rickety kitchen units, a red Rayburn cooking range that also ran the central heating, and a large food pantry. This larder had been painted dark purple by the previous owner. It was the size of a small bathroom, and as well as holding up the ceiling, it was our only food store.

"Where was it?" I asked, edging cautiously forwards.

"On the right, behind the cereal," she whispered. "It was just sitting there!"

A quick search revealed nothing. Not even any droppings.

"Are you sure?" I asked, somewhat innocently.

Silence.

Casually I turned around. Lesley's face told me I was in

trouble. Never question your wife's eyesight, particularly when it's cold and your dressing gown has come undone. Thinking quickly, I regrouped, and covered my embarrassment.

"You probably scared it away," I explained. "It was probably just a mouse."

"It was a rat!" she snapped fiercely.

"Okay. I'll go to the village and get some mouse traps as soon as I'm dressed."

"And some rat traps," she growled.

"And some rat traps," I agreed.

That afternoon, I busied myself with a bucket of mortar and several cans of expanding foam, filling in every visible gap and orifice in the walls throughout the house. Not only would this simple task deter a further intrusion from our hapless rodent, but with the holes blocked, the constant draught had lessened considerably, making the house noticeably warmer. Next I baited several traps (chocolate hazelnut spread works best) and placed them in areas of the house where they would be accessible to vermin, but not curious dogs. My final task was to leave a couple of traps in the loft.

Balancing on the ladder, with a small torch clamped firmly between my teeth, I lifted the trapdoor with my head and carefully slid the rat trap onto a rafter. No sooner had I climbed down and removed the ladder than I heard the distinctive *snap* of the trap activating.

"Blast!" I said.

"What's the matter?" Lesley called from the sitting room below.

"I've just shut the loft hole and that trap has gone off," I shouted. "It's got a real hair trigger. The change of temperature has probably set it off. I'll have to set it again."

"Mind your fingers!"

"Thanks," I laughed.

I reset the ladder and climbed back up.

"Blimey!" I said as I saw the trap.

"What?"

"There's a huge rat in it!"

"Already?" Lesley exclaimed. "It's only been up there for a few seconds."

I showed her.

"Eeeww!" she cried. "Get it away!"

I disposed of the body, replaced the trap, and put the ladder away. Just as I came back indoors, Lesley called out.

"The trap has gone off again!"

"You're kidding!" I said.

She was right. Two dead rats in 20 minutes. We are both animal lovers, but there is a limit to our benevolence. Hoping our vermin problem was solved, I replaced the trap and waited. It didn't take long.

***

Early in our married life, Lesley and I came to accept that the secret to domestic bliss lay largely in sleeping in separate rooms. No longer were our nights a misery of snoring, elbow pokes, and the constant fight for the covers that had previously decorated our disturbed sleep. Now we could luxuriate in the empty space of our own double beds, able to sleep early or read late, and rise as soon as the mood took us, without disturbing our spouse.

That night, as I lay reading in my bedroom, three rat traps in the loft space above my head went off in quick succession. An hour later I was rudely awoken as the trap behind the wardrobe went off. Unfortunately, the creature was not killed instantly, and it spent the next ten minutes running around the room and crashing into things, before gradually succumbing. Picturing something much larger and more ferocious than the medium sized brown rat that had found its way into my bedroom, I bravely hid under the covers until the morning.

Four rats in one night. Clearly we had a serious vermin problem that could take a little while to solve. The following night, I went outside with a powerful spotlight and spied several large rats running along our gutters.

A little internet research revealed that, when faced with a prolonged period of heavy rain and flooding, vermin will naturally move to higher ground. In this case, higher ground was our loft and roof. The huge stone walls of our property were probably inundated with burrows and rat runs. Other than protecting the downpipes with wire, buying some clever electronic deterrents, and keeping the traps baited, there was little more I could do. Oh the joys of country living and owning an old house!

"Perhaps we should get a cat?" I suggested, as I emptied another trap the next morning.

"I'd love one too, but no," Lesley replied firmly.

"Why not?" I'm a sucker for kittens and puppies. "Amber would love a playmate."

"I'm sure she would, but no."

"Why?" I asked again. "It would solve our vermin problem."

Lesley shook her head. "It *may* solve our vermin problem, but a cat would *definitely* chase off the wild birds. And that won't do at all."

I knew she was right. When we first arrived, there were disappointingly few wild birds around, mostly because our house is remote and built at an altitude of around one thousand feet, so the growing season for their natural food of bugs, berries and seed is relatively short. Quite early on I decided to build a large bird table, using up some scrap wood and roofing felt. It stands on a stout post, protected from the worst of the wind, in the centre of the courtyard, close to the trees and overlooked by ten windows. Because the house is so remote, this single dependable food source has quickly attracted a large variety of birds – and probably several rats. By the end of spring, we were getting through forty kilos of bird seed a month, and a dozen fat balls, trying to keep up with the ravenous hordes that sit in the trees and fall on the food before I can step away from the table.

Lesley has spotted at least 18 different species of birds at the table, including finches, dunnocks, tits and thrushes. We were delighted to see our first house sparrows. They are a very common bird in Ireland, but not at this altitude. Presumably they heard about the free food and decided to make the trip up the hill from the valley. Occasionally the local sparrow hawks will buzz the table, in the hope that a tasty young bird will fly into a window in panic and fall to the ground stunned. When they do, the lightning fast sparrow hawk is on it in an instant.

Eventually the rodent problem was solved with traps and

vigilance, but not before we killed 22 rats in a ten-day period. Such slaughter is difficult to live with, but when the population of vermin gets so far ahead of the population of predators something has to be done.

***

One mystery that took a while to solve was that of the elusive flying ghosts. After a hard day building the pump house, I thought I'd ease my aching back and take a walk around our land. As dusk fell, I climbed the hill on our meadow in the hope of spotting the International Space Station flying over. It was a pleasantly warm and cloudless evening. The twilight sky was still coloured amber from the glorious sunset, but quickly fading blue to black. Already, in this half-light, I could see the major planets and the early flickering of a thousand stars.

Later in the year much of the bird song would fall silent, but this was mating season, and the dusk sky was a delicious ruckus of competing songs and calls. I walked west, towards the fading sunset. This would take me to the highest point of our land, where I would have the best view of the night sky and the ISS as it flew over. Although I knew this route well, I took care to stay well clear of the black yawning mouth of our quarry. It is only an acre in size, but the walls are sheer and high and not something I would enjoy falling down.

Thrusting my hands deep into my pockets, I lifted my eyes to the sky and took a deep breath of the finest air on the planet. Just then, I heard a most peculiar noise. It was a sound as large as the call of a humpbacked whale and yet as quiet as the wind rustling some leaves. The sound seemed to resonate around me, but as fast as I could turn an ear to follow, it was gone. Curious, I stood my ground and slowly turned my head. There it was again. As if someone had just thrown a boomerang close to my ear, but that would make a different noise. This sound was huge. In my vivid imagination, I pictured several hang-gliding elephants, doing ghost impressions whilst playing the low notes on pan pipes. This eerie noise seemed to circle my head and reverberate around the valley, without following any discernible path. It is such a deep and warm sound that, although it resonated down into my chest, I never felt in the least bit threatened. With the International Space Station forgotten, I ran back to the house and dragged my reluctant wife to the top of the hill, so she could share in my wonder and excitement. Ever the enthusiast for standing in the dark and being cold, she complained all the way to the top of the hill.

"What?" she whined. "What is it?"

"Shush," I whispered. "Listen."

"Just tell me." she hissed.

"Shhh."

Silence.

More silence.

"What?" Lesley snapped.

I huffed in frustration. I really wanted to share my mysterious discovery, but now it was gone.

"There was this sound…it was huge…and really quiet." I was babbling like an overexcited idiot.

"Was it a UFO?" she asked.

I imagined my dear wife was now looking at me sideways, somewhat concerned for my sanity. Fortunately, it was now pitch dark and I couldn't see her scepticism. Disappointed and embarrassed, I led the way back to the house. Two days later, the same thing happened again, although this time I wisely left Lesley indoors.

Just after sunset, I was up on the hill throwing a ball for Amber when the hang-gliding elephants returned. Although I was fascinated, turning my head to try and locate the sound, Amber seemed unaware of this ghostly noise. Or perhaps she was just more interested in retrieving the ball. Whatever the cause of this mystery was, the strange noise continued for a further half-hour, unperturbed by Amber's incessant barking. Back indoors, I repeated my description of this mysterious sound to Lesley. As I ran around the lounge with my arms spread and making *woo-woo-woo* sounds like a demented toy train, my wife watched me with impassive indifference, although I suspect she was trying to remember where the family straitjacket was kept.

As luck would have it, a few days later we got chatting to a passing walker. He announced himself as David, an amateur ornithologist. We talked about our new home, explained why we had moved to Ireland, took turns complaining about the weather and the government, and then moved onto the wildlife. Always keen to revisit my glory days treading the boards as an actor, I mentioned our mystery sound and launched into my description. David watched my overly-energetic performance, momentarily horrified. Perhaps he was assessing if I was about to leap our gate and bite his ankle. Then his face broke into a wide smile. I fell silent as he held up a finger.

"It's a snipe," he exclaimed.

"A what?" I asked.

"A common snipe drumming," he replied, then added, "it's the mating call of a bird."

So the monster behind this seasonal haunting was the common snipe, a ten inch short-tailed bird, with a face like Pinocchio lying about his expenses. This diminutive wader's mating display involves swooping dives at dusk, with its tail feathers extended laterally into the airflow, an action which creates the ghostly drumming noise that had so intrigued me.

I was grateful to David for this valuable information, it solved an intriguing puzzle, and convinced my wife that, at least for now, she didn't need to call the nice men in white coats to take me away.

***

As it was such a beautiful morning, I decided to take the dogs on a walk that was a little longer than usual. This picturesque track took us in a wide clockwise loop, up through the forest, across a field and then down to the lane that would take us back towards the house. Romany was trotting along at my side, occasionally stopping to sniff a stick, or pee on a tuft of grass.

Little Amber had finally tired of chasing her ball, which was currently leaking doggy slob into the lining of my coat pocket. She was now leading the walk and making her little *hup-hup-hup-hup* noises as she ran excitedly from bush to bush. Nearing home, the forest path opens into a field with extraordinary views across the valley towards the villages of Bodyke and Tulla. At the bottom of the field, our path joins another at right angles. The path to the left leads through a meadow and on towards the village of Feakle, but our journey would continue to the right, through another field and on to a single track road that leads back towards the house.

Bouncing along some fifty yards ahead, Amber suddenly spied something on the left. I could see from her body language she was about to run after whatever had attracted her attention.

"Amber," I shouted in an encouraging tone of voice whilst pulling the soggy ball from my pocket. "What's this?"

She glanced in my direction momentarily, but her eyes quickly swung back towards the field.

"*Aaamm-berr!*" I called again, adding an implied threat to my voice.

The little dog looked at me again as she weighed her alternatives.

"Good girl!" I called, with a smile in my voice. "Come here!"

After one more glance in my direction, and a stoic shrug that suggested *Oh well, what the heck!* the little dog took off like a rocket and sprinted into the meadow. I ran forward to look for her, but the knee high grass hid the action from my view – but not the sound. Oblivious to my angry shouts, the little terrier was racing around the field barking wildly. Something was going on, but I couldn't see what. The motivation behind this kerfuffle was a mystery until a large hare suddenly burst from the field, quickly followed by a ball of angry beige fluff. The hare was casually lolloping along the path, hotly pursued by Amber, clearly delighted to be pursuing something that was almost twice her size. As the chase passed from left to right, directly ahead of me, the scene played out in a series of slow motion images.

First I saw the hare, calmly trotting along with its ears up and white tail bobbing, as if it was enjoying some gentle exercise in the countryside. I imagined it was quietly singing *dum-de-dum-de-dum*. A few yards behind came Amber. With her head down and ears back, the little dog was running flat-out, but slowly losing ground on the much faster hare. Although Amber was visibly running out of energy and panting hard, the terrier in her DNA was clearly unwilling to admit defeat so early in the pursuit.

Behind this chase, and unseen by the little dog, a second hare emerged from the field. Spotting its friend in the distance, it casually trotted along behind Amber, as if they were all out on their usual Sunday morning jog.

As she passed by, Amber turned her head and looked into my

eyes. Her grinning face proudly said, "Look at me Daddy, I'm a mighty hunter!"

At that moment the second hare decided it was time to catch up with its mate. The European hare is a large animal that can run at up to 35 miles per hour. Amber cannot. Like a Ferrari overtaking a tractor, this magnificent beast lengthened its stride and easily accelerated past the diminutive panting dog. Poor little Amber was still looking at me and smiling, when the previously unnoticed hare crossed her field of vision and, dismissive of any potential danger, easily accelerated away. In that instant, I saw Amber visibly deflate, gradually slowing her stride as she came to terms with the hopelessness of the pursuit. As the two hares joined up and effortlessly bounded away, Amber came to a halt, head down and panting like a heavy smoker. I laughed so hard I got a stitch.

Somehow it all became my fault, and even after I had stopped laughing and dried my eyes, Romany glared at me accusingly and Amber snubbed all my attempts to apologise. Presumably, the hares were feeling a little guilty as well. As we walked towards the house, they repeatedly offered themselves to be chased again, but poor little Amber was inconsolable. Despite staring at their enticing white tails and muscular legs, she stubbornly refused to have anything further to do with them. By the time we got back to our land she had perked up a little, taking a few moments to chase a butterfly and woof at a passing aircraft, but it was only a half-hearted effort, lacking any real expectation of success.

6. Stovepipe blues

It was early in the morning and I was walking with Romany and Amber along the narrow road leading back to our house when a dark blue car came along. Chasing a dozen yards behind was a gangly black dog with several white patches, as if it had been accidentally daubed with paint. I realised the rising sun was shining directly along the road, making us almost impossible to see. Swiftly stepping aside, I pulled the dogs behind me and told them to sit. They both complied – albeit somewhat grudgingly. I needn't have worried. As it approached, the car slowed, eventually pulling to a stop opposite where we were standing. A moment later, with a growl and a woof, the dog lolloped past. Fifty yards ahead, it dived into a gap in the hedge and waited, like a tiger preparing to pounce on an unsuspecting deer. Seeing its wild and excitable eyes, foaming mouth and lolling tongue, it would have been understandable had I felt a twang of fear as this dog approached, but I didn't. I knew the score.

With a sound akin to fingernails dragging across a blackboard, the driver cranked down his side window.

"Well hello, young feller," he said, smiling.

The car was weather-beaten and old, as was the driver. I guessed his age to be somewhere north of 70. He had snowy white hair, a ready smile and sparkling blue eyes that spoke of kindness and mischief in equal measure. I saw so much of my late father in these features that my heart skipped a beat. Regardless of that unanticipated association pulling at my very core, I knew immediately I would like this man.

"You must be Tom, Lesley mentioned you," I replied, pointing up the road, "and I'm guessing that was Patch."

Tom nodded. I offered a handshake and introduced myself and the dogs. Tom pointed to Amber.

"You'd better keep her close, or the Travellers will have away with her."

"Travellers?" I was unfamiliar with the term.

"Pavees," he replied. "Itinerants."

I shrugged and shook my head.

"Knackers, tinkers," he said. "You know, gypsies."

"Really?" I exclaimed, finally understanding his meaning. "Why would they steal my dog?"

"They'd rob a terrier like that in a heartbeat. They use them for rooting out badgers."

"Oh, right. Thanks, I'll try to keep her safe then."

"Best if you do," Tom replied.

"Lesley told me about Patch. I see he's still chasing cars."

"Aye." He smiled. "I've tried to stop him, but whatever I do doesn't work."

"Oh yes." I laughed. "Lesley told me about some contraption you hung around his neck. She said it looked like a coat hanger with bells on."

"That's right. It were supposed to bang on his front legs and put him off chasing stuff. Didn't work though." Tom smiled. "He just ran sidewards. Then I tied a football to his collar, so it'd get in the way like."

"And that didn't work either?" I asked.

"Nope!" Tom shook his head and smiled. His face lit up. "Patch just held it in his gob and ran with it."

"Well, he's resourceful, I'll give him that."

Changing tack like a yacht on a windy day, Tom pointed towards my house. "Your wife says you're fixing up your house yourself."

"That's right," I replied. "It seems like the best option."

"Couldn't get a builder?"

I could see he already knew the answer. I pulled a pained expression and shrugged. "You've heard."

"They're all surfing the wave of the Celtic Tiger. Me, I calls it 'Stupid people getting into debt'. Right now they're laughing all the way to the bank, but they won't be laughing when the Sheriffs come 'round to take away their Mercedes."

"Are Sheriffs like bailiffs?" I asked.

"That's right." Tom nodded. "Ireland still puts people in jail for not being able to pay their debts."

"Good grief!" I exclaimed.

"Aye." Tom gave me a wink, filled with humorous evil. "When things go wrong, some of them new rich will be wishing their mothers had never met their fathers."

"You could be right," I agreed, quietly pleased Lesley and I were determined to stay debt free.

"It'll be nice to see the old place fixed up. How's the DIY going?"

"Oh, okay," I replied guardedly. "I've just built a pump house for the new well. Yesterday the water was finally connected."

"Good water is it?"

I nodded enthusiastically. "Cold as ice and as sweet as peach juice. The best I've ever tasted."

"That's good." He nodded appreciatively. "You built it yourself then?"

"Yep!" I smiled proudly. "It was a sort of proof of concept, just to verify I could do it. Soon I'm going to start on the cow shed."

"You're not keeping cows are you?" Tom's bushy eyebrows disappeared under his bushy white hair.

"Nooo!" I laughed. "We're going to make it into a guest wing. It'll be somewhere for Lesley and I to live while we're doing the renovations on the house, and later, accommodation for visitors."

Tom nodded towards a small herd of scraggly cows grazing on my meadow. "Them's not yours then?"

"No. They belong to Jim, from down the hill."

"Ah yes. Jim." Tom nodded knowingly. "Jim has a very flexible approach to fences and the like."

I spotted the misunderstanding. "Oh, it's not like that. I agreed that he could graze his cattle on my land. He's going to pay rent."

"Jim's going to pay rent?" Tom snorted so violently, I thought he had swallowed his dentures. "Good luck!"

With a wave, he drove on. Patch waited patiently until the car had passed before joyfully taking up the chase once more.

***

With the well and pump house completed, the next thing on my 'to do' list was the fireplace in the sitting room. Once the internal chimney had been removed with the help of Peadar, the burly builder, I had laid a tiled plinth, ready for our new wood-burning stove to be slid into place.

The following day, two weeks later than expected, I finally received the phone call from the shop telling me our stove was on the way. Predictably, the delivery driver had no idea where our house was, so we picked a mutually-recognisable meeting place and I set off in my car. The crated stove was the size of a rabbit hutch and as heavy as a car engine. The lopsided, rusty, white delivery van was clearly struggling under the weight, so I took the least arduous route back to the house. Once the van had parked near our front door, the driver and his mate climbed out.

"Blimey!" he exclaimed. "I'd never have found this place on my own."

"That's why I came out to meet you," I replied. "Maybe one day Ireland will get postcodes."

"Ha!" he snorted.

The driver's mate was squinting at our house and scratching his head.

"I don't know where we are," he said, "but I've definitely been here before." He had an Australian accent.

"At a guess, you were probably at a party," I suggested.

He clicked his fingers and pointed at me.

"You're right!" he exclaimed. "I remember! Man, that was a wild night. There was this hot blonde girl–"

"Enough!" I laughed, holding up my hands. "I have to live here."

We'd only been at Glenmadrie for a few months, but in that short time we had met a disturbingly large number of people who claimed to have enjoyed drug and alcohol-induced revelry at what was now our home. There were other, more lurid, tales of what went on as well, but I didn't want to hear them. Quickly, I changed the subject.

"Let me show you where the stove will go. I'm afraid there's a few steps and doors for you to negotiate. I can help, if you like."

"We'll manage," the driver said confidently.

And they did, but only just. With the stove still in its protective crate, it was loaded onto a heavy-duty sack barrow and pulled onto the van's tail lift. Once it was lowered, the two lads pushed and shoved the barrow across the gravel, levered it up two steps and through the front door. The barrow rolled quite smoothly across the rough concrete of the cow shed and coped quite well with the two small steps leading into the conservatory. The first real difficulty was negotiating the large step down into the alcove leading through the low kitchen door.

"Mind your head," I advised, a fraction too late.

There was a sickening crash as everyone let go of the stove and took interest in other things.

"Bugger!" the driver shouted, clutching his head and bending over.

"Strewth!" his mate squealed, sucking his skinned knuckles.

After some medical TLC and a bit more swearing, they squeezed the crate through the kitchen door, and climbed two more steps into our sitting room. With the cardboard and wood of the crate stripped away, we could finally inspect our new stove. Lesley was the first to spot a problem.

"This is not the stove we ordered."

"It must be," the driver replied.

"This is not the stove we ordered," Lesley repeated.

"You must be mistaken," he said rather firmly.

Not wanting to become collateral damage, I swiftly stepped aside. Fortunately, my wife only indicated her displeasure with a glare. All the same, it was a vicious glare – the sort of glare that can make a grown man feel guilty at 50 yards.

The driver, perhaps sensing the gravity of his error, paled visibly and fumbled in his pocket before pulling out a sheet of paper. "I'll check the delivery docket." Peering over his glasses the driver squinted at the numbers on the docket, then compared them with the model number on the remains of the box.

Lesley tapped her foot.

"This is not the stove you ordered," he confirmed. "I'll have to phone the shop."

Because of the thick stone walls at Glenmadrie, he went out to the van to make his call. When the driver returned he confirmed what we already knew. They had indeed delivered the wrong stove. This one would be returned to the shop. A replacement was now on order, but it would take 14 days to arrive. It was frustrating, but we took the delay with better humour than the delivery driver and his Aussie mate, who skinned knuckles, banged heads and cracked shins several times before the stove was safely back in the van.

"Sorry about that," he said as they climbed back into the van.

"Not to worry," I replied. "Anyway, you'll be happy to know the correct stove is even bigger."

He was sucking his bruised knuckle, so I didn't hear his reply, which was probably a good thing.

***

"You won't believe what just happened." Lesley had arrived back from the local shop.

"What?" I asked.

"I was chatting to the lady at the deli counter and I asked her if she knew where I could get some offal to cook up for the dogs."

"Oh yes," I nodded, delighted at the prospect of Romany having even worse wind.

"Anyway, she asked me what kind of dogs we have and I told her. But when I was describing Amber, I said she was a little toe-rag." Lesley raised her eyebrows.

"So?" I asked. Toe-rag was a term of endearment quite commonly used in Lesley's native Birmingham.

"There was a dreadful silence and I realised everyone was staring at me, open-mouthed."

"Oh dear," I exclaimed. "What does toe-rag mean in Ireland?"

"I have no idea." Lesley shrugged. "I didn't ask, or wait to find out."

It seemed an odd reaction to an apparently harmless phrase, especially as so many people in Ireland casually use the F-word as a precursor to both verbs and adjectives, but reserve the official Irish swear word *feck* for polite profanity. Lesley's accidental misuse of an expletive was particularly ironic, given what happened later that day.

My wife was strolling along the farm track at the back of the house, returning from walking our dogs, when she encountered an extremely large black bull. I had seen this creature before. It was five feet high and six feet wide, with ominous looking horns and testicles like two basketballs in a sack. This two thousand-pound behemoth was ambling its way up the hill, clearly on the scent of some fertile and willing cows in the fields behind the house. For a moment, Lesley had considered standing her ground in the mistaken belief that the bull, wanting to avoid confrontation, would return meekly to the field from whence it had escaped. It quickly became frighteningly obvious that the bull was not to be deterred, either by the wildly yapping dogs or the mad English lady who proved to be surprisingly spritely for her age, as she dived over a nearby fence.

A short while later, our friendly but geographically distant neighbour, Jim, walked along the lane with three of his children in tow, looking for his lost bull. Spying us in our garden, he stopped by the gate and waved politely.

"Hello, sir. How are you and missus sir, today?"

"Fine, Jim," I replied. "We're both just fine. How are you?"

"Ah we're grand. Fecked off though, me bull's escaped again. Have ye seen it?" he asked.

"What colour was it?" I teased. Lesley poked me in the side with her elbow.

"It's a big black one, it is. Went right through the fence again. After the cows it is."

Lesley chipped in. "Yes, Jim, it came up here an hour ago. I tried to stop it, but it didn't want to know." She smiled. "I had to jump over the fence to get away."

"Oh ye don't want to get in his way," Jim confided. "He's a big, black …" Jim used an impolite word reserved for a woman's reproductive organs, but delivered with virulence more appropriate to a Glaswegian football hooligan, renaming the judge who has unjustly sentenced him to twenty years' hard labour for an unpaid parking ticket.

I heard Lesley take a sharp intake of breath. "Really?" she enquired with a fixed smile.

"Oh yes," Jim replied, and he proceeded to describe his bull's Houdini-like escapology, coloured with generous applications of the same expletive.

My wife is no prude, but as each profanity landed, I watched her eyes become ever wider and her smile more fixed, until she looked like a waxwork model about to topple over backwards. Slowly she raised her arm, pointed a shaking finger towards a distant field and mumbled, "He went that way."

"Ah that's grand," Jim said, giving us another friendly wave. "See you soon!" And with that he set off in pursuit of his bovine escapologist, with his children following obediently behind.

My wife shook her head and went indoors for a lie down.

***

Two weeks later, our new stove was due to be delivered. It was the beginning of the school holidays and I was out all day teaching a group of junior golfers, so I missed the fun. Returning home, I strode excitedly into the sitting room, only to be confronted by an empty plinth.

"Where's the stove?" I asked.

"The driver took it back." Lesley rolled her eyes and tutted dramatically.

"Don't tell me they sent the wrong model again."

My wife shook her head. "No. It was the right stove, but the wrong driver."

"Huh?" I frowned in confusion.

"It was the correct stove, but they only sent one driver," she explained. "He was a little guy, smaller than me. He probably weighed about seven stone. I think they expected you to be here. I told him I had a bad back and I couldn't help, so he tried to unload it himself."

I momentarily closed my eyes in despair. "He dropped it?"

"Yep." Lesley nodded. "It fell from the tailgate and snapped one of the legs clean off."

"So we've got to wait for another stove to be delivered?" Lesley nodded.

"Another 14 days?" I asked.

Lesley nodded again.

I may have uttered a profanity.

***

Actually, it was three weeks before the replacement-replacement stove finally arrived. In the capable hands of two burly delivery men, it was safely transported through the house and onto the plinth, without even a skinned knuckle. Once the packaging had been removed, I admired our new purchase for a moment before asking the obvious question.

"Where's the chimney?"

The delivery driver pointed to the hole in the wall that led to our external chimney.

"No," I explained, "I mean the metal pipe that connects the stove with the chimney."

"Oh. You mean the stovepipe."

"Yes!" I clicked my fingers. "The stovepipe. Where is the stovepipe?"

He carefully checked the delivery docket before shaking his head.

"It's not on here." He shrugged. "Sorry."

When they had gone, I took a deep breath and telephoned the shop to report my missing stovepipe. The manager was polite, but unapologetic.

"I'm looking at the order here and the problem is, you didn't order a stovepipe," he confirmed.

"But I expected it to be included with the stove," I explained. "We have been waiting for this stove for weeks."

"Yes," he laughed. "A lot of people make that mistake."

"Why don't you just ask people if they want a stovepipe?"

"Well, sir, had you decided to use our stove-fitting service, our engineer would have supplied a stovepipe at the time of fitting."

"But you wanted to charge me €400 to stand the stove on the plinth that it is already standing on!" I replied.

"And to fit the stovepipe," he pointed out helpfully.

"Oh, so now I understand. The cost of the stovepipe is included in the fitting?" I asked.

"No, sir, the stovepipe and the fitting would have been extra," he told me happily.

"That's ridiculous. Where did you think the smoke was going to go without a stovepipe?"

"It's not our job to think, sir. If you wanted a stovepipe, you should have asked for one when you ordered the stove," he explained, as if he was talking to a child.

"Well, I know that now, don't I? Can you please order one as soon as possible?" I pleaded.

"Yes, sir, I will be delighted to. It should be here in around 14 days."

Even though it was summer, or what passes for summer here in Ireland, when the stovepipe arrived, I couldn't resist lighting a small fire, just to prove it worked. The carefully-fitted and sealed stovepipe worked splendidly, whisking the smoke up the chimney and helping the fire to draw in fresh air. Unfortunately, we hadn't anticipated the horrid smell and acrid fumes caused by the new paint slowly burning off the outside of the stove. This would pass, but not for a few days. So, with all of the doors and windows open to avoid suffocation, and the house slowly filling with moths, midges and mosquitos, Lesley and I sat in front of our new stove and enjoyed our evening watching television. Although we were sweating like a couple of sumo wrestlers, with watery eyes and raw throats, we were both happy to finally have our new stove – the heart of our home.

7. Playing Chicken

"Well, that was an interesting drive!" I exclaimed, walking into the kitchen.

"Why?" Lesley asked.

My wife was chopping vegetables and feeding them into a large pot on the stove, her witch's cauldron, as she prefers to call it. The air was thick with the delicious aroma of onions, garlic, pepper and several root vegetables slowly turning into soup. Apart from the bowl we would have later, soon it would all be frozen, ready for the winter.

"Every nutter and his dog was out on the road," I replied. "Perhaps it's just coincidence, but some days I can drive to Ennis without a problem, and the next I have to do an emergency stop every half mile."

"And today was one of those days?"

I nodded. "First there was Patch, attempting to commit suicide. Then a succession of homicidally-driven cars, all trying to kill me. It was like they were playing a game of vehicular Chicken. Twice I had to put a wheel off the road to avoid a collision. The second time some bushes scraped along the car. They scratched the paintwork."

"How can you tell?" Lesley quipped.

"The new scratches are a slightly different colour to the old ones," I explained. "I know a couple of new scratches don't really matter, particularly as I'm getting shot of that Ford shortly, but if I hadn't been on my toes, there could easily have been a crash."

"Don't be so dramatic," Lesley said, either to me, or the potato she was peeling. "What happened to Patch?"

"Old Tom's car was parked at the side of the road, on the flat bit before the cross."

"I don't know where you mean," Lesley said.

"It's about a mile along the road, there's a gun club sign. Just near where we saw that Marsh Harrier on Sunday," I explained.

"Oh yeah, I know now." Lesley nodded.

"Anyway, I think Tom has a field up there. I couldn't see him, but his car was there. I guessed Patch was hiding somewhere nearby, so I slowed down as I passed Tom's car. It's a good job I did, as that dog suddenly shot out from behind the car and ran straight in front of me. I left a lovely set of skid marks on the road trying to miss him."

"Silly dog!" Lesley said.

"The worst of it was, once I'd gone by, Patch started to chase me." I laughed. "My goodness that dog is fast. It took a while to lose him. I thought he was going to follow me all the way to Ennis."

"He's certainly seems fit enough to run that far," Lesley quipped.

I smiled and nodded. "Anyway, changing the subject. You know the new bit of road they're building near Spancilhill, down on the main road?"

"You mean the never ending roadworks with the temporary traffic lights?" Lesley asked.

"Yes, that's the one."

"Can't say I've even noticed them," my wife replied, in a rare moment of sarcastic wit.

The short stretch of tarmac engineering, to bypass a dangerous bend, had apparently been stalled since we moved to Ireland. This road was our only route to Ennis, unless we took a long detour. The traffic lights and long queues of traffic were an unusual sight in rural County Clare, but frustrating all the same.

"Any-who," I said, "there's a big orange warning sign at the end of the roadworks. It says 'Slow Excavation'. Today I noticed that someone had added the word 'Very' to it."

"Very droll." Lesley rolled her eyes.

"But wait!" I held up a finger. "This is not your British graffiti, daubed on with a felt pen or spray paint. This was a handmade sign, of exactly the same colour orange, written in the correct font, and lovingly attached to the top of the original sign with little legs."

"Good grief!" Lesley exclaimed. "Someone has too much time on their hands."

"Well, I think it's brilliant," I replied. "And the fact that the site workers had left it alone, shows what a great sense of humour we have in Ireland."

Lesley smiled then peered out of the window. "Did you get the chickens?"

"Three point-of-lay reds." I nodded, and then added. "As instructed."

"Don't be like that," she chided. "We don't have room for any more than six."

"It wasn't that. The Chicken Lady had some little white baby ducks," I explained. "And they were so cute!"

Lesley gave me a sideways glance, as if I'd suddenly expressed a desire to wear frilly pink underwear.

"Maybe later, when we have a bigger pen," she said, firmly. "For now, six chickens are plenty. Did you remember to take a box this time?"

"Ha!" I sniggered. "I'm not making that mistake again. Although next time, I'll park a little closer, or drive to Gort." The 'Chicken Lady' sold her wares twice a month, first in the village of Gort, and later in the day at Ennis market.

"Did you have a problem?" Lesley asked.

"I didn't realise there was car parking so near to the market, so I left the car behind Dunnes supermarket and walked across town."

"That's not very far to walk," Lesley commented.

"No it isn't," I agreed. "But on the walk back, I took a shortcut through Dunnes. Just near the back door, I almost bumped into this woman. She was coming in the opposite direction and we did that little dance where we couldn't decide which way to go. Suddenly she stopped and stared open mouthed. When I looked down at the box, I saw one of the chickens had stuck its head out to see where we were going."

"Perhaps it was bored," Lesley suggested, smiling. "So what did you do?"

"What could I do? From her face, I don't think the lady had ever seen a live chicken before. So I gently pushed its head back down, gave her a smile and a nod, and went on my way."

Lesley giggled. It sounded like distant wedding bells.

"Shall we introduce them to the flock?" she asked, drying her hands.

"Sure," I replied. "Let's do it!"

My home-built, self-contained chicken coop was theoretically perfect accommodation for three healthy chickens, but even moving it every day, couldn't stop our front lawn from looking like a battlefield. The solution had been to let the chickens out every day, where they could forage and scrape for food over a wider area. The risk of fox attacks was admittedly rather high, but they were cautious chickens and kept close to the house. When Diarmuid arrived to drill the well, his lads helped me move the coop to our meadow, where there was much more space. 'Out of sight and out of mind' is great territory for hungry predators, but likely to shorten the life of a chubby chicken to no more than a few hours. So, I visited our local hardware store, purchased several angle iron posts, two rolls of chicken wire, a packet of cable ties, and set about building a large cage to protect our flock.

To make more space, I left the original coop on the outside of the pen. The chickens had access to their new play area via a door, which we could leave closed if we were ever staying out late. Our three chickens, called Little, Nugget and Drumstick, had critically examined their new run and declared it to be well-constructed and of adequate size. In their gratitude, they even endured their first wing clipping with hardly a squawk of complaint. This involves catching each chicken in turn and trimming the flight feathers off one wing with a pair of scissors. It is an entirely painless process (at least for the chicken) although the operative is likely to get scratched and pecked a few times. Chickens can fly surprisingly well, and ours would easily have escaped their enclosure had we not grounded them.

With a larger pen at our disposal, we had decided to double our flock. Six chickens were not exactly extreme farming, but nonetheless, these were exciting times.

I collected the box from the car and carried it to the coop, where Lesley was waiting, along with Little, Nugget and Drumstick, who were patrolling the wire and hoping for a tasty treat. When we entered the cage, Lesley sprinkled some wild bird seed at one end of the enclosure, while I carefully placed the open box at the other end. Being the dominant hen, Nugget excitedly barged through the crowd and began selecting the best seeds to eat. Confident there was enough food to go around, the more laid-back Little casually sauntered along, pecking unhurriedly at whatever happened to be nearby. And the ever-friendly Drumstick, ignored the seed and squatted at Lesley's feet, with her neck arched and wings splayed, hoping to receive a fuss.

At the opposite end of the cage, I was trying, somewhat

unsuccessfully, to introduce our new chickens to their future home. Although they had been unceremoniously shoved into the box by the Chicken Lady, the hens now appeared to regard it as home. Aside from that brief moment of curiosity while I was walking through Dunnes, these new hens were showing no interest in leaving the secure warmth of their cardboard box. One of them had even laid an egg. I put it in my jacket pocket, making a mental note to avoid creating an accidental omelette.

"They don't want to come out," I said to Lesley.

"You'll have to pick them up."

"Owww!" I squealed. "One of them nipped me."

"They're probably not used to being handled," my wife said. "They might be a little defensive for a while."

"You think?" I mumbled, sucking the blood from the back of my hand.

"Tip the box a bit," she suggested.

I did. There was a scrabbling sound, but the chickens remained in situ.

"Give it a shake," she advised.

I did. Again, nothing happened. I imagined the chickens linking arms and bracing their feet against the walls as they fought against the laws of gravity. Tipping the box upside-down, I gave it a violent shake. Their makeshift home suddenly became three chickens lighter. There was a squawk, and an ominous thud.

"They're out," I said casually.

At the sudden appearance of three interlopers to her territory, Nugget spun around, fluffed up her feathers to appear as large as possible, and eyed them suspiciously. At the same time, Drumstick hid behind Lesley's legs, peering out uncertainly. The ever-casual Little just shrugged in indifference and continued feeding. The untidy pile of new hens quickly sorted themselves into a sub-flock, with legs at the bottom and heads at the top. For a couple of minutes they pecked about uncertainly. Then, as if by common consent, they huddled into a group and sat down in a patch of damp mud.

"They're probably not used to being outside," Lesley observed.

I tried waving my arms and shooing them along, but they just hunkered down and glared at me accusingly.

"Perhaps if we leave them for a while, they'll relax a bit and join the others," I suggested.

"I guess so," Lesley shrugged. We went indoors.

A little later, it began to rain. I checked on our new chickens several times throughout the afternoon, hoping they had integrated into the flock, but they remained stubbornly huddled in a group, looking sullen and damp. Around dusk, I checked again. Nugget, Little and Drumstick had gone to roost in the coop, but the new chickens were still sitting in the same puddle. I couldn't leave them outdoors all night, at the mercy of foxes, pine martens and owls. There was nothing for it, I would have to move them into the coop by hand.

"Oh, now you decide to run about!" I growled as the chickens scattered before me.

If I could only herd them into the caged part of the coop, then I could shut the door. The hens would still be wet and a little cold, but safe from predators. They may even climb the ladder and roost with the other hens. Using a slow walk combined with some cooing and a little gentle arm flapping, I set about herding the group of hens towards the coop. We almost made it, but at the last moment, Nugget descended the ladder to investigate the kerfuffle. In an instant, the flock split apart, moved to opposite corners of the cage, and eyed me suspiciously. Happy her work was done, Nugget returned to her bed.

For the next ten minutes I chased our new hens through a succession of geometric shapes. We did squares with rounded corners, straight lines, a trapezoid, a convex octagon and finished with a very pretty irregular decagon, all without ever getting my stretched fingers within an inch of a tail feather. Eventually, I tired of walking like an ape under a low tree and gave the whole idea up as a bad job.

Indoors, my wife glanced up from the chicken husbandry book she was reading and eyed her mud-speckled husband.

"Leave them until it gets dark," she said, tapping the page with her finger.

And she was right. In complete darkness, aided only by the failing glow from my bicycle lamp, I was able to pick up each hen in turn and transfer them to the safety of the roost, without so much as a squawk or ruffled feather. In the morning, all six chickens were feeding and scrapping at the earth as if they were lifelong friends.

"Shall we call them Faith, Hope, and Charity?" Lesley suggested.

"That's not what I called them last night," I growled.

"Be kind," she chided, nudging me in the ribs.

And so, despite the fact that they all looked identical, our new hens acquired names.

***

"That was an interesting drive!" I said, arriving back home from another long day of teaching golf. Lesley was still crippled with back pain and she wasn't getting out much, so I liked to bring home the odd interesting story to brighten her day.

"Go on," she said. "I'll bite."

"On the way to Ennis, I saw Tom's car parked at the roadside. I knew Patch would be hiding somewhere in a nearby ditch, preparing to spring out like a ninja greyhound. So I slowed down and got ready. Suddenly there he was, chasing my little car and trying his best to seize the bumper. He's incredibly fit and determined. I could see his eager face in my wing mirror, tongue lolling and eyes sparkling as he revelled in the chase. But in my rush to get away, I missed a gear change and he almost caught up with me. He equalled my pace and ran for several hundred yards, until I finally got onto a downslope and managed to open up a gap."

Lesley laughed. I continued the story.

"Just then another car passed, travelling in the opposite direction. Looking in the rear-view mirror, I was horrified to see Patch perform an athletic back-flip into the ditch, as if he had been struck by a bolt of lightning."

"Oh no!" My wife brought her hands to her face. "Did he get hit by the car?"

"That's what I thought, until I saw Patch was unhurt and chasing after the second car. I realised the aerial acrobatics were only his brain trying to change direction, without consulting his body."

"Silly dog," Lesley shook with laughter.

"There's more," I said.

"Go on." She pointed at the kettle.

I nodded. "When I got to the roadworks, I noticed the 'Very' amendment to the 'Slow Excavation' sign had changed. There was another perfectly manufactured addition. This one said 'Particularly'. I guess today was sign switching day or something, because when I was driving home I realised the sign addition had changed again. It was yet another impeccably crafted add-on that changed the sign to read 'Painfully Slow Excavation'. Isn't that just hilarious?"

"The workmen must be furious," Lesley smirked.

"You'd have thought," I replied, "but apparently not. There was a couple of guys wearing yellow safety jackets and hard hats taking a picture of it."

"You have to appreciate their sense of humour."

"Anyway," I continued. "I wish I'd had my camera handy a little later."

"Why?"

"As I was stuck behind several cars and two tractors, I decided to turn off and take the low road back to the house. The drive was going along swimmingly, until I encountered another traffic jam at the primary school."

"Surely the school is shut for the holidays?"

"There must have been some sports event on. Perhaps a hurling camp for the kids. The road was a minefield of haphazardly triple-parked cars and buses, chatting parents and wildly running children. All the traffic in both directions was stationary and the pavements outside the school were crowded with dozens of primary school children. The youngsters were all laughing and pointing, despite being held back by the hapless teachers and some parents desperately trying to block their view."

Lesley frowned. "What on earth was going on?"

I explained. "There were two dogs fornicating in the centre of the road."

My wife rolled her eyes. "I'll bet that went down well, directly in front of a Catholic school."

"That wasn't the half of it," I said. "Picture this. The female dog, was a pretty black collie. She had her head hung low and turned away, as if in shame. Meanwhile, the male dog, a scruffy beige mongrel with his tongue lolling and cross-eyed in ecstasy, proudly went about his business with everyone watching."

"Oh my goodness!" Lesley sniggered prudishly. "You'd have thought the audience would have put him off."

"Not at all," I added. "I think he was encouraged by the presence of the unplanned audience as well as the elderly nun, who was beating him on the bottom with her umbrella."

Lesley shook her head. "I don't believe you. It can't be true."

"Like I said," I shrugged, "I wish I'd taken my camera!"

8. New friends

Making friends can be difficult, particularly when you live somewhere new. Moving away from England and the people we knew, to begin a new life, friendless in a foreign country, was a daunting prospect. On our first scouting trip to Ireland, the landlady at our B&B (who we had lovingly named Mrs Menopause) gave us fair warning of the likely problems ahead.

"If you don't go to church, or hurling, or the pub, or the local livestock mart, you'll have trouble meeting people," she explained. Then she added, "We Irish are very friendly folk, but don't be surprised if we're not your friend. People here tend to keep a close circle. In Ireland, we put family first."

Forewarned, we started with low expectations, only to be pleasantly surprised.

Typically, friendships are formed because of shared interests, a similar history, or because of common values. With that in mind, it is not shocking that we have made friends with people who are immigrants, or have British accents, or share an interest in golf or gardening. My first friendship in Ireland was formed over the telephone.

Andrew Rich is a fellow golf coach. He lives close enough for us to meet, but not so close as to be a competitor. Convenient geography for a potential friendship. Initially, my telephone call was strictly business. Andy was just another name on my list. I was trying to pull together a group of similarly-minded colleagues, to share best practice, war stories, and perhaps to negotiate some better deals for consumables and insurance. We hit it off immediately, chatting about business, family and the weather. The conversation moved on to golf swing theory, at which point we became quite heated and passionate about our conflicting opinions. At the conclusion of that two hour-long conversation, we were already mates and arranged to meet.

It may surprise you to learn that golf coaches don't play much golf. Spending so much time on the course teaching leaves little room in the diary for golf as a leisure activity. When professional golfers play for money, either in competition or paid as a coach, we are working, so we take the game very seriously. But, if there ever is time, it's nice to kick back, play golf with like-minded friends, and perhaps take a few moments along the way to smell the roses.

Andy was waiting for me in the golf club car park. I'd pictured a tall and dashingly handsome man with an aquiline nose and great hair. In reality, he was somewhat shorter and a little wider than anticipated, with a thick shock of almost white hair, small ears, a rounded rubbery face supporting a bulbous nose and thin lips. For a moment, we eyed each other cautiously. I offered a tentative handshake, and as we clasped hands, Andy gave a huge smile and pulled me into a full-on man hug.

"Nick!" he bellowed in my ear. "Howareya?"

"Fine, fine," I wheezed, gasping for breath. "It's nice to meet you."

"And it's good to meet you too." He pointed to the boot of my car. "Get your clubs out, we're on the tee in ten minutes."

"Can't we hit a few balls first?" I asked, conscious of my stiff back, but Andy was already walking towards the clubhouse.

"Just to get warmed up," I pleaded.

He glanced over his shoulder. "No time for all that nonsense. Come on, hurry up!"

I heaved my kit out of the car, slipped on my golf shoes and sprinted after my new friend. A few minutes later, slightly sweaty and still panting, I fired my tee shot deep into the trees. I wasn't surprised, but I was disappointed. I'd hoped for better.

For a guy in such a hurry, Andy took an inordinate amount of time to hit his shot. I could easily have hit several golf balls, and done a still-life painting, while he stood twitching, shuffling, and waggling his club as he processed several mental checklists. Finally, he took a swing. Instinctively, I leaned backwards as his shot passed close to my nose, soaring majestically into the distance, but at right angles to the intended path, over some trees and out of bounds.

"Oh well," he said, smiling shyly. "You wanted to visit the practice ground."

His second effort took even longer, but delivered a marginally better result, landing somewhere within the grounds of the golf course. Game on!

After what turned out to be a relaxing and enjoyable morning playing some golf, we spent an hour on the practice ground discussing swing theory and shooting some video for the training session we were planning. Once our equipment was stowed, we headed indoors for a bite to eat. Unlike the cloistered red leather, oak-panelled silent rooms of old, this clubhouse bar was lively and bright. It had a high ceiling, light wood furniture, and huge windows providing panoramic views of the course. No white gloved toilet attendants, members' bar, or newspapers on sticks here. I smiled at the relaxed atmosphere. It was a refreshing change. Perhaps I was looking at the future.

Andy and I found an empty booth by the window, overlooking the first tee. I took a moment to take in my surroundings. Even though it was only Tuesday, the room was packed to the gills. Casual dress seemed the order of the day, with the emphasis on jeans and t-shirts. There wasn't a tweed jacket or military tie in sight. With so many people talking, and several children playing an ad hoc game of chase amongst the tables, the bar sounded like a school playground. I had to lean forward and raise my voice to be heard.

"Is it always this busy?" I asked.

Andy nodded, then pointed discreetly at the first tee. "Watch this," he whispered.

A gent in his mid-forties was making several energetic practice swings. His technique appeared quite sound. I looked at Andy and frowned. He mouthed, "Wait for it," and flicked his eye towards the tee. I looked again. The man was now preparing to hit his shot. As he addressed the ball, the casually confident athlete was suddenly transformed into a waxwork statue. He stood stiff and unmoving, for fully thirty seconds. Just as I began to speculate that he had suffered a seizure and was only waiting for a gust of wind to blow him over, the swing began. With an ugly lurch like a man attempting to kill a snake in a wardrobe, he heaved himself at the ball. A huge clod of earth flew up, making rather more forward progress than the ball, which bounced along the ground before hiding under a bush.

"Good grief!" I exclaimed.

"He's as rich as God," Andy whispered. "If he would only book some golf lessons, I could put my kids through university."

There wasn't much on the menu. Most people were eating

toasted sandwiches with huge piles of chips. The kids were just eating chips. Andy opted for an all-day breakfast. Being vegetarian, I chose egg and chips. The food was excellent. As we ate, Andy and I had the opportunity to share our experiences and chat about Irish culture.

"I ran a junior summer camp during the holidays," he said. "It was the usual format. Twelve kids, two hours a day for five days. I usually split the groups into two or three teams, each with a captain. We had little challenges and competitions throughout the week."

"But somehow, it always comes down to the last putt, on the last day?" I suggested, smiling.

"That's right." Andy pointed at me with his egg-stained fork. "It's a trick, but it keeps them engaged throughout the week and lets everyone contribute to the team success."

"That sounds like a good idea," I commented. "I'll have to think about doing a camp next year."

"There's a school holiday in the autumn. You could try doing one then," he suggested. "If you talk to the editorial team at the local paper, they'll usually put a free mention in their What's On section."

"Thanks. That's good to know."

"Anyway," he continued, "on the Friday morning, I asked the two team captains if they wanted to gee-up their troops with an inspirational speech. The first lad came forward and made a commendable effort, praising his team for their skill and perseverance, and promising victory if only they would continue to apply the lessons of the week."

"Oh very good," I exclaimed. "How old was he?"

"Only around 12," Andy replied. "Anyway, the second team captain stood in silence for a moment, presumably gathering his thoughts. Then he stepped forward, looked sternly at his troops and said, 'Don't cock it up!' Honestly, I laughed so hard, I thought I'd broken a rib!"

"Kids are so funny." I shook my head and wiped the laughter tears from my eyes. "Who won?"

Andy shrugged. "I don't remember."

I finished my last chip, savouring the flavour. They really were very good. In reality, I was just stalling for time, there were some delicate questions I needed to ask, but I was unsure of the best approach. Ireland is a Catholic country and I didn't want to upset my new friend. Mentally I shrugged, In for a penny…

"I wanted to ask you something. A cultural question of sorts," I said cautiously. "Are you religious?"

"Am I the feck!" Andy laughed.

"Oh good." I relaxed a little. "Tell me, what's gay football?"

Andy frowned. "What?"

"Gay football," I repeated.

"No idea." He scratched his head. "Where'd you hear that?"

"Some juniors I teach every Thursday after school. They're often late arriving, but they insist on leaving by five, because they have to go to gay football. I wondered what it was."

Andy started shaking, his eyes watered and his face turned pink. Suspecting he was choking on a piece of poorly-masticated sausage, I was about to render assistance, when he let out a laugh so loud that several people stopped talking at turned to look.

"Gay football!" He shook his head and wiped his eyes. "Gay football! Oh that's class, that is."

"What?" I was flabbergasted.

"It's not gay football, it's G-A-A football." Seeing my embarrassment, he added, "But a lot of kids would pronounce it in a way that sounds a bit like gay. The Gaelic Athletic Association or GAA, is an Irish international sports and cultural organisation. Their task is to promote indigenous Gaelic games like Gaelic football, camogie, and hurling, which is pretty much the national sport."

"Oh." I grimaced.

"It's an easy mistake to make," he confided, then added, "still bloody funny though."

I smiled. It was good to have a golfing buddy again.

Andy is a great guy. The sort of friend you can really depend on when you need a helping hand. Even though he had spent a good bit of his formative years living in England, he hadn't quite come to understand the British tradition of 'gallows humour', particularly in the event of someone's untimely death.

On our next meeting, as we waited for lunch at the golf club where I teach, I spotted a newspaper headline reporting the demise of some unfortunate, attempting to swim in the storm-tossed seas off the coast of Cork. Gleefully, I showed the paper to Andy.

"Look at this," I said, pointing to the headline. "Cork Man Drowns."

"Oh, how dreadful," he said.

"Well, yes," I admitted, "but it's funny though."

"Why's it funny?"

"Well, you know, Cork man drowns?" I said, with some emphasis.

"I know people from Cork tend to be a bit above themselves," Andy replied seriously, "but laughing seems a bit harsh, like."

"Yes, but he's a CORK man," I persisted, "you'd expect he would float."

Nothing, not even a hint of a smile.

"He probably couldn't swim, most people here can't." He glanced at the paper. "What was his name, perhaps I can get to the funeral."

I gave up. It was a price well-worth paying for his continued friendship.

***

"You must be Nick." The husky voice was female, distinctly British, and came from behind me. For an instant, I pictured a tall brunette, dressed in a slinky black cocktail dress with white gloves and a matching silk scarf. I imagined she would be wearing sunglasses, holding a cigarette in an ivory and gold holder, and sipping a martini. "Are you Nick?" The throaty question was repeated.

I looked over my shoulder, expecting to see the face of a movie star with lips the colour of cherries, but there was no one there. How strange. I was standing in a queue at the checkout of our local convenience store. Ahead was the liquor counter and beyond that, the frozen food section. I turned my head to the front again. A few yards away to my right, I could see Lesley by the newsstand. She was reading a gardening magazine while she waited for me to pay for our shopping.

"I see Lesley is waiting, so you must be Nick," the mystery voice said, almost in a whisper.

I turned again. Apart from an elderly man looking at the beer section, I was alone.

"I'm Christine," the voice said. It came from below.

I looked down. Looking up expectantly was the face of a short, round woman, with blonde hair, wearing a light beige raincoat. I'm not a tall man, just average height. Certainly not basketball material. But the top of Christine's blonde head hardly reached my chest. No wonder I didn't see her. She had dark blue eyes and a small nose. Suddenly, her face lit up with genuine warmth as she hit me with a full-beam smile.

"I'm sorry," I blurted, shaking my head. "You caught me off-guard. Yes, I'm Nick." I offered a handshake. "Lesley mentioned you."

Christine looked past me towards my wife. "Cooeee!" she shouted.

Several people turned to look. Lesley wasn't one of them. Giving her a gardening magazine is like sitting a toddler in front of the television and expecting them to notice an earthquake.

"Cooeee-Lesleeey!" Christine yelled, even louder.

My wife turned towards the noise and frowned in confusion.

I waved to attract her attention and pointed to Christine who was peering out from under my armpit.

Lesley beamed a smile in return, waved back and mouthed, "I'll wait outside."

I nodded and turned to face Christine. "I hear you work at the–" I began, only to be interrupted by a passing shopper.

"Hello, Christine. How's your daughter?" the lady asked, hardly breaking stride as she strode past.

"Fine, Geraldine. She's fine," Christine replied to her receding back.

"I believe you work at–" I began, only to be interrupted once more.

"Hi, Jenny!" Christine shouted, suddenly waving to someone I couldn't identify. "Are you coming on Sunday?"

"Of course," a distant voice replied. "I wouldn't miss it for the world."

As the queue shuffled forward, I tried chatting with Christine again, but soon gave it up as a hopeless task. She was clearly a popular and well-connected lady, who knew everyone in the shop by their first names.

I loaded my purchases into a spare box from behind the checkout and politely waited for Christine to finish her conversation with the cashier. The process of scanning the contents of Christine's shopping bag slowed appreciably as they chatted. At one point it stalled completely while they discussed the relative merits of probiotic yogurts. I marvelled at the patience of the other shoppers in the queue, who were not only unperturbed by the delay, but openly taking an active interest in the conversation. Such an unwarranted delay occurring at a supermarket checkout in England would surely have led to a riot. An involuntary smile spread across my face. Ireland was truly a wonderful country.

Christine's purchases were mostly liquid and her shopping bag clinked tellingly as we headed towards the exit. Lesley met us outside, and there I stood for the next 20 minutes. With my arms weighed down by our box of groceries, and too courteous to interrupt or walk away, I waited in silence while the two women chatted. Their conversation was animated and wide-ranging. Like any dutiful husband, I nodded respectfully and tuned them out.

We were in the centre of the village, standing on a wide section of the pavement to one side of the shop. Behind me was one of several pubs in the village. It was dark in colour with a low roof and a single door. The windows were blacked out, giving the building a foreboding appearance. It was probably a delightful place, but to me it appeared rather uninviting; reminiscent of a private members' club. Across the street was a large, blocky, grey building. A hulking gothic structure. There was no visible signage, just a string of leftover Christmas lights decorating the gutter. The building could have been a library, a court house, or a Masonic hall. It was a mystery. To the right was the hardware store that supplied everything we needed for our renovations. To the left was a second, smaller, hardware store. This shop sold everything imaginable that the first store did not stock. Should space aliens ever land their faulty ship in the centre of the village, I imagine one of these wonderful emporiums would have the part necessary to see them on their way.

As people passed, I heard snippets of conversations. It was like standing at an airport, except here everyone made eye contact and smiled. A few yards away, two women paused for a moment to chat.

"My goodness, isn't the traffic awful today?" one lady said.

"And the parking!" the second lady tutted. "I had to drive around twice, before I found a spot."

I counted. There were 11 cars parked in the village, with room for maybe 20 more. At one point, during my last week as an employee in England, I had been stuck in stationary traffic on the M4 motorway heading towards London. Aware of my intended route, my Satnav gleefully informed me that the traffic jam extended all the way to my home. A distance of 56 miles. I smiled inwardly at the comparison, happy to live somewhere considerably less congested.

Hearing my name, I tuned back into the conversation.

"Is that alright?" Lesley had asked.

I nodded. "Yes, dear." It seemed like the right thing to say. Lesley frowned.

Perhaps I was mistaken. Time would tell.

"But surely you drink cider?" Christine insisted.

"Sometimes," I lied, trying to avoid confrontation. The last glass of cider I'd drunk was probably when I was a student. My previous job had involved a lot of client lunches and team meetings. These were usually well-lubricated affairs held at expensive hotels or fine restaurants. Although Ireland has a culture of social drinking, since moving here, my alcohol consumption had fallen considerably. Boozy lunches, vintage port and expensive red wine were now a thing of the past. Admittedly, I had acquired a taste for Guinness, but three cans in a week would now be my definition of excess.

"Try this. You'll love it." As if it wasn't already heavy enough, Christine shoved a three-litre plastic bottle of cider into my box.

"Thank you," I grunted, "but you shouldn't."

For a moment we did the 'let me pay you – no, you won't' dance. I gave up and accepted the gift. The contents appeared to be cloudy and slightly green. The label read 'Devil's Bite'. In retrospect, it should have carried a better health warning. That evening, I casually consumed a pint as we watched television. In the morning, I couldn't make a fist, and my teeth were itchy.

"My goodness. That stuff's got some kick to it," I mumbled over my morning cup of tea.

"You said that last night," Lesley replied, rather louder than I would have wished. My head was pounding.

"Next time I'll use a wine glass."

"You said that last night too."

"Did I?" I asked.

"Yes!" Lesley shouted, or so it seemed.

I winced

"Now, hurry up and get dressed. We're having lunch at Christine's."

"Are we?"

"Yes!" Lesley rolled her eyes. "She invited us yesterday. You said it was okay."

So that's what I was agreeing to.

"Oh, right," I nodded (carefully). "Can we stop at the shop and buy some more of that cider?"

My wife tutted dramatically and rolled her eyes again.

9. Best laid plans

"We should make a plan," I suggested.

"Why?" Lesley asked, visibly frustrated.

I cannot function without my long lists with multi-level bullet points, three dimensional schematic drawings, and carefully calculated plans. My wife despises such restrictive covenants and dismisses them as meaningless trinkets designed to smother her free spirit.

"We need a plan," I persisted.

"There's so much to do. What's the point of drawing up another of your lists? Can't we just get on with it?"

I shook my head.

"It's because there's so much to do that we need to draw up a plan." I paused for a moment, trying to gather my thoughts. "Look at it this way. What do we want to get done this year?"

"Oh, what's the point?" Lesley growled and waved a hand dismissively. "Do your list, if it makes you happy."

I guessed my wife was probably feeling overwhelmed by the sheer size of the renovation job we were facing. Her bad back seemed to be considerably worse, despite her course of injections. Furthermore, my teaching business had become unexpectedly busy. With up to ten hours coaching a day and a commute, it was fortunate I didn't work weekends, or the renovation would never get done. Speaking softly, I put a calming hand on her arm.

"Humour me for a minute. Please."

Lesley huffed and began listing the jobs, each on a separate finger.

"I want a vegetable garden. The bit you've fenced off is the right size, but the ground is full of rocks and builder's rubble. I'd dig it over myself, but just now I can hardly tie my own shoelaces, let alone use a spade."

"Okay." I wrote it down. "What else?"

"I need a greenhouse and a polytunnel. It's too cold up here to grow much without some cover."

I nodded and added another item to the list. It wasn't the final list, just my provisional list, but it was a start.

"What else?"

"The garden needs to be landscaped and all the damage from the well digging needs to be levelled, so we'll probably have to get several loads of top soil."

"Mm-hmm." I nodded and added another note. "It sounds like we'll need another digger, probably for a few days."

"If we got a digger, would you be able to clear that embankment away from the south wall of the house?" I could see Lesley was warming to the planning process.

"I guess so," I replied. "I'd have to get a bigger machine. We'd probably need a rock breaker as well. That embankment isn't there for decoration. I suspect there is a load of rock under the soil."

"You're probably right. Old Tom said the front lawn was once a huge hill, until someone dug it out."

"There you go then." I added a three-ton digger and a dumper truck to my list. "If we time it right, I can do the front lawn, the landscaping, and clear that embankment over a long weekend."

"Don't forget all that old concrete needs to be removed from the courtyard entrance. You'll need to lower the floor level as well. Otherwise, you'll be banging your head once the roof is replaced."

"Okay. I'd better plan on keeping the digger for a week." I made a note. "Anything else?"

"The wing, obviously."

"Already on the list." I tapped pen on paper.

"Does that help?"

"Hang on a mo…"

While Lesley made a pot of tea, I squinted at my notes and gradually rearranged them into a workable list. It had numbers and headings and even a few little arrows. Workflow heaven.

"Okay," I said, "here's how I see it going."

My beloved wife held up a hand. "Just stick to the main points."

"O-kay!" I conceded. "First, we need to get the vegetable plot dug over."

"And quickly," Lesley added, "otherwise, it'll be too late to grow anything."

"The other day at lunch, Christine said she knew an odd-job man who would do a bit of digging. Cash-in-hand and all that. Can you phone her and ask for his details?"

"Are you sure?" Lesley asked, frowning. "I thought we were

trying to avoid spending on workmen."

"We are, but as long as he costs less per hour than I charge for golf lessons, it makes sense."

"Fine by me." She nodded at my list. "What's next?"

"Well, we need a sheltered area for storing firewood and building materials. So replacing the roof on the coverway is rather a priority. If I put a flat clearlight roof on the goat shed as well and connected it all together, we'd have around 500 square feet of covered workspace. What's more, if I added some doors, the goat shed would double as a pretty good greenhouse."

"That would work," Lesley nodded, "but what about removing all that rubble and concrete? Would the digger fit under the roof?"

"No." I pointed at my list. "That's why I drew this little arrow, and the clock."

Lesley tapped her finger impatiently. It was a warning. "Just get to the point."

"We need the digger first, so I can do all the landscaping and clear the rubble."

Lesley gave me a suspicious look. "You just want to play with the digger again."

"The delivery is half the cost," I pleaded, "so doing it all at once will save time as well as money."

"Boys' toys." She shook her head. "You're such a child."

"Honest." I tapped my list with the pen. "It's right here."

"You'd better hire the digger then."

"I'll have to source some topsoil first, and don't forget your mother is coming to stay. I'll try and arrange it all for just after she's gone back to England. How long is Muriel staying?"

"Just a few weeks," my wife replied nonchalantly.

"Weeks!" I squealed.

Lesley glared.

"Oh, how nice," I added.

"Okay," Lesley shrugged. "Is that all?"

"I guess so. By then we'll be into autumn and I won't be as busy teaching, so I can start work on the wing."

"Don't forget the water leak on the south wall." My wife tapped my list with her spoon. It left a little brown stain. I rubbed it with my thumb.

"I'll add it, but I'm hoping the water leak is fixed. I did it when you were away," I responded. "On the understanding that water flows downhill, I started at the top. There was no obvious leak, although there were some bird nests in the loft and the felting was damaged. It's a good chance that's where the water was getting in. I've removed the nests, blocked up the holes where the birds were getting in and patched the felting. Hopefully it's fixed."

"Hopefully?" She frowned.

I shrugged defensively. "Until it rains again – I mean proper Irish rain – we won't know for sure."

"Damn this fine weather," Lesley joked.

At this point, I should explain that there are 236 different types of rain in Ireland, ranging from light drizzle, to lashing fire hoses and everything imaginable in between. On this emerald isle, we can experience the soft humid mists which gently caress us on a warm day. Or big fat rain drops that instantly soak through my shirt when I've forgotten my umbrella. There's vicious cold-steel rain, which only falls when I'm wearing my best suit and trying to change a flat tyre.

Because Glenmadrie is at altitude, we are privileged to receive a very special version of the rain that, when wind assisted, can travel sideways and occasionally upwards. On the days when the house is enveloped in cloud or hill fog, the wind can push the water around, and even under, the best fitting doors, leaving large puddles in the porch, which we incorrectly used to blame on the poor dogs. This kind of soft mist can last for days, particularly when I need a dry day to cut the grass or paint the outside of the house, and over time this unrelenting moisture will cause any exposed or untreated wood to swell and warp. On "wild days" the rain will unremittingly pound the south end of the house, as if it were an ancient sailing ship rounding Cape Horn during a winter storm. This kind of weather will find even the smallest crack or cranny and force water into the house, and because water can easily follow unseen gaps in the stonework, leaks can be very hard to repair.

***

The following Monday morning, a dilapidated car pulled into the driveway. It was an ancient Toyota hatchback, so old the red paintwork had faded to a dull pink, except for the bonnet and roof, where the underlying rust had added a tinge of brown. I stepped outside, just as the driver was climbing out. He was a scrawny fellow, with long brown hair and a shaggy beard. He wore hiking boots, jeans tied at the waist with orange twine, a pink vest, and a green waxed jacket. Around his neck was a red knotted silk scarf, an exact match for the one he wore on his head. Although his attire was hardly suitable for a debonair scarecrow, it was adequate for digging Lesley's vegetable plot.

As I approached, he nodded and turned to face his car. I stood at his side and watched in fascination as the vehicle chuffed, wobbled and shook, like a poorly-balanced pink washing machine.

"I presume you've turned it off," I said, trying to break the ice.

He gave me a sideways glance and dangled his keys. "Fer a car that's so hard to start, it's surprisingly reluctant to stop."

His accent was English, with perhaps a hint of Welsh. The car thrummed, surged, rumbled and shuddered, then with a final wheezy cough, it slipped into silence.

"Should I call the undertaker?" I joked. "Or perhaps a mechanic?"

"Can't be wastin' money on mechanics," he said. "I've only just got it workin' right."

"You must be Ed, Christine's friend." I said. "You're here to do some digging."

"That's right," he replied, rubbing his hands together. "Where do you want me?"

Just then our front door opened and Lesley hobbled out. She was swiftly overtaken by Romany and Amber, both keen to meet the new visitor. As I was on my way to work, I made the introductions and left Lesley to direct Ed in the mysteries of digging.

Two hours later, I was back. I made Lesley a mug of coffee. She was lying on the bed, reading a book and trying to rest her back. Somewhere outside, music was playing.

"You were quick," she said.

"The lesson was cancelled," I explained. "The client phoned just as I got there."

"Oh, how nice," Lesley said sarcastically.

"I've got another lesson this afternoon, but it wasn't worth waiting so I came home."

"I wish I'd known," Lesley moaned, "You could have gone to Dunnes. I need strawberries."

"I can go after I finish teaching this afternoon," I suggested. "Why do you need strawberries?"

"I was going to make jam. Check to see if there are any short-dated strawberries on the reduced counter."

"Ooh lovely!" My wife makes the best jams and pickles. "Do we need any other shopping?"

"I'll make a list." She sat up, wincing in pain.

I grimaced. "How's your back feeling?"

"Sore." She nodded towards the window. "I tried to sleep, but that music was keeping me awake."

"How's Ed getting on?" I asked.

"You'd better check."

I found Ed leaning on a garden fork, smoking a suspiciously aromatic cigarette and bouncing his head to the rhythmic sounds of Bob Marley blaring out of an old battery-operated radio.

"Hello, Ed," I said, quite loudly.

He took the hint and turned the music down slightly.

"I thought you was working," he said.

"Me too," I replied. "It was rather a wasted trip. The guy called to cancel, just as I got to the golf club. Apparently, he suddenly remembered he had to go to a funeral."

"More like he just heard about a funeral," Ed sniggered.

"I don't understand."

"Over here, funerals are like a big social gathering," he explained. "Lots of free food, and a chance to catch up with mates and the local gossip."

"And comfort the grieving relatives," I added.

"Oh sure. That too. If the queue isn't too long. Most times there'll be a couple of hundred people."

"Good grief," I said, "that's a lot of invitations."

"They don't send out invitations. It goes in the paper and gets announced on the radio. You must have heard the Death Notices by now."

"Oh yes!" I snapped my fingers as the penny dropped. "We'd heard them, but I thought they were just like the obituaries in English newspapers. I hadn't realised they were an open invitation."

"So your guy was off to a party of sorts," Ed explained.

"Well, I guess it's nice that the relatives get so much local support."

"I suppose," he shrugged indifferently, "although I don't hold with it myself."

I changed the subject. "How's the digging?"

"Hard." He kicked at a small pile of rocks and rubble. "It seems this area was a dumping ground for any old rubbish. Apart from this lot, I've found several bottles, plastic bags, bailing twine, and these old glass syringes. I'm guessing the farmer did his own livestock injections. It's pretty common around these parts."

"Actually, this used to be a goat farm," I explained. "At one time there was a thriving business here, selling milk and cheese. Until it went out of fashion. These walls behind me were part of the old milking parlour. And the area you're digging was once the paddock, so the soil should be pretty fertile."

"That would explain the bones I keep finding." Ed picked a jawbone out of the rubble pile. "I hope this was from a goat and not some unfortunate what got killed up here."

"Perhaps we should call the police," I joked.

Ed flicked the bone over a hedge. "Too late now. That's gone and so are the goats."

"Not true," I said, holding up a finger. "Apparently, when the goat farm closed, the owner just opened the gate and let the goats run free. I see them sometimes, up on the cliffs overlooking the moor. They've gone feral, so they're rather shy, and cautious of boisterous dogs."

"I'm surprised they don't come back here looking for food," Ed said.

"Funny enough, one turned up just a few days ago. It was a large billy goat. We found it just sitting in the middle of our driveway."

"Was it friendly?"

"He was quite calm and inquisitive, but obviously cautious as well," I explained. "We decided he was head of the original herd, and simply decided to pay us a visit. That sort of thing is quite common around these parts, or so we've found. If it's okay for the previous owner to let himself in and make a cup of tea, why can't a billy goat drop by unannounced?"

"Seems fair," Ed laughed. "Did you get close to the goat?"

"Not really. I have never found goats and sheep to be particularly appealing creatures, perhaps it is the odd shaped pupils that give them a slightly alien expression, so I was being a little cautious," I confessed. "But this fellow was truly magnificent. Physically, he was very large, with a long grey coat, and he had the biggest set of goat horns I have ever seen. They came out horizontally about three feet, before curving up for another foot and a half. Including his head, the span of his horns was easily seven feet. If we could have tamed him, we would have had a unique and interesting way of drying our laundry."

"Did he say for long?" Ed asked.

"Not really. I guess we were rather a disappointment." I shook my head and frowned. "We tried to make friends, but he just huffed and casually walked away. I've seen him from a distance, over on the moor, marshalling his harem toward safer ground, but that visit remains a one-off."

"His loss."

I look at the vast expanse of, as yet, undug garden. "How long do you think this will take?"

"Oh, a while. Mustn't over-do it," he said, smiling, "health and safety and all that."

I laughed, but he wasn't joking.

Ed looked at his watch. "Time for lunch. I'm off to the pub. I'll crack on with this when I get back."

It seemed the digging would be a leisurely affair.

***

Later that afternoon, I finished work and headed into Dunnes. I am not an enthusiastic shopper. To me, grocery shopping is a chore, a necessary evil, something to be done with efficiency and alacrity. The only saving grace is the opportunity to converse with so many happy and talkative people. Another benefit of living in Ireland.

Armed with just a wire hand basket, I completed my small shopping list and headed to the reduced counter in search of strawberries, only to find I had struck pay dirt. Before me were some 30 punnets of perfect strawberries, reduced to less than half price. But how many should I buy? Despite my careful training and loving guidance, Lesley persists in populating her shopping lists with things like 'marg' and 'apples' when she actually wants 20 one-kilo tubs of Stork cooking margarine in the yellow plastic tubs and five kilos of cooking apples. Well aware that any failure on my behalf to return with the correct products or quantities can seriously affect my jam privileges, I decided to phone my wife for guidance. For a change, she answered on the second ring, demonstrating that she actually understood the concept of both 'phone' and 'mobile' – although previous evidence would suggest otherwise.

With surprise, I said, "Oh, you've answered!"

"Yes, you rang. What do you want? I'm busy," she replied. Always the loving wife.

"How many punnets of strawberries do you want? There's loads here, and they're all reduced."

"Get as many as you can, I'll make jam tonight."

I had a quick count.

"There's about 30 punnets, is that okay?"

"Oh yes! That'll be fine."

Clearly the little wire hand basket was no longer up to the job. I left the basket, along with my shopping, on the floor by the reduced counter and jogged to the front of the store where the trolleys are kept. Two minutes later, I returned to discover a Trainee Manager laboriously moving the strawberries into a low green wheelie bin.

"Hi," I said, giving him my least threatening smile. "I've just got this trolley so that I can buy those strawberries."

"Can't."

"Sorry?"

"Can't buy them," he said firmly.

"But I just went to get this trolley, so that I could buy them," I pointed at my basket that was on the floor by his foot. "Look, here's the rest of my shopping."

He inspected my basket of shopping as if he were trying to figure what type of exotic meal I was planning to construct with caster sugar, a block of cheese, toothpaste, four pints of milk, a can of air freshener, and some pile ointment.

"That stuff's okay, but you can't have the strawberries. Them's out of date."

"But I was just going to buy them, but I needed a bigger basket – well a trolley. See?" I gently rocked the trolley to demonstrate.

"Can't," he said, more firmly. "Out of date."

Before I was able to draw breath, he had a little eureka moment. He held up a finger to make his point.

"Health and Safety!"

I sighed.

"Look, they were on sale not three minutes ago, and if I'd had a trolley then they would all be in it by now, and I would be over there at the till paying for them right now."

"You're right," he said, "but now they're in my bin, and you can't buy them."

"Why?" I pleaded.

"Out of date," he repeated.

"*Caveat emptor*," I suggested.

"Cravat what?" he asked.

"It means, let the buyer beware. I'll take the risk."

"No. Rules is rules."

"But I don't care!"

"Doesn't matter." Then he repeated his mantra. "Health and Safety."

"Oh look, this is ridiculous. I want to buy all of your out-of-date strawberries. Just put them in my trolley and they'll be gone, and so will I. Poof! No worries!" Again, I tried my best reassuring smile. "By tonight they will be turned into the best homemade jam."

"Can't," he said again.

I shook my head, defeated in the face of intractable officialdom.

"So what are you going to do with them? Please tell me that they are going to feed the homeless or something."

"No," he said, "they've got to go in the bin. It's orders."

"You're joking!"

"No."

"So I can't buy them, but you're going to throw them away? Isn't that a dreadful waste?" I asked.

"No," he said, firmly, "it's Health and Safety."

My shoulders slumped in defeat, and then I had an idea.

"Not to worry," I said, "I'll just go around the back and pick them out of the bin."

"You can't do that!" He stared at me as if I had just cocked a leg and broken wind. "That would be stealing!"

I had a hard job explaining to Lesley why I came home without her strawberries. I did my best, but I'm not sure she believed me.

10. Delays and distractions

Even though we regularly visited Lesley's mother when we lived in England, and shared family holidays when our daughter was little, Muriel's first visit to Ireland was rather an unanticipated disruption to our routine.

When they were younger, Muriel and her late husband spent most of their free time at the pub. Not just for the drink, but for the company and chat as well. In the 15 years since she was widowed, Muriel had retired, stopped visiting the pub and gradually become less active, hardly ever leaving the house. Now she spent most of her days happily reading the newspaper, chatting with her neighbour, doing jigsaws and playing solitaire. It had been an effort to convince her to pack a bag and visit our new home. To ensure Muriel could have a worthwhile holiday, the originally planned weekend trip had morphed into a three-week stay.

Lesley had been eagerly looking forward to her mother's visit, anticipating some sightseeing trips, long walks with the dogs, and working together in the new vegetable garden. Quality time. The reality was so different it was almost shocking.

"I'm really worried about her," Lesley said.

It was Saturday morning and we were walking the dogs together.

"She seems fine to me," I replied.

"That's hardly surprising," Lesley huffed. "You've been out at work all week, from dawn to dusk. Apart from when we eat, you haven't seen her."

"I'm sorry I've been so busy. Do you want me to clear my diary for a bit?"

"It's not that. She won't do anything. All she's interested in is playing cards, she won't even read the paper."

"Why not?" I asked. "She reads the paper at home. I made a special trip to get a copy of The Mirror, just so she would feel welcome."

"You got her the Irish Mirror," Lesley explained. "She wanted the British paper."

"Oh. Sorry. But surely it's almost the same?"

"It doesn't matter," Lesley shook her head. "I think she's

struggling to concentrate. Being the wrong paper was just an excuse. We tried playing cards, but she got all muddled up. She's not even 70 yet."

"Oh."

"And she won't walk anywhere. Did you know Joanne had to get her a wheelchair at the airport? It was the only way to get her on the plane."

"But that's only a couple of hundred yards," I said. "Surely she could walk that far?"

Lesley shook her head. She seemed cross, but in reality she was upset to see her mother's health declining.

"The same thing happened when we went to Bunratty Castle on Wednesday," she said. "Luckily they had a wheelchair we could borrow, or that would have been a short trip."

"You pushed her around all day?" I exclaimed. "That can't have been good for your back."

"It wasn't," she snapped. "And now she doesn't want to go out again."

"She's probably embarrassed." I pulled Lesley into a hug. "I'm sorry, love."

"It's so frustrating!" Lesley sighed into my chest. "I thought we'd spend this time together in the garden. Mum loves gardening, or she used to. All she wants to do now is sit and play cards. Once, just once, I got her to come outside. I even got her a sun lounger to sit on. I thought we could chat while I worked. It lasted ten minutes and then she went back indoors. At this rate I'm never going to get my vegetables planted."

"Well, you can only do so much," I said. "I'm sure she realises you have work to do. Make the offer. She can join in, or not. It's up to her. You're not her babysitter. Otherwise, she can sit and watch television."

"I tried that, but she moaned that she was lonely. It made me feel so guilty."

"I'm sorry. I know it's tough seeing her get old."

"What if she gets worse, when she's back at home? How will she cope?"

"I think we're a long way from things being that bad, but when the time comes, we'll sort it out."

"How?" Lesley pleaded.

"I guess we could always move her over here, once the renovations are done," I suggested. "The wing could be a good granny flat."

Lesley buried her head in my chest. "That wouldn't be my first choice," she mumbled.

"Probably not Muriel's either, but at least we will have enough space," I said. "Let's go back. I'll ask her if she wants to go to the pub. She might enjoy a drink and some Irish music."

"I doubt it," Lesley huffed.

"Come on, don't be like that." I gave my wife another hug. "Let's try and make the most of her time here. She'll be home soon and you may not see her for a while."

Muriel agreed to go to the pub, albeit reluctantly. I picked a local bar, well known for its traditional Irish music sessions. We set off as soon as we had finished our evening meal. It was still light when we arrived and the pub seemed quite busy. As there were no nearby parking spaces, I dropped Lesley and Muriel at the door and left my car a hundred yards up the road. The evening was pleasantly warm. Several people were sitting on the benches outside the pub, listening to the music blaring from the windows. As I jogged up, an elderly man with a straggly grey beard, and wearing a leather Stetson hat, raised his glass in mock salute.

"No rush, sonny," he shouted. "There's plenty of beer left."

"Was it like watching a gazelle, striding across the plain?" I joked, slowing to a walk.

"More like a pregnant hippo," he mumbled into his beer.

Inside the pub, the noise was deafening. Despite the warmth of the evening, there was a peat fire burning in the hearth. In an alcove near the door, a group of sweating musicians were playing an Irish jig. There was a young girl with a fiddle and a slightly older lad with a guitar. An elderly man wearing a flat cap was playing a small black concertina with white ivory buttons. Next to him, another girl was playing a tin whistle, and a wild-haired man, with excitable eyes, was drumming the beat on a bodhrán. To my untrained ear, traditional Irish jigs seem to have a delightfully circular quality, with the themes rotating around endlessly, as if there was no defined ending or requirement to find one. For a moment, I closed my eyes and imagined the musicians flying around my head like a beautiful swan. At the head, the fiddle was leading the way, with the concertina breathing like lungs. On the wings, the guitar and tin whistle kept the tune aloft, while the bodhrán pumped the blood like a mighty heart. No wonder I was tapping my feet.

I helped Lesley carry our drinks to a marginally quieter spot at the rear of the pub. A blind man was sitting alone on a bench seat by a table. He was rocking his head and tapping his white stick in rhythm to the music.

"Is anyone sitting here?" I asked.

Eyes blank behind dark glasses, his pale face turned towards the sound of my voice.

"Sit where you like. I'm on my own." His accent was English, probably from somewhere north of Milton Keynes.

"Thank you."

Lesley and her mother squeezed onto the bench, I sat opposite on a hard wooden chair. An elderly man sitting on the next bench leaned towards Muriel.

"Are you enjoying the music?"

She looked away and sipped her drink.

"You're not from around here are you?" he asked.

Muriel nodded and sipped her drink again. The man shrugged stoically, drained his glass and headed to the bar.

"What's the matter?" Lesley asked, leaning towards her mother.

"I can't understand these Irish accents," Muriel complained.

"That's because he was German," I explained. I'm not sure she believed me, but he was.

The music stopped. To my untrained ear, there was no melodic conclusion to mark the cessation of the tune. As if by some prearranged signal, the musicians just stopped playing and took a drink. Everyone clapped. This being Ireland, they may have been applauding the beer. The music began again. It may have been exactly the same tune, I couldn't tell, but I didn't care. It sounded just fine to me. I tapped my foot and the blind guy tapped his cane. He leaned forward.

"The music's great."

I nodded. Silly me. "Yes," I shouted. "Very good." Why was I shouting at a blind person?

"Are you on your holidays?" he asked.

"No. We live here, but my mother-in-law is visiting."

"Where are you from?"

"Essex," I replied. "And you?"

"Manchester," he said, "but I've been here since '98."

"We just moved at the beginning of the year," I explained. "How do you find it over here? Can you get around okay? It must be hard."

"It's grand really. I don't have any work just now, but the social welfare is pretty good. I hitchhike most places."

"That's a lost art in England. Probably too many axe murderers," I joked. "I see lots of people hitchhiking over here though. Even young girls. I'm Nick, by the way."

"Garry." He drained his glass and went to stand.

"I'll get that," I said. The room was crowded. Perhaps he would appreciate avoiding the crush at the bar.

"Thanks." Garry sat back in his seat.

Over the following hour, I bought Garry another drink and we chatted about nothing in particular. Lesley joined the discussion. She's from Birmingham, so they shared some geographical DNA. Muriel remained stubbornly silent, resisting any attempt to draw her into the conversation. The music stopped and the players began packing away their instruments. People were leaving.

"I'd better get going," Garry said.

We said goodbye and I moved my chair to make space. A few minutes after Garry had left, I noticed he'd forgotten his white cane. I spoke to the barman.

"Excuse me. The blind guy left his white cane behind. Do you know where he lives?"

"What blind guy?" he asked, frowning.

I pointed to the corner. "He was sitting there. His name is Garry."

"Garry?" he exclaimed. "He's not blind!"

"But the cane…" I stammered.

The barman glanced to the corner and sniggered. "That's a stick for opening the roof vent."

"But he was wearing dark glasses," I pleaded.

"He thinks wearing sunglasses at night makes him look cool," the barman explained. "Garry's not blind, he's just an eejit!"

105

***

A few days after Muriel returned to England, the topsoil we needed to resurface the garden arrived. This was the last item on my list before I could order the digger and begin landscaping. With Ireland's economy booming, there were new roads and houses popping up like mushrooms on a compost heap, so I had no difficulty sourcing 20 tonnes of unwanted topsoil – for a price. After several back-and-fourth phone calls, I successfully guided the driver to Glenmadrie.

The lorry was huge. Not articulated, but long and high, with a triple rear axle. I doubted it would even fit up our curving driveway, but the driver did a magnificent job backing up and turning, ready to dump our soil in exactly the right spot. The top of the lorry was open, like a dumper truck and I could see the soil piled high above the hopper.

"Blimey!" I said to Lesley as we stood watching. "We may have too much soil."

"Don't worry," she replied, "we'll never have too much top soil. I'll always find a use for it on my vegetable garden."

"Here we go," I pointed. The driver was manipulating some buttons and, with a hiss of compressed air, the hopper slowly began to tilt. For a while nothing much happened, then with a whoosh, the soil poured out the rear flap. Lesley and I shared a look.

"Where did it all go?" she asked.

I had been expecting a huge pile. Not quite on the scale of an Egyptian pyramid, but high enough to encourage some climbing and perhaps the planting of a flag. In reality, once tipped, 20 tonnes of fine topsoil was little more than a muddy nipple, ten feet long and about as high as my hip pocket. Looking at our expansive, battle-scarred lawn, and then at our pile of top soil, I did a quick mental calculation.

"We're going to need another load," I said.

"Several," Lesley added, confirming my fears.

"I'd better phone up and postpone the digger."

***

To fill my time before I could begin landscaping, Lesley tasked me to repair our fences. At one time our property was fenced well enough to keep hungry goats in and curious cattle out. Over the years since the farm closed, much of the fencing had fallen into a state of disrepair. Furthermore, we wanted to create an effective barrier to separate the grazing on the meadow from our vegetable garden and lawn. Feeling all macho and manly, armed with several rolls of fencing wire, dozens of wooden posts and various hammers and nails, I strode off to do some fencing work. Left to my own devices, it would take an afternoon to complete the task, but Romany had other ideas.

As an older dog, Romany avoids strenuous exercise, preferring to sleep all day, snoring like a drunken sailor, or sitting in her favourite spot on the hill and watching over her territory. Often she will just woof at the world and then at her own voice, as it echoes from the cliffs on the other side of the valley. Lhasa Apsos have a stubborn streak about a mile wide, and Romany is always eager to demonstrate her obstinate nature, particularly when she is confronted with a closed door.

Imagine a nice warm summer's day. I'm climbing around on the roof doing something important and Lesley is taking a bath to ease her aching back. Without fail, and at this most inconvenient moment, Romany will go out the open back door, have a pee, and walk all the way around the house to the closed front door. There she will stand, pig-headedly barking until someone lets her in. She will never walk back around the house to the open back door, but will remain rooted to the spot, barking at this inconvenient obstruction. Try as I may, this persistent *ark, ark, ark* cannot be ignored as it will not stop, or even change in tone or frequency. So I find myself climbing down from the roof to let her in, usually at exactly the moment Lesley climbs out of her bath to do the same thing. Oblivious to our dagger-like stares, Romany will trot past us and into the lounge where, after circling her bed three times, she will flop down with a satisfied grunt and instantly fall asleep.

"Perhaps she needs some training," Lesley suggested, "so she learns to go back to the open door herself."

"What do you have in mind?"

"Next time she does this, just leave her alone. In the end she'll just give up."

"I doubt it," I said, bravely contradicting my wife, "but we'll give it a try."

And so it was while I was happily repairing fences up on the meadow, Romany circled the house and started barking at the closed front door once again. Lesley was away shopping in Limerick, and I was theoretically far enough from the house to be unaffected by the persistent barking, so I decided the time was right to enact our plan.

At first I ignored her barking, just as Lesley had suggested. But even at such a distance the sound seemed to carry remarkably well. Furthermore, each bark was amplified by a following echo as the noise reverberated from the cliffs on the moor. How can such a small dog produce such a loud bark? Initially the noise was just annoying. Then it became grating, and soon each *ark, ark, ark* made me flinch in shock, like cold water on a sensitive tooth. I tried singing some popular songs to cover the noise, but this presented two problems. First, my singing voice is not my greatest strength. In truth, it doesn't even make the top twenty on Nick's List of Assets, and probably sits somewhere below 'doesn't moan much when forced to go shopping'. Secondly, Romany's incessant barking had induced some sort of temporary amnesia in the part of my brain where I store song lyrics. After two renditions of 'Happy Birthday to Me' and three of 'God Save the Queen' I gave it up as a bad job.

I'm a doggedly-determined individual, but the determined doggy was winning this battle. After an hour of relentless woofing, I finally cracked. I was getting a headache. Each bark was now digging into my brain like a hot needle. I could take it no longer. With a sigh of defeat, I downed tools, climbed the fence and trudged my way back down to the house. At the front door, Romany eyed me with open contempt for daring to delay her journey. With the door open, she trudged indoors, circled her bed three times, and snuggled down for her afternoon nap. I took two headache tablets and made a cup of tea. In the blessed silence I made a pledge – whenever Romany is woofing at the door, I would let her in. Sometimes it's good to know when you are beaten.

11. Breaking ground

With our final load of topsoil delivered, it was time to start on the landscaping. With some determined negotiating, I got a special price to hire a three-ton digger with caterpillar tracks and a rock breaker attachment. Along with it came a large dumper truck, so I could move any excess rubble up to the quarry. Even with my discount, the rental and delivery cost was more than I paid for the uncomfortable Ford car I brought over from England. Such an outlay was going to put a dent in our renovation budget and it couldn't be repeated. I cleared my diary for the week, so I could complete the task.

Dressed in my purple overalls, ear defenders and Wellington boots, I got to work. I had never driven either type of vehicle before, but I soon got the hang of things. The digger was, in principle, the same as the machine I had used to dig the trenches, only on a much bigger scale. The dumper truck was enormous, with a powerful engine that sounded like an American sports car. It had rear-wheel steering, which was a bit fiddly to master, but I soon got the measure of things and had tremendous fun roaring around like a proper builder. It was all very macho. Unfortunately, the novelty wore off pretty quickly.

Barely an hour after I began work, the low, steel-grey cloud split open like an over-ripe tomato and cold rain began pounding the soil. The weather was miserable. It lashed down with freezing rain every day, turning the garden into a sea of sticky mud. Although I was protected from the rain inside the unheated cab of the digger, every fifteen minutes I had to drive the dumper truck to the quarry so I could empty another load. Sitting high up and fully exposed to the elements, I was soaked through in a matter of seconds. Returning to the relative warmth of the digger was a blessed relief. But as I squelched my soggy bottom onto the seat, the evaporating water quickly fogged up the windows. Soon I was cold, miserable and covered in sticky mud. After a couple of hours, I was shivering so hard I could hardly operate the controls.

"This is madness," Lesley said, as I stripped off my clothes and tried to rub some life back into my limbs with a fluffy towel.

"G-g-g-got to c-c-carry on," I said through chattering teeth.

"W-w-w-we've only got a week to finish this."

"Wait until the rain stops," Lesley suggested, poking the soggy pile of clothes with her slipper.

I shook my head. "T-t-this is forecast to carry on all week. I'd b-b-better keep g-going."

"You can't keep getting soaked like this. You'll run out of clothes."

"Y-you're right." I held up a wrinkled finger. "I've g-g-got some old g-golf waterproofs somewhere. I'll d-d-dig them out. They'll keep me d-dry."

Actually, I had two rain suits, which was even better. While I wore one, the other could be drying off indoors. As I sloshed and slid my way through the landscaping work, Lesley fed my wet clothes into the tumble dryer, and kept me supplied with hot drinks and encouragement.

There were four tasks on the 'must do' list and one 'would be nice'. The walkway around our courtyard was an untidy and illogical muddle of concrete platforms and steps, much of it more than two feet thick. Removing it would allow me to lay a new floor, much lower than before and all at the same level. The second job on my list was to dig out a 30 yard trench through the head-high embankment leaning against the south end of the house. This would create a new path into the house from the garden, and remove a possible source of dampness. My third task was to level a 250 square foot area of land ready for our polytunnel and a second vegetable garden, Finally, I needed to repair the damage done by the drilling crew and spread over a hundred tonnes of top soil.

The weather was truly miserable, yet I had no choice but to crack on. By working gruelling 16 hour days, constantly cold and wet, I finally completed each task on my list. Along the way I shifted several tonnes of rock, concrete, shale, and rubble to our quarry, where it became no more than a rocky dimple, hidden within the walls of that huge excavation.

My boys' toys were due to be collected by the hire shop on Monday morning, and with all the landscaping finished, I had just enough time on Sunday to address the final item on my to do list.

Both of our previous homes had garden ponds, which are excellent for attracting wildlife like frogs, newts, and dragonflies, so we were keen to have something similar at Glenmadrie. However, as we now had much more space, this pond would be considerably larger. There was a perfect location in the boggy south corner of our land, where there was a natural spring just beneath the surface. I figured if I dug a big enough hole, it would gradually fill with water and become a permanent feature. Lesley wanted the pond in a doughnut shape, with a little island in the centre, which would give predator protection to any visiting wildlife. Using some wooden stakes, Lesley had marked out an area of around 40 by 30 feet.

Starting the digger, I scooped my first load of soil, only to meet with some unexpected resistance. As I was quite close to several large trees, I assumed I'd snagged a root, so I decided to press on until it snapped. I was happily working the controls to manoeuvre the digging arm up and down when something odd caught my eye. With each tug of the digger, a telephone pole on the road above was rocking a full six feet. I was obviously pulling on an underground telephone cable.

A quick inspection revealed the problem. To take the shortest route from the telephone pole at the roadside to the pole by the house, the engineer had simply buried the cable under four inches of soil as it ran across my land. As I broke ground for the pond, I had unwittingly snagged it with the shovel on the digger. As the telephone reception seemed no worse than usual, despite the cable being stretched by three feet, I just buried it again and started my pond two feet further to the west.

By bed time on Sunday night, I had created a large circular pond with gently sloping shallow sides, deep areas down to five feet, and a nifty island in the middle. As if by magic, the following morning our pond was full to the brim with crystal clear water and already home to some happy pond skaters, several frogs and a couple of ducks. Job done!

***

Living in such a remote location, far from the convenience of city shopping and the security of knowing help is only minutes away, can have its drawbacks. But after a few early mistakes, we soon learned to plan ahead for essentials like milk, butter, bread and fuel. On the up-side, the land around our mountain-top home is an oasis for wildlife.

As summer arrived, each day brought a fresh sighting; the exciting discovery of another species sharing our new home. Close to the house we have seen deer, foxes, mink, and pine martens, as well as the tracks of badgers. The trees in our wood and the nearby forest, and the beautiful but desolate moorland, provide good nesting for kestrel, merlin, game birds, and several species of owls and ducks. Sometimes, we have caught a glimpse of the ever-elusive hen harrier.

This rare raptor is surprisingly large, but rather shy. When we spot the male, it is usually just a fleeting impression of a white flash on black wings, as he whips past our heads and disappears over the hedge. Such a sighting is a sure sign his lady is nearby, hidden amongst the heather. The male will dodge and weave and swoop above her in a display of his aerial prowess, gradually winning her appreciation with his low-level acrobatics. As a closing token of his affection, he will bring her a gift. Not a ring for his love, but a dead rodent. Once she accepts, the union is made and they will fly together until she has laid her eggs. On a fine Sunday morning, Lesley and I were privileged to see this mating pair riding the thermals. With our heads back and necks aching, we watched for an hour as these beautiful birds bonded in flight, spiralling slowly upwards. Like newly-weds dancing together for the first time, they turned in lazy circles, rising on a column of warm air, until they were just a dot in the azure sky.

Perhaps my favourite aerial artist is the skylark. These tiny birds are as synonymous to summer as strawberries, sunburn, and ice-cream. After wintering in the valleys, they become active in early summer, when insects are prevalent. Easily heard, but difficult to see, a tiny spot hovering high above the moor. In an untidy mass of fluttering wings, they hang almost stationary for minutes on end, whilst delivering the most beautiful songs I have ever heard. A skylark's tune is so melodic, complicated and beautiful, even the most talented of violinists would fail to emulate it.

Whenever I hear a skylark, I am instantly transported back to a Sunday morning during the hot summer of 1975, when I was still a lanky teenager, all knees, elbows, pimples and hormones. It was during a round of golf with my father near Cromer, in Norfolk, England. We were taking a break from the heat to drink some tea from a flask and eat a sandwich. As we sat together on a grassy mound by the cliffs overlooking the sea, we watched a skylark performing its eloquent rhapsody, and my father told me exciting wartime tales of his time as a Mosquito pilot. Seeing a skylark today refreshes my memory and makes me ponder if some small part of him is in that tiny bird, singing in delight as he swoops through the air.

While the skylark is the musician of the sky, the swallows are the undisputed masters of feathered flight. Lesley was gardening when she spotted our first pair. Their tweeting calls, like small screams of delight, caught her attention. By the time I arrived home from work, their number had swelled to six, swirling around the house, searching for a suitable nesting spot.

"I'm so pleased we have swallows," Lesley said. "They are such fun."

"I know," I said. "It's remarkable to think they've just flown all the way from Africa."

"Watch where they nest," she said, with a note of warning. "And make sure the renovations don't deter them nesting again next year."

"Don't worry, I'll be careful."

Our growing community of swallows are endlessly entertaining, as they swoop and whirl, like fighter pilots defending their airfield from the attacking hordes. However, the greatest flying displays at Glenmadrie are provided by a tiny mammal.

I spotted them first. It was just after dusk one warm summer evening, when I noticed their silent fluttering flight, like leaves floating through the air. Excited as a child on Christmas morning, I summoned my wife. Emerging from the bright lights of the house into the comparative darkness of dusk, Lesley squinted at the sky.

"What?" she demanded.

I pointed skywards. "Just watch."

"I can't see anything."

"There!" I jammed my finger at the sky.

"Where?" she asked. "I can't see anything. What am I looking for?"

"Bats!" I declared, proudly. "We have bats."

Over the following week we identified two bat colonies on our land. One group roosts within the roof at the north end of the house and the second had made its home somewhere in the rock of the old lime kiln, overlooking our quarry. These welcome friends can eat millions of the devilish midges each night, by diving and twisting in delightfully energetic aerobatics. I love to stand and watch the little pipistrelle and brown long-eared bats, engaging in their adventurous displays, particularly when the air is so still I can hear the clicks and whistles as they chase down their prey. Bats are harmless creatures and welcome to nest in our loft, although we were slightly disgruntled the night one broke into the house.

It was a hot night, or what passes as hot here in Ireland. About 2 am, I was rudely awoken after a young bat climbed in through an open window, and began flapping in panicked circles above the bed. Lesley came to investigate the cause of the kerfuffle, adding Romany and an over-excited Amber to the confusion. With the dogs locked away, we discussed our options.

"Perhaps, if you leave it alone it will fly out by itself," Lesley suggested.

It didn't.

"We'll wait until the morning. Once it's roosted, I'll be able to catch it and put it outside," I said.

"You can't do that. If it isn't back in its roost tonight, it may die."

"Well then. We'd better catch it!"

It was half an hour before we managed to snag it with a tea towel and gently return it to the safety of the night air. Bats are lovely creatures, but up-close, this little pipistrelle had a face only a mother could love. It was like a small bulldog crossed with a fish and wearing Mr Spock's ears. A triumph of evolution. What interesting creatures.

That first year we spotted many new arrivals at Glenmadrie. Every bush and tree seemed alive with birds, either nesting, feeding, or looking for a mate. Some even took to the roof.

The first was a pied wagtail. I was on a ladder cleaning the guttering when this cheeky fellow came over to see what I was doing. Fresh back from his winter holiday in the south of France, this little black and white bird was wandering around on the roof when my head popped up. For a few minutes, I watched in fascination as he trotted up and down the roof, sometimes within inches of my face. He picked at the moss, looking for bugs, and made sudden lunging runs whenever something tasty flew by. Their name comes from their distinctive tail wagging, which he demonstrated to great effect.

The thick green moss on our roof is a popular attraction for several species of birds – all apparently on a rota. Whereas the magpie has the morning and the wagtail the afternoon, one less welcome individual chooses to visit during the night.

The nesting season at Glenmadrie is heralded by the arrival of dozens of cuckoos. Each calling for a mate, in an ever-louder competition that reverberates around the surrounding hills. These are fascinating birds. The parasite of the avian world, planting their eggs in the nest of some unsuspecting birds who will eventually raise the young as their own. Cuckoos are so well evolved, they even lay eggs of the exact colour as those of the birds they have chosen as surrogate parents. When I'm working up on the meadow, it's great fun to mimic their call with a cheeky whistle. There is an instant and confused silence, followed by an angry reply.

"How dare you come into my territory?"

Sometimes a cuckoo will fly over, trying to spot the interloper, not suspecting it is me. If I'm in a particularly wicked mood, I'll keep up the game for several hours. It's very entertaining, but payback can be a bitch.

A few days later, we were treated to a visit from a night cuckoo. This dubious honour involves the bird sitting on our roof and delivering the loudest imaginable calls throughout the night, regardless of any amount of shouting and swearing by the occupants. The star-crossed bird will continue this insidious torture every night for up to a week, pausing only long enough for us to drift into sleep for a few moments, before he delivers an extra loud cuck-oo to startle us awake again. Oh, the joys of country living!

***

In Ireland, late night calls are not the exclusive preserve of the cuckoo. The harsh ringing of the house phone startled me into some semblance of wakefulness. I turned on the light and squinted at the bedside clock. A few minutes before 12. "This can't be good news," I thought, dragging on my dressing gown and heading for the stairs.

"The phone's ringing," Lesley shouted helpfully.

The dogs joined in, adding their barks to the clamour. Sprinting across the lounge, I grabbed the handset.

"Hello?"

I listened in dread. Was my mother ill? Or Muriel? God forbid something had happened to Joanne.

"Nick?" A familiar voice. It had an Irish accent, but I couldn't place it.

"Hello?" I repeated.

"Nick!" The voice said. "You're a hard man to find."

"Who is this?" I asked, rubbing the sleep from my eyes.

"It's Vincent," he replied, as if he were a close relative. "From the golf club. You gave me a lesson yesterday."

"Who is it?" Lesley whispered from halfway down the stairs. I waved her back to bed.

"Oh yes, I remember," I said, doing my utmost to be polite. "Vincent, from the golf club."

"I wanted to ask you which was the best driver for me to buy," he said.

"Isn't it rather late?" I asked, hoping he would get the clue.

"Not at all!"

"I was in bed," I added.

"Are you ill?" he asked.

"No, I'm…" I took a deep breath and spoke calmly and politely. "Clients don't usually call me at home, and certainly not at this time of night."

Vincent laughed. "Ah, not to worry. You're in Ireland now!"

It took another 40 minutes to end the call without upsetting Vincent, or causing an international incident. After three more similarly rude awakenings, I had to temporarily unplug the phone. Vincent, and several other well-meaning clients, continued to make midnight calls on my mobile phone, but that device was switched off at bedtime.

There is an unwritten rule in Britain that, except in an emergency, you don't phone someone before 9 am or after 9 pm. Within the financial services industry, this is actually a written rule. As we were quickly discovering, Ireland has a somewhat more relaxed attitude to such infractions. Lesley was scathing at my politeness in the face of such an apparent breach of etiquette. She demanded I tell Vincent to stop phoning at such a late hour, and became rather annoyed when I declined. Later she refused to believe that he had acquired our home phone number by simply calling directory enquiries. I solved the problem by changing our number and going ex-directory, but it was a thorny subject for a while and Lesley remained unforgiving. However, what comes around, goes around.

Two weeks later, I was awakened again by the insistent ringing of the house phone. "This can't be good news," I thought. "It's a new number. Only family would call at this late hour."

"Hello?" I said, cautiously.

"Nick!" The voice bellowed in my ear. It was familiar, female and obviously slurred.

"Hello, Christine," I said.

"What a co-hinsidence, you calling! I was jush thinking about you," she laughed.

"You phoned us!" I pointed out.

"Did I?" She sounded quite drunk and very confused. "Is Lesley there?"

"Who is it?" Lesley whispered from halfway down the stairs. I waved her forward.

"She's right here, Christine." I handed over the phone and mouthed, "She's your friend."

With an evil smile, I headed back to bed.

12. Amber's addiction

"Why don't you come in for a cup of tea?" Lesley asked.

Even though the hill-walking season was drawing to an end as autumn closed in, on nice days like this, we would still see a few groups every Sunday. Most would pass with a cheery wave as they trudged up the lane behind our house. Others would walk by quickly, determined faces staring at the path ahead, perchance aided by Amber, growling harmlessly at their heels like an overgrown hamster. But sometimes they would pause a moment, take in the scenery, and rest their weary legs after the arduous 800 foot climb. Any group of strangers looking over our fence would immediately attract the attention of two excitable dogs, and sometimes become engaged in casual conversation by Lesley or me. We considered such interruptions to be a delightful feature of our more relaxed lifestyle and an opportunity to make new friends.

"I've just made a fresh batch of scones," Lesley added, perhaps conscious we could easily be mistaken for deranged axe murderers.

The family of walkers shared a knowing look. Obviously the mention of fresh scones overrode any lingering doubts they may have had about our sanity.

"That would be lovely," the lady said.

While the kettle was boiling, we made our introductions. The family had been visiting County Clare for a holiday, and decided to finish the week off with a strenuous hill walk. Nikki was English, a nurse from Oxford, now working in a hospital in Waterford. Her husband, Brian, was originally from County Cork and a computer technician. His job involved a lot of driving, so he liked to put on his hiking boots whenever he could. They had two daughters, twin sisters, around 12 or 13 years old. They both had bright red hair, blue eyes, pale skin and freckled noses. They couldn't be more Irish if they were wearing green and dancing a jig.

We all sat at the kitchen table, but once the scones were consumed, the two girls knelt on the sitting room floor and played with Amber.

"Your daughters are lovely girls," Lesley said, "and so polite."

"Thank you," Nikki replied.

"Since we moved to Ireland, we've noticed how the children here are much better behaved," I said.

"Perhaps it's the Catholic schooling," Brian suggested.

"Oh yes. I remember!" I said, laughing. "I went to a convent school in Scotland. It was a bit violent at times, but it taught us to be polite. You don't mess with those nuns."

"A whack on the head with the blackboard rubber?" Brian suggested.

"Usually it was a hard slap on the knuckles with a ruler," I explained.

"Those were the days," he said quietly. I don't think he was feeling particularly nostalgic.

"How long have you lived here?" Nikki asked.

"Almost nine months," Lesley said. "We're just getting used to it."

"So you're still Blow-ins then?" Nikki joked.

"And always will be," I replied. "I suppose you are as well."

"Absolutely! Even Brian is considered a Blow-in, being a Cork man living in Waterford."

"So you haven't experienced St. Patrick's Day then?" Brian asked.

"Not yet," I said. "It's in March, isn't it?"

"The 17th," Brian nodded. "Out here there'll be lots of parades and marches, with floats for the kids. St Patrick's Day is great craic. But in the cities, it seems to be an excuse for some folk to get absolutely hammered and act the maggot."

"Get drunk and be stupid," Nikki translated. "I expect by now you know what craic means?" She pronounced it krak.

"Craic means enjoyment, doesn't it?" Lesley asked.

"Pretty much," Nikki said.

Brian nodded. "Craic is a Gaelic word. There's no exact English translation. Some people think understanding what craic is all about is a good test of your Irish credentials. But it's not just about having a good piss-up. I guess the closest definition is fun, but there is an implied element of social connection as well, and perhaps a lot of dancing. The Irish phrase *ceoil agus craic*, meaning music and fun, is probably pretty close to the best definition."

"Thanks," I said. "That's one mystery solved."

"Tell them about Martin," Nikki said.

Brian frowned in confusion.

"When he went to Boston," she prompted.

"Oh yes!" Brian smiled. "My brother went to America for St. Patrick's Day. He was with a couple of Irish mates. There didn't seem to be much going on, other than the parade, so they went into some side streets in hunt of a good party."

"As you do," Nikki added.

"So they're going about asking these strangers, if they knew where they could find a good party, when this guy pulls out a gun and arrests them."

"Good grief!" I exclaimed. "Whatever for?"

"It was an undercover DEA sting," Brian explained. "Apparently, the police thought they were asking for crack cocaine. A group of Irish lads asking, 'Where's the craic?' and, 'Is there anywhere around here where we can get some good craic?' was too good to miss."

"What happened to them?" I asked.

"It all got sorted out pretty quickly. Someone looked craic up on the internet. The police were very apologetic. Afterwards, they showed them to a good pub and even joined them for a drink."

We laughed.

"Lesley had the opposite problem," I said.

"Did I?" she asked.

"Sure you did. The guy with the polytunnel," I prompted.

"Oh that." She smiled. "I was talking to a chap in the post office. A scruffy, middle-aged sort. Anyway, he was complaining that the police–"

"Guards," Nikki corrected. "Or Gardaí, or Garda."

"What's the difference?" I asked.

"*An Garda Síochána* is the national police service of Ireland," Brian explained. "Garda is singular and Gardaí is plural, but many people also use the English version, Guard."

"So which version should we use?" Lesley asked.

"All of them." Brian smiled. "Everyone else does."

Lesley frowned and shook her head.

"Don't worry, Lesley." Brian laughed. "Carry on with your story."

"This guy said the Guards had stolen his grass. I said I was sorry for his loss and left it at that. After he had gone, I was trying to figure out why the polic– sorry, *Gardaí*, would steal someone's lawn. But then the postmaster explained. It wasn't his lawn they took, it was the cannabis crop growing in his polytunnel."

"That's not uncommon around these rural areas," Brian said laughing.

"We're getting a polytunnel," I announced, giving our guests a thumbs-up.

Lesley gave me a loving punch on the arm.

"Oh yes?" Nikki exclaimed with joking suspicion.

"I will only be growing vegetables and salad crops," she said, and then pointed at me. "But if I did grow cannabis, this one wouldn't recognise it anyway."

"Yes I would."

"No you didn't," Lesley said, winking at Nikki.

I frowned. Lesley explained.

"In England, we often had cannabis plants sprouting up around the bird table. It's from the hemp seed in the wild bird food. He never spotted them."

"Ooh! Home grown weed," Nikki exclaimed. "What did you do with them?"

My wife shrugged. "I pulled them up and put them in the composter."

Nikki pulled a face consistent with the death of a close relative. Further conversation on the subject of accidentally home-grown drugs was thwarted by an excited yelp, which diverted my attention towards the sitting room, where the girls were still playing with Amber. For the first time I realised how exhausted the little dog looked.

For a while the youngsters had sat on the rug, taking turns throwing a ball for Amber to chase. Every few seconds the ball would roll across the polished wood floor of the sitting room and bounce down the stairs into the kitchen, hotly pursued by a scrabbling ball of beige fluff. Sometimes she would catch the ball, before she slid into the kitchen table, and sometimes she wouldn't. Regardless of any minor injuries, seconds later she would return the ball, panting heavily and with her eyes twinkling with mischief, ready and willing to go again.

Caught up in our conversation, I hadn't realised Amber was no longer crashing into the kitchen every few seconds. The game had switched to an ad hoc version of 'piggy in the middle', with Amber as the canine version of piggy. The twins were sitting at opposite ends of our sitting room and throwing the ball to each other. The children laughed in delight when Amber scrabbled for grip on the shiny wooden floor and they squealed in excitement as she performed acrobatics of Olympic proportions, in an effort to snatch the ball as it sailed repeatedly past her nose. It was well-intentioned fun and would have been harmless with any other dog. But Amber is a terrier, and inclined to make up for her diminutive size with courageous displays of pig-headed determination. The little dog was totally exhausted and barely able to walk. I called a halt to play before Amber's tiny heart exploded.

The two girls were disappointed, like typical teenagers, making a big show of crossed arms and pouty faces, until Nikki brought them back in line. On the other hand, despite gasping for breath, staggering on wobbly knees, and being just a few calories away from collapse, Amber begged for a continuation of the game, long after they had left to finish their walk.

Further evidence of Amber's rough-and-tumble character can be drawn from a technique she has developed for playing with one of her favourite toys. It is a hard rubber ball attached to the end of a stout piece of rope. Somewhat reminiscent of a medieval mace, it is hardly a suitable toy for an excitable puppy, but she knows what she likes. If nobody will consent to join in the fun, the little dog will play on her own, putting on a show that is captivating, terrifying, and quite dangerous.

Taking centre stage in the sitting room, Amber will grasp the end of the rope and begin turning in circles, like an Olympic hammer thrower. As her pivots become ever faster, those of us with previous experience, will involuntarily flinch, lean away, and even cover our faces in preparation for what is to come. Once the maximum speed of rotation and centrifugal force has been achieved, Amber will suddenly release the rope. On bad days, this missile might hit a window, smash some crockery, knock over a hot drink, or wound a visiting friend. Alternatively, the ball will harmlessly rebound off of walls, furniture, or just ricochet off someone's head. Whatever the outcome, the bouncing ball will immediately be chased down by Amber, with her usual gusto. Once she has grasped the rope again, the petite dog will growl and shake her head violently, causing the hard rubber ball to repeatedly bash her on each side of the head. Such a pounding must surely hurt, but she remains remarkably unaffected, emerging with only a bad hairdo, slightly cross-eyed and with a momentary wobble in her step. Silly dog.

Like many children of her age, Amber has had several toys, but her favourite is a small, fur-covered pyramid. She will lie for hours sucking on one corner, even falling asleep in the process, just like a child sucking its thumb. We call this pyramid Amber's Sucky Toy.

"It's no good," Lesley said. "I'll have to wash it."

"Wash what?" I mumbled, looking up from my book.

"Amber's Sucky Toy."

"Oh that," I said. "Yes, it is rather gross."

"Gross is an understatement."

"She won't like it," I warned. "Amber's become very attached to her little pyramid."

"If you take the dogs for a walk, I'll wash it while you're out. It will be dry in no time."

"Okay," I shrugged. "It's your funeral."

"Don't worry," Lesley said. "Just make it a long walk."

As instructed, I took Romany and Amber on a lengthy hike. Following the logging road, I made a wide circle around the hill at the rear of the house. Switching to a second path I cut through a field and then followed a farm track down the hill and onto the road leading back to Glenmadrie. It was a slow walk, broken by periods of sniffing and several games with a stick. Romany trudged along, stoically hiding her antipathy for unnecessary running around. By way of contrast, Amber woofed excitedly for me to throw the stick and then sprinted after it as if she were in a competition.

As she tired towards the end of our walk, we switched to a game of tug which, by common consent involved several periods with Amber dangling in the air. To any casual observer, this activity could seem cruel, but Amber thinks it is great fun. Once she has a good grip on the stick, I can lift her a few inches in the air. There she will hang, like a fish on a line, shaking and growling in delight, until I gently lower her to the ground.

Back home, the cunning plan had hit a snag.

"Joanne phoned," Lesley explained, as if receiving a telephone call from our beloved daughter was a satisfactory excuse for depriving Amber of her favourite toy. "I've washed it, but it won't be dry for a while."

"Oh dear!"

Oh dear indeed. Within minutes, Amber realised that Sucky Toy was missing. At first she searched the sitting room, checking under furniture, and sniffing the floor like a miniature Hoover. Next, she went upstairs, investigating each room in turn – again without success. Finally, she returned downstairs where she spotted the love of her life, all bright and clean, but just out of reach, gently drying on top of the kitchen radiator. Lesley was preparing lunch. Amber began barking a series of irritating yips.

"You can't have it," Lesley insisted.

Amber hopped up and down, leaving muddy footprints on the white paint of the radiator.

"Get down!" Lesley snapped.

Amber whined and scrabbled.

"No! It's not dry yet," my wife explained.

Amber howled.

"I'll put it in the tumble dryer," I suggested.

"It's a waste of electricity," my wife replied sternly. "She can wait."

"I disagree," I said, grimacing. "Look at her."

Amber was panting hard, almost frantic with stress. Circling and pacing, her little black eyes, somehow conveying her desperation.

"Go on then," Lesley agreed.

The little dog saw me pop her beloved pyramid into the tumble dryer. She had no choice but to wait. It was hard going. Unable to sit still, Amber was like a furry drug addict in withdrawal, endlessly pacing the kitchen and staring gloomily at the door of the tumble dryer. Twenty minutes later, like someone expectantly peering through an airport crowd in hope of spotting a long lost friend, Amber stood on her hind legs and watched me open the dryer. As soon as I turned in her direction, she hopped up and delicately plucked the still warm toy from my fingers. With her head held high, she trotted into the lounge and flopped onto her bed. Holding the pyramid between her front paws and with her eyes closed in ecstasy, Amber sucked contentedly on a fluffy corner until she slipped into a deep sleep.

Lesley and I watched from the sitting room door.

"Well isn't that a remarkable sight?" I whispered.

"It's like a comfort blanket."

"Let's hope we don't have to wash it too soon."

"Let's hope we never lose it," Lesley joked. "I don't think Amber could take the strain."

Romany was watching impassively from her bed. She yawned expansively, stretched and let off a loud fart.

"Fair comment," I said.

***

"When are you going to start working on the wing?" Lesley asked.

We were in the kitchen, clearing away the plates after lunch.

"As soon as I get back from England," I replied cautiously.

"When's that?" she snapped.

"I haven't booked a flight yet, but my mum's birthday is in a couple of weeks. I'd like to go then."

My wife did her trademark huff. It was fair warning she was becoming impatient.

"Can't you just get on with it?" she demanded.

"I will. As soon as I get back," I promised. Sensing Lesley's frustration had not been placated, I tried a different track. "First I need to draw up some plans. Perhaps we can do that now. Together?"

"Okay." My wife smiled.

I knew she would have preferred to just launch ourselves at the old cowshed with pickaxes and crowbars, but drawing up a plan was at least some kind of progress. The renovation was likely to be a trifle tricky, particularly if we were going to retain the character of the old cowshed, with its arched windows and rough stone walls. To my mind, having a plan was essential, as well as being my favourite bit. I grabbed a pencil and a pad of paper and joined Lesley out in the cowshed. Left unattended for almost a minute, she had slipped back into immediate progress mode.

"Can't we just knock it down?" she pleaded.

"We can, but then I'd just have to build it again. And at what cost?" I replied.

"What do you mean?"

"This place is bigger than some bungalows. It would cost a bundle to rebuild, and it would be a waste of money," I explained. "Except for that bit over there, these walls are fine as they are. I've already found a company that can manufacture curved windows to fit in here, so this side will still match the courtyard, and I can easily repair the wall on the other side. The electrics are sound, but I'll need to add some new power points and lights. I'll also have to extend the heating and water. You see, there's no need to knock it down."

"Can't we take the roof off?" she asked. "That's got to go anyway."

The roof was constructed from an ad hoc arrangement of wooden beams of indeterminate age. Many of them were rotten. The whole thing was sagging under the weight of the corrugated iron sheeting. Several lengths of rope and dozens of spiders' webs appeared to be the only things holding it all together.

"You're right," I agreed. "It does need to come down, but not yet. First I want to repair the walls, and I'll need the roof for shelter."

My wife grimaced in frustration, then she smiled. Although she was keen to get on, Lesley recognised the need for a workable plan. Particularly if we were going to keep within our limited budget.

We spent a happy hour measuring and pacing, and then drawing lines in the muddy floor with a stick. Before us now was the rough outline for a wet porch, a utility room, a two room apartment with a bathroom, and a connecting corridor. Once we were both satisfied with the results, I transferred it all to paper.

"What about this?" Lesley gently kicked at a free standing internal wall. It bisected the old cowshed.

"I'll have to knock it down," I replied. "It looks like it's made from rough river gravel mixed with cement. They probably put up wooden boards and poured it in place. I'll have to get a pneumatic drill so I can break it up."

"Can you use the rubble to fill some of the floor, before you lay the concrete?"

"I guess."

I could see Lesley was still keen to do something to signify progress. I suspected she wanted to get a sledgehammer, or perhaps some dynamite.

"This wall looks a bit wobbly," she remarked. "Can I give it a shove?"

The wall was 20 feet long, ten feet high and six inches thick. Several tons of concrete. We were safe.

"Sure." I shrugged. "Have at it."

My diminutive wife put her hands on the wall, braced her legs and pushed. To my amazement it rocked once and promptly fell over. There was a mighty crash and we were engulfed in a cloud of grey dust. As the air gradually cleared, I coughed and wiped my face. The wall had disappeared, broken into a thousand tiny pieces of rubble. We were both covered in grime. Lesley looked like a coal miner finishing a shift, but she was smiling proudly.

"Now we're making progress!" she said, beaming like a Cheshire cat on drugs.

I looked at my wife suspiciously.

"You're stronger than you look!" I said, awestruck.

What else could I say?

13. Car Wars

Police checkpoints are a common sight in Ireland. They pop up without warning, on country roads, in town streets, and even on busy stretches of motorway. In many other countries, a couple of police constables stopping every vehicle on the road would likely lead to traffic chaos and a near riot. But in Ireland, such inconveniences are endured with passive restraint. Since peace has broken out on the Island of Ireland, the Guards are primarily looking for expired tax discs, traffic violations, and the illegal use of agricultural diesel. But sometimes, particularly if the driver of a vehicle appears to be a little tired and emotional, they may lean forwards and have an exploratory sniff for alcohol fumes.

I was driving towards town when I encountered one of these pop-up checkpoints. Summer had long gone and it was raining hard. The Guard on my side of the road looked soggy, cold, and thoroughly miserable. Nonetheless, due to my British number plate, I expected to be waved through the checkpoint as usual, but this time I was confronted by an upraised hand. Confused, I stopped the car. The Guard walked forward and motioned for me to lower my window. Perhaps he thought I had been drinking.

"Where are you going?" he asked.

"Into town." I pointed ahead. "I need to do some shopping."

"Are you on your holidays?" he asked. It was a common question whenever someone recognised my English accent.

"No. We live here," I replied proudly.

"Is this your vehicle?" He pronounced it ve-hik-al. It's a Guard thing.

I nodded.

"How long are you here for?"

"Since March."

The Guard sucked his teeth expressively and shook his head. Suddenly I was worried. Had I misunderstood the immigration laws? Where was my passport?

"Any resident of Ireland, importing a motor vehicle, must register said vehicle and pay any due taxation within seven days of the date of importation," he said somewhat firmly.

"What?" I asked.

He repeated his statement, this time rather more sternly.

"But I'm English," I explained. "And this is an English car."

He shook his head. "As soon as you become resident here, you are required to register your vehicle. If you fail to do so, said vehicle can be seized and crushed."

"Oh!" I gulped.

The Guard was about to say more, but I interrupted him with a snap decision. It was something that had been niggling at the back of my mind for a while.

"Look," I said. "I'm taking this car back to England. I'll go next week. It's my mother's birthday. You'll never see this vehicle again. I promise."

He chewed on his lip, toying with his options. In desperation, I played my trump card.

"Frankly, it's a piece of crap. If you want to crush it, go ahead. You'll probably be doing me a favour." I gave him my best smile.

The Guard smiled and rolled his eyes.

"Okay. Off you go," he said. "But if I see this car again, and it isn't heading towards Dublin port, you'll be walking home."

And with that, he waved me on my way.

Although that little Ford car had performed well, given its accident history and low purchase price, I never grew to like it. Whatever I tried, I was unable to find a comfortable driving position, the steering was vague, the rear suspension sloppy, the boot space unsatisfactory, and in Ireland the insurance would have been prohibitively expensive. As promised, the following week I took the Ford back to England where a friend took charge of arranging the sale. Despite its valiant efforts, I was happy to see that car gone.

After a few days visiting friends and family, I flew back to Ireland and began the search for a replacement vehicle. I wasn't worried, I was just buying a car. How hard could it be?

***

If space aliens were ever to visit our quiet corner of the universe, or examine our insignificant blue planet from afar, it is conceivable they would conclude the dominant species here is the motor car. It would be an understandable mistake, given how much time, affection and money we humans expend in caring for our cars. I understand our obsession with the infernal internal combustion engine: the joy of speed, the thrill of power and that new car smell. I get it. But owning the most expensive, shiny, new, super-fast status symbol in County Clare is akin to putting lipstick on a pig. No. The narrow potholed roads here in rural Ireland are best tackled in something slow and previously dented.

As a child, I learned car maintenance by helping my father, back in the days when a few spanners, a screwdriver, some emery paper, and a pot of fiberglass body filler were all that was required to keep an aged automobile roadworthy and apparently rust free. We were not a wealthy family. Living in austere times, and still engrained with the wartime 'make do and mend' mentality, cars were seen as a necessary purchase, best acquired with the minimum of expenditure. In time this attitude became part of my DNA and fed into our plans for a simple, debt-free life in Ireland. With this in mind, I began searching for a decent and reliable second-hand car.

"Well, this can't be right," I said, refolding the newspaper.

"What?" Lesley asked.

"None of the car adverts in here show any prices."

"Paul said about that. He had the same problem when he was looking for his digger. A lot of big ticket stuff doesn't show a price in the adverts."

"So how are we expected to know how much things are?" I asked. "All these adverts show is the make, model and year."

"I guess you'll just have to ask," Lesley replied. "By the way. When I told Christine we were looking for a car, she said to watch out we don't get charged the 'English price'."

"Surely that's just a myth."

My wife shrugged. "I'm just telling you what she said."

"How do I avoid getting charged extra, just because I have an English accent?"

Lesley just shrugged again. "We'll have to get a second car, even if it is expensive," she said. "This house is too remote to get by with just one. Particularly with you out teaching every day during the summer."

"Okay. You're right." I stood and waved the newspaper. "This may not tell me the prices, but at least we know where they are.

Come on, let's go shopping for cars."

"Ooh!" Lesley flashed her eyes seductively. "You really know how to show a girl a good time."

By combining our trusty tourist map of Ennis with the adverts in the newspaper, we successfully navigated our way to an out of town road with several car dealerships. Like bank robbers casing the joint, we cruised slowly past, made a U-turn and drove by again. Somehow the grey sky and the steady slap of the windscreen wipers made the whole scene feel rather depressing and industrial.

"They all seem to be selling new cars," Lesley said.

"I'm sure they have second-hand cars as well." I pointed to a sign. "Look, it says trade-ins welcome."

"I suppose we'd better ask."

The rain was easing, so I parked at the first dealership on the road and we went inside. The showroom was all bright and shiny. It smelled of new cars, rubber and floor wax. There were six new cars on display, neatly parked like fighter jets waiting for battle. I guessed they represented the full range of new models for that particular brand. None had any price stickers. At the rear of the building was a row of glass-fronted offices. In the centre office, I could see a middle-aged man wearing a crumpled brown three-piece suit. He was smoking a cigar, drinking a coffee, eating a burger and talking on the telephone. For a moment we locked eyes. He raised a hand momentarily, before swivelling his chair to show me his back. Perhaps his multitasking didn't extend to dealing with customers.

"Ooh! I like this one," Lesley squealed, running her hand along the immaculate paintwork of a huge black SUV.

"Yes, dear," I said, keeping my voice deliberately neutral, "but it's not really what we're looking for."

"I expect it will be dreadfully expensive," Lesley admitted.

"Especially as we'll probably use it for transporting cement and compost." I looked around for a sales assistant, but apart from the guy smoking a cigar in the middle office, no one was in sight. I scratched my head in frustration. "Let's try looking outside. Perhaps they keep the second-hand cars around the back."

There was a light drizzle falling so we stuck close to the building for some shelter. The weather wasn't helping my mood and the feeling we were wasting our time. I hunched my shoulders and thrust my hands deep into my pockets. Lesley was walking ahead. At the corner of the building, she stopped and beckoned me forwards.

"There you are." My wife pointed at a sign above the gated enclosure. *Quality used cars.* "That's what we're looking for."

There were perhaps 20 cars parked haphazardly in the lot. They were caked in grime and several had flat tyres. My mood was becoming as dark as the sky.

"This looks more like a breaker's yard," I growled. "Or staff parking."

"They've got 'For Sale' stickers on the windscreens," Lesley pointed out. She gave my elbow an encouraging squeeze. "Come on. Let's have a look."

We explored the lot for about 20 minutes, peering through windows and kicking tyres. Once I'd eliminated the executive limousines, the huge SUVs, Jeeps and people carriers, we'd narrowed our selection to just four cars. None had prices.

"I don't recognise the badges. What make are these?" Lesley asked.

"These two are Toyotas. That one's a Fiat and this is a Renault."

"No Fords?"

I shook my head. "It's interesting how much more eclectic the scope here is. Much more continental, particularly in the mid-range. I don't recall seeing a Ford dealership anywhere, and Vauxhall is called Opel over here. It's the European brand name."

"Does it matter?" Lesley asked.

"Not to me," I replied. "As long as it gets the job done, I don't care what make it is. The only benefit of owning a Ford in Essex was the availability of cheap parts."

"That's hardly surprising," Lesley said. "Ford did used to have a factory in Dagenham."

"Did you know the first Ford factory in Europe was built here in Ireland?"

"Really?"

"1917," I said. "It was down in Cork. First they built tractors and by 1921 cars as well."

"Wikipedia?" Lesley asked, raising an eyebrow.

I shook my head. "Discovery channel. I watched a documentary about Europe."

"My car's a Citroën," she said.

I laughed. "There you go. We're Europeans already."

"I think I've figured out how the number plates work over here."

"Really? Do tell."

"Well, if I'm right, it's much simpler than the British system." She pointed at the Toyota. "I think the first two numbers are the year of registration. The letters must be the county. CE is for Clare, W for Waterford—"

"Or Wexford," I suggested.

She shook her head. "That would be WX, like that Mercedes. D is for Dublin, and C is for Cork."

"Oh, I get it. So that BMW was registered in 2002 in Dublin."

Lesley nodded, happy to have solved the puzzle. We were both getting cold, so I suggested returning to our car and trying another garage. Just then, the man in the brown three-piece suit came striding around the corner. He was puffing on his cigar and walking fast. The way the smoke billowed and his arms pumped brought to mind an image of a rusty steam engine. He waved cheerily.

"Hello. Hello. I'd have come out sooner, but I've been up the wall." He rolled his eyes dramatically. "Me head's wrecked."

I smiled stiffly, my lips numb from the cold. We introduced ourselves and I explained what we were looking for.

"You're English," he said.

My heart fell. *Here we go. Buckle up for the English prices!*

"Yes, we're from England," Lesley replied. "But we live here now."

"I'm Seamus," he said, shaking my hand enthusiastically and completely ignoring my wife. "Don't you worry, I'll sort you out."

"I hope so," I replied, glancing at Lesley. She grimaced and shrugged. It wasn't the first time she'd encountered misogyny in Ireland (or in England for that matter). Seamus had a pleasant face, a ready smile, eyes twinkling with humour and a tendency to finish each sentence with a cheeky wink. Despite his attitude towards my wife, I couldn't help liking the man.

"We've the best range of cars in Ireland," he exclaimed.

"You'll not be disappointed. I'll do you a great deal."

"Good, good," I said, my spirits lifting.

"Now look at this Mercedes," he said, striding away.

I held my ground. "We're not really looking for an executive car," I explained.

"But you must!" he declared, as if he were quoting the law. "A smart-looking man like you should have an executive car. You deserve something special."

"Sorry, Seamus." I pointed towards the Toyota. "We're only looking for a reliable and inexpensive family run-around."

"B-but!" Seamus was flabbergasted. "But, a Mercedes says everything about you!"

"What does it say if you're wearing overalls and loading bags of cement in the boot?" Lesley interjected tersely. She was getting cold as well.

"Can we see this one?" I asked, swiftly redirecting the conversation.

"Of course. The door is open. Climb in and try it for size."

The interior was damp and smelled of mildew. There was a puddle of water in the foot-well and the windscreen was dripping with condensation.

"It seems rather wet," I observed.

Seamus waved a hand dismissively. "Someone probably left the windows open. It'll soon dry out."

The steering wheel was sticky and I was sensing some dampness seeping through the seat of my trousers. I squinted over my glasses, trying to read the mileage displayed on the odometer. It was misted up, but the numbers were clear enough.

"Good grief, 266,000 miles!" I exclaimed. "Is that correct?"

"Ah!" Seamus smiled and pulled a crumpled sheet of paper from his crumpled suit pocket. He narrowed his eyes. "Yes. That's right."

"But it's only ten years old."

He sensed my consternation. "You must expect that. Ireland has the highest mileage per capita of any European country."

"I know, but…" I shook my head in dismay. Apart from taxis, I'd never seen a car with such high mileage. "How much is it?"

Seamus looked me up and down, presumably trying to judge the girth of my wallet. "Well now, Nick, how much do you think it would cost?"

"What? Err, I don't know, why don't you just tell me?"

Seamus smiled like a school teacher confronting a naughty but likeable child. "Ah now, go on with you, have a guess."

I did some quick mental arithmetic. "Oh I don't know, perhaps €800?" I suggested hopefully.

Our baggy little salesman staggered back in mock horror.

"No, sir, not even close!" he laughed. "You'd be robbing me."

"I'm sorry. I was thinking what I'd pay in England for a car with this much mileage," I explained. "How much is it?"

"This one's just €9,500," he said proudly. "Terrific value."

"Good God!" I was genuinely shocked. It seemed an outrageous price.

"We can easily arrange finance," he suggested, gripping the cigar in his teeth and smiling.

"No, thank you. That won't be necessary." I was about to put an end to the conversation, when Lesley spoke up. She had drifted over to the Renault.

"What about this one?"

"Ah!" Seamus beamed at Lesley, as if he were noticing her for the first time. "You have a good eye. Sit inside, both of you."

Despite being the victim of the earlier slight, my wife smiled demurely at the compliment. At first glance, the Renault appeared a better choice. It was a little larger and somewhat less dented than the Toyota, with almost half the mileage, but the interior was sticky and gross. It reeked of tobacco, stale sweat and something else that may have been goat related. I gagged and we quickly climbed out. Lesley and I shared a knowing look. She was involuntarily wiping her hands on her jeans.

"€12,000?" Seamus suggested, hopefully.

I shook my head. "Thank you, but no. I think we should shop around for a bit," I explained.

We shook hands and parted amicably. It wasn't his fault. The story was repeated almost word for word at the next three dealerships we visited. Obviously, the car prices in Ireland were substantially out of step with those in the UK. Lesley captured the conundrum perfectly.

"Isn't it odd how the car prices are so high here, but the houses were so much cheaper?"

"We may have to rethink our budget," I said. Empty-handed, we were heading for home.

"I still can't get over the difference in prices," Lesley said, shaking her head. "That last car was more than we paid for my Citroën, and it was twice the age."

"I guess the registration tax they have here on new cars pushes up the price a lot and that feeds through to the second-hand market as well."

"I'm sure you're right, but knowing it doesn't make it better."

"Like I said, we'll just have to rethink the budget."

Silently, we chewed on our own thoughts. I was just wondering what other financial shocks were coming our way, when Lesley suddenly pointed to my right.

"Look! There's a Ford dealership."

"Do you want to stop?" I asked.

My wife shrugged. "Sure. Why not?"

Another showroom, another salesman. This one was called Don. He listened as I explained what we were looking for, and after only one half-hearted attempt to sell me a new car on credit, he led us out through a rear door.

"This is where we keep the trade-ins," Don explained.

My heart fell as I cast my eyes over yet another group of potentially over-priced and under-serviced wrecks. We looked at a couple of his least despicable offerings, but our interest was at best half-hearted. Even Don seemed embarrassed at the quality of his offerings. He beckoned us to move closer and glanced furtively towards the office.

"Look, I'll tell you the truth. We've recently had a big trade-in event. Most of these cars will probably go for scrap – as they should. I would avoid them myself." Don smiled. The laughter lines on his face aligned appealingly. I suspect he smiled a lot.

"Thanks for your honesty," I replied, offering a handshake.

Don held up a finger. "But there is one car…" He smiled again and pointed to a silver hatchback in the far corner of the lot. Just then, the sun broke through the overcast, bathing the car in a golden glow.

"We've had it a while," he explained. "Admittedly it's an older model, but it has low mileage and a full service history. For €1,500 I'll even throw in a six-month warranty. It may be just what you're looking for."

And it was.

The following morning I was giving my new toy a wax and polish, when Lesley came out and stood by my side. Something was troubling her. She narrowed her eyes and tapped a finger on pursed lips. The tension was palpable. Finally, she broke the silence.

"Isn't this exactly the same as the car you've just returned to England?"

"No, no, no!" I laughed, shaking my head at her mechanical inexperience. "That one was blue."

14. Stormy weather

Our first eight months in Ireland had been a frenzied whirlwind of activity. We had moved in, learned a good bit about our new home and country, and entertained several guests. Outside, we had cleared away tons of rubbish and concrete, had a well drilled, built a pump house, landscaped our garden and dug a pond. We had also demolished a chimney and installed a stove. At the same time, I had established a thriving business and conducted hundreds of golf lessons. Now the unseasonably warm summer had turned into a depressing procession of cold and wet days, sending even the hardiest golfers away. Suddenly, my time was my own, and there was no longer an excuse to put off what had to be done. Winter had arrived at Glenmadrie and it was time for me to get stuck into the renovations.

Working under the welcome shelter of the old cowshed roof, I had demolished any of the walls that were unstable and, after digging new foundations, began the rebuilding process. Aided only by my trusty DIY manual and a new electric cement mixer, I was gradually replacing a thirty-foot section of haphazardly constructed external wall with a smart, double layer of concrete blocks, complete with cavity wall insulation and three windows.

Despite my best efforts, I had yet to master the builder's trowel. A proper bricklayer will casually deliver the perfect amount of mortar into exactly the correct place with a deft flick of the wrist. Conversely, I looked more like a drunken monkey attempting to eat soup with chopsticks. Not for the first time I had just wasted half a load of mortar whilst attempting to manoeuvre the requisite amount into the correct place. With a growl of frustration, I gave in and reverted to using my rubber-gloved hands, like a child making mud pies. I had just cleaned up the mess, in preparation for mixing another load of mortar, when Lesley came out to deliver some bad news.

"There's water leaking into the studio," she said sullenly. "And the floor in the bedroom above is wet under the window."

"Blast!" I growled. "I was hoping I'd fixed it."

"Well, it's definitely leaking from somewhere."

"Is there much water getting in?" I asked.

Lesley bit her lip and grimaced. "Sorry. It sounds like someone has left a tap running."

"Alright!" I sighed. "I'd better come and have a look."

She was right. The leak was much worse than I had expected. The floorboards under the bedroom window were soaking wet, and in the old music studio below there was a steady stream of water dripping through the ceiling. I shook my head in dismay and confusion.

"Where on earth is the water getting in?"

"From the roof?" Lesley suggested.

"I'm sure I fixed it," I reiterated.

A quick trip into the loft space above the bedroom proved I was right. It was bone dry. Logic dictated the next step in the investigation, but I wasn't happy. Lesley had just finished decorating the bedroom. I softly tapped the studwork wall that surrounded the window.

"I need to remove this wall," I said.

"Why?" Lesley groaned.

"This is a false wall." I tapped it with my knuckle again. "Behind it there should be some insulation and a vapour barrier, and behind that the concrete wall. I need to remove this studwork so I can find where the water is getting in."

"Can't you just make a small hole?" she asked.

"Not really." I shrugged apologetically. It was the end wall of the house. A twenty-foot wide section of freshly painted plasterboard. "Anyway, I'll also need to replace these floorboards."

Lesley huffed. "Go on then."

"I'll have to leave the wing and get on with this," I warned.

"Fine," she sighed. Obviously it wasn't.

"Do you have any of this paint left?"

"About two litres."

"Good," I said. "Once I've fixed the leak, I'll put up new plasterboard. With a lick of paint, you won't even see the join."

"You'd better get cracking," she replied. "I'll go and put the kettle on."

Even though I took extra care to avoid any unnecessary damage, it took me less than an hour to remove the plasterboard from the end wall. Once I had cleared away the debris, I could see the gravity of the problem. Although the rain had temporarily stopped pounding against the windows, the concrete wall was still slick with moisture and the floorboards below were wet and softened by rot. Despite the plasterboard being removed and the evidence revealed, I still couldn't figure out where the water was getting in.

"This makes no sense!" I complained, shining my torch into the darkest corners. "There's obviously a serious leak, but where is it?"

"Perhaps it's condensation," Lesley suggested.

"That's a hell of a lot of water for condensation," I snapped.

Lesley looked hurt by my sudden outburst.

"Sorry," I said quickly. "I'm just frustrated by this." I waved my hand at the wall and the growing puddle of water on the floorboards.

"You said there should have been insulation and some sort of barrier, but there wasn't any. Wouldn't that cause condensation?" my wife asked.

"Yes, a vapour barrier," I replied. "You're right. But a missing barrier wouldn't cause this much water. It's pouring in from somewhere. But where?"

Lesley shrugged and looked sullen. "Missing insulation, no vapour barriers, leaky walls. This is the newest part of the building." She nodded towards the rest of the house. "What are we going to find out there?"

"God knows," I replied. "But whatever it is, we'll fix it."

I stood and we shared a hug.

"Oh look!" Lesley was pointing at the wall.

While we were talking, the rain had returned. There was now a steady trickle of water running down the wall from just below the window. I dropped to my knees, and using a torch and screwdriver, began probing for the source of the leak. Suddenly I had it.

"Good grief!" I exclaimed. "Look at this."

"What?" Lesley asked, moving closer.

"These windows aren't fitted to the concrete. They're actually attached to the wooden frame of this fabricated wall. There's a big gap between the window frame and the external wall and someone has filled it with plaster and some newspaper. No wonder the water was getting in."

"Why would someone do that?" Lesley asked. "Especially on this end of the house. It's exposed to the very worst of the weather."

"It's beyond me," I replied. "Perhaps the builder didn't have the correct equipment to drill holes in the concrete, so he just bodged it."

"Now I'm really worried about what else we're going to find."

"Me too," I replied.

"Can you fix this?" Lesley asked, pointing to the windows.

"Sure, it's easy. I'll just move them to the correct place. It looks like they'll fit without any problems. I'll have to drill a few holes in the cement for the fixings and fill the edges with proper mastic, but after that, we'll be as dry as a bone."

"If it's that easy, why didn't they…?" Lesley's voice trailed off in frustration.

I shrugged. "You tell me. It looks like these windows have been reused from another house. Perhaps they didn't think they would fit."

Lesley stood back and stared in silence at the windows. Her eyes were darting back and forth as she plotted. The silence was almost painful, but I resisted the temptation to fill the void. Finally she spoke those dreaded words.

"I've been thinking."

I closed my eyes and waited for the other shoe to fall.

"I hate these windows," she added.

There were four sets of double windows, fitted in pairs on either side of a two-foot thick central pillar. They had chunky brown wooden frames and a lattice of heavy leading that almost obscured the glass. I didn't like them either.

"How hard would it be to remove that pillar?" my wife asked matter-of-factly.

"Probably pretty easy. I've got a disc cutter, but I'd need to rent some scaffolding…" I stopped as soon as I saw the trap, but by then it was too late.

"Wouldn't it be great if we had one huge window here?" My wife beamed. "Just think of the light, and the views!"

Of course she was right.

It would have been beyond madness to remove the pillar during the winter, so I temporarily refitted the windows in the correct place and sealed them against the weather. To confirm the leak was finally fixed, we agreed to leave the internal wall bare until the spring. My final task was to calculate the dimensions for the new window and add it to the six I had already ordered for the wing. With the mess cleaned up and the wall apparently dry, I was able to return to building the wing.

This was our first winter in Ireland and the weather was going out of its way to make an impression on this mad English couple. Even with the protection of the old cowshed roof and a large sheet of blue tarpaulin, I needed to take regular breaks to thaw out my numbed fingers and strip off my damp clothes. Lesley was typically unsympathetic about my plight. Sitting toasty warm by a roaring fire, she was reading the paper.

"You need to work faster," she suggested. "It's no wonder you're cold."

"It's not like I'm laying bricks you know," I complained. "Those concrete blocks weigh about twenty pounds. If I lay more than two layers before the mortar has set, the weight makes the wall go all crooked."

"You must be doing it wrong," she observed helpfully.

"Probably," I agreed. "Those heavy blocks are an Irish peculiarity. There's no mention of them in my DIY book."

"Well, as long as it doesn't fall over," she warned.

"It'll be fine," I replied. "I'd get on a lot quicker if this foul weather would break."

"Not much chance of that," she laughed, pointing to an article she had been reading in the paper. "Listen to this. *Things have got so bad that, as part of a project to raise awareness of potentially dangerous weather events, Met Éireann, the Irish National Meteorological Service, have started naming storms. With the help of the public, they selected names like Clodagh, Gertrude, and Henry. Sadly the alternative suggestions of Leaf Shaker, Tree Stripper, Branch Wobbler, Trunk Trembler, Root Ripper, and Armageddon, did not make the final list.*"

We both laughed at this example of Irish humour.

"Are you sure that isn't just a joke?" I suggested.

"No, it's right here." She tapped the paper with her fingernail. "Anyway, if they're going to start naming storms over here, we might have to buy a boat."

"Ooh a boat," I exclaimed. "What a great idea. What with all the lakes around here–"

"No!" My wife glared at me.

My sudden dreams of being a captain shattered, I pulled a sad face. Lesley pointed towards the wing.

"Go, slave! Get back to work."

As always seems to be the way when the weather service has predicted storms, we had a short period of dry and unseasonably mild weather. I made good progress on the renovations in the wing and even managed to fit in a couple of games of golf with Andrew.

When Mr Rain finally reappeared at Glenmadrie, we discovered he had invited his two superhero friends, Gale and Storm, to help him make up for lost time. They soon set about flooding the meadow, battering the house, knocking over trees and randomly disconnecting our telephone and electricity, always at the most inconvenient of times.

Our chickens were suffering too. Their pen became a quagmire of sticky mud. They stopped laying eggs and spent their days huddled under the shelter of their coop, staring gloomily at the lashing rain.

Superhero Gale is cold at heart and insisted on pointing out all of the places where she could get into the house, by howling through every gap in the walls and blowing dust down through the ceilings. I used up several more cans of expanding foam, trying to keep her out of the older parts of the house. In the end, I had to temporarily box off the spiral staircase, just to keep the draughts in the living room below hurricane force.

Conversely, Storm is a moody cow, inclined to violent tantrums, moaning and wailing all night long and stealing anything that isn't well secured. I always thought superheroes were supposed to be a force for good, but these wicked sisters soon set about re-educating me. Lesley was back in England visiting her mother on the day the weather took a turn for the worse, demonstrating the full force of an Atlantic storm.

It was late in the evening when both Gale and Storm decided to pay a visit. I was working under floodlights, laying a few more blocks to use up the last of the mortar I had mixed. First, the trees around the house started to thrash alarmingly and there was a ghostly moaning from the hill opposite. The wind and rain increased to a startling ferocity, as the unseen squall approached. The roof of the wing is five hundred square feet of corrugated steel, with a frame of timber and tree trunks, yet it was shaking and bouncing as if there were an earthquake. As the winds peaked, the entire roof suddenly reared up, like the lid on a giant toilet seat, balancing precariously on one edge. I stood transfixed, watching what was probably a couple of tons of rusty steel and rotting wood hanging motionless above me, apparently unsure of which way it should fall.

In an instant the wind subsided into an eerie silence, and then, to my horror, the roof slowly dropped towards me. Yelping in a far less manly fashion than I would have liked, I covered my head with my arms and threw myself onto the ground. With a mighty crash, complemented by a shower of rust and dead spiders, the roof came down. As the dust cleared, I cautiously peeked out from behind my fingers and gaped in amazement. The roof was perfectly positioned on top of the wall. Some ropes I had used to attach the tarpaulin had acted as a hinge, fortuitously ensuring the whole thing fell back into its original position, rather than squashing me like a bug as it would surely otherwise have done.

In time, the winter storms gave way to better weather. The lack of frost allowed me to complete the walls and by Christmas week I had moved on to digging up the floors, ready to lay the sewage pipes for the bathroom. Lesley and I are not particularly inclined to celebrate Christmas just because some retailers say we should, although we would make a special day of it if we had guests. So we had no special plans for our first Christmas at Glenmadrie, other than a roast dinner and perhaps a glass of wine to complement the inevitable television re-runs of classic Christmas movies. But the Irish weather intervened again.

On the morning of December 25th, I opened the curtains to discover the altitude and meteorological conditions had combined to deliver a special Christmas treat. We were shrouded in a thick layer of snow. The heavy white blanket suppressed noise and made the branches on the trees hang low. With visibility reduced to less than fifty yards by the hill fog, it felt like we had been wrapped in cotton wool, or maybe it was Santa's beard. I put the kettle on and lit the fire. After telephoning our friends and family, I cooked our traditional Christmas breakfast of thick slices of French toast with lashings of maple syrup. Personally I prefer my French toast smothered with strawberry jam, but it seems that this dietary quirk is unacceptable in polite company – unless you happen to be pregnant.

Once we were washed and dressed, we set out like two polar explorers with mismatched dogs for a walk in the forest. Amber ran, rolled and jumped in the snow with a childlike delight, chasing after every puff disturbed by our boots. Occasionally she would dive headfirst into a drift, in pursuit of some particularly devious snowflake, only to emerge moments later, eyes dancing and grinning widely, with her face covered in snow.

Romany had seen it all before. She trudged along with grudging indifference, collecting ever larger snowballs on her feet and underside, until finally she could walk no further. There she sat, stubbornly refusing to move until one of us held her upside-down like a turtle, and the other risked frostbite while breaking off the lumps of ice with our fingers. Back home, happy but exhausted, we warmed ourselves by the fire. Amber still wanted to play, but Romany fell instantly asleep, despite steaming gently as the remaining ice melted from her fur.

As it was too cold to work outside, I took the rest of the day off. Lesley and I sat together, watched some television, read a little, ate too many mince pies and then dozed on the couch until it was time for bed. The snow lingered for two weeks. Rural roads in Ireland are seldom gritted or ploughed, and the lanes at Glenmadrie were soon impassable. Such a confinement caused us little inconvenience. We have two large chest freezers well stocked with frozen milk, bread, and other essentials, so we got by.

Glenmadrie quietly slipped into the New Year, without ceremony or the usual barrage of fireworks, which seems to punctuate every party in England from mid-October through to the end of January. Just after midnight, I let the dogs out before bedtime. While I waited for their return, I stood in the deep crisp snow, revelling in the silence, and breathed deeply of the deliciously pure air. As I stared in awe at the star-filled vista of a crystal clear sky above me, I took a moment to remember my father, it would have been his birthday, to think of our friends and family abroad, and to give quiet thanks for our new life in Ireland.

15. A bad first impression

The snow was deep and crisp and even. It was beautiful and romantic, but it hung about like the smell of boiled cabbage in a care home. Some days it snowed a little more and some days it melted slightly, only to freeze solid overnight. The thick white covering of snow and frost soon lost its novel appeal.

I was waiting for a break in the weather to replace the roof on the wing. Only then could I fit the internal walls and lay in the electrics and plumbing. Until the weather improved, I couldn't do anything but potter and wait. Perhaps sensing my frustration, or hoping to escape her own crisis of cabin fever, Lesley made a suggestion.

"Nick?"

"Yes, dear?"

"I've been thinking."

Oh those dreaded words again. What now? Would my lovely wife ask me to dig up our newly-laid concrete floor? Did she want to open a cattery? Or had she discovered a previously unknown desire to live in Russia? The wing had but one exit and Lesley was blocking my escape. With a sense of foreboding, I slowly raised an inquisitive eyebrow.

"We should go out for a drive," she said.

"Out?" I exclaimed. "There's a foot of snow and the road is sheet ice. Why should we go out?"

"Well, we both need a break," she explained, "and there's the January sales."

I removed my hat and scratched my head. It made a squeaking sound. Perhaps she wanted me to buy a wig.

"What do we need in the sales?" I asked. It seemed a fair question, particularly as we were trying to live on a budget.

"Everything!"

"Everything?" I exclaimed in a startled voice. "What do you mean, everything?"

My wife extracted a sheet of paper from her pocket, took a big breath, and began reciting her shopping list.

"Floor tiles for the kitchen, floor tiles for the wing, kitchen units for the utility room, wall tiles for the bathroom, a shower, a sink, a toilet, a kitchen…" She paused and smiled.

"That's a lot of shopping," I said. "And a lot of money."

Lesley held up a calming hand.

"I know what you're thinking, but hear me out. I was watching the TV. Loads of retailers are having their sales, and two in particular are offering a double discount for today only. If we went now, we could order almost everything we need. It's on sale at less than half price. We'd save a fortune."

"Where would we put it all?" I asked.

"In the studio." She pointed and smiled. "Now you've fixed the leak, it will be perfect for storing things like the kitchen units until we need them."

I couldn't argue with her logic. Perhaps somewhere in the back of my mind I'd been hoping we would never need to buy all the big ticket items she'd listed. But that's just me.

"You'd better get your coat," I laughed.

My wife clapped her hands like a child waiting for sweeties. Lesley hates shopping almost as much as me, but I guess her huge list was less retail therapy and more to do with advancing our renovations and creating the illusion of progress.

It was still snowing, so we elected to wear coats, hats, gloves and Wellington boots. As a precaution, I checked the charge on my mobile phone and put a shovel, a blanket, and a towrope into the boot. We set off just after 11 am. The first three miles were torturous. Even at walking pace, it was all I could do to keep the car in between the ditches. Clearly the only traffic passing this way had been tractors. The thick snow had been crushed to sludge and frozen harder than steel.

"This is ridiculous!" I growled. "It'll take hours to get to town. We'll probably end up sleeping in a ditch."

"I'm sorry, you're right," Lesley sighed. "It was a silly idea. Let's go back home."

"I can't turn around here, there's just no room. I'll have to drive on until we reach the crossroads."

We crept on, crunching cautiously over the ice for another mile, but as we reached the crossroads, the white covering abruptly disappeared. There was no gradual thinning of the snow, just a line of separation. On one side of the road it was deepest winter, and on the other, green grass and a hint of spring.

"Good grief!" Lesley exclaimed. "How bizarre."

"It must be because of the change of altitude," I suggested. "Usually, the snow cover would diminish gradually, but I guess the temperature gradient was quite profound just here."

Lesley waved her hand forwards. "Drive on!"

"Well, we're certainly noticing some variances in the weather here," I said. "It's amazing how just six hundred miles can make such a difference. The storms come crashing into the west coast of Ireland, but by the time they reach the east of England, the lashing rain is no more than a light drizzle."

"If that," Lesley replied. "Essex is almost a desert these days."

As we drove lower down the hill, the sun came out and the temperature climbed. At the next junction, I pulled over so we could remove our coats.

"We're going to look like proper chumps dressed up like polar explorers on such a fine spring day," Lesley laughed.

"At least we can catch up on the shopping. We're getting low on milk and bread." I had a thought. "Don't forget Joanne and Rebecca are coming to stay soon. We'd better get some extra groceries."

"And booze," Lesley added. Rebecca was our daughter's flatmate, a lovely girl, despite her proclivity for consuming copious amounts of alcohol.

"We can get a few bottles of that cloudy cider Christine suggested. What was it called?"

"Devil's Bite," Lesley replied. "But the girls won't drink it."

"Their loss," I said, smiling wickedly.

By the time we reached Limerick, the sun was shining and the temperature had risen markedly. It was as if we had started our journey in Antarctica and finished in Spain. As we parked, a small crowd surrounded our car, perplexed by the thick layer of snow still coating the roof. Some children even started an ad hoc snowball fight. Still wearing our Christmas jumpers and stomping along in green wellies, we emerged from our car and edged our way through the crowds towards the shops.

"We must look like a right couple of idiots," I hissed.

"It's still quite cold. I wouldn't want to take my sweater off," Lesley said. "Anyway, we're English. People will understand."

Of course she was right. Despite our inappropriate attire, we were treated with politeness and courtesy. Perhaps it helped that we were spending several thousand euro and giving two lucky sales assistants a hefty commission boost to start the year, but I prefer to think it was just a good example of Irish tolerance and understanding.

By the time we set off on the drive home, we were both sweating like racehorses, despite stripping off as many layers as we could whilst still remaining decent. Lacking air conditioning in our car, we drove along with the windows down and the wind whistling across my bald head and through Lesley's hair. Although the sun was still shining, as we began the climb up the hill towards our house the temperature dropped noticeably. At the crossroads we entered the snow field again, and by the time we reached Glenmadrie, the car windows were closed and the heater was on full blast. Staring at the thick snow and ice-shrouded trees, it was hard to believe a few miles away people were saying, "Feck, but it's fierce mild today!"

While I unloaded our groceries, Lesley lit the fire and fed the dogs. Once my wife had her feet up and a coffee in hand, I returned to the kitchen. There, in celebration of our successful shopping trip and the money we had saved, I prepared a favourite meal of ours. First I popped a budget frozen cheese and tomato pizza into the oven. Then I finely chopped some red and green peppers and sliced three mushrooms, which I added to the top of the now-defrosted pizza along with a sprinkle of garlic, black pepper and a generous drizzle of extra virgin olive oil. Once the deep topping of mushroom and peppers was cooked, I added a hefty covering of grated mature cheddar and returned the pizza to the oven until the cheese was bubbling and golden brown. The entire meal took just 25 minutes to prepare, and combined with a side salad, made a welcome treat for two weary shoppers.

"I have to admit, buying all those bits for the renovations feels like some kind of progress," I said.

"Here's to progress!" Lesley held up her coffee mug in salute. I clinked it with my glass of cider.

"And to the money saved," I added, taking a sip of cider. "Phew! This stuff's got some kick."

"Then it's a good job you're drinking from a wine glass," Lesley laughed.

"I'm not making that mistake again." I smiled, remembering my first encounter with Devil's Bite. "Tomorrow, I'll make some space in the studio so we can store the kitchen and other stuff."

"*When* it arrives," Lesley warned. "It won't be here for a while."

The kitchen supplier had predicted a delay of three to four months.

"I'm not too worried about the kitchen units," I explained, "but I'll be ready to fit out the bathroom and utility room pretty soon."

"That quick?" Lesley asked.

I nodded. "Provided the weather improves."

But it didn't. The snow hung around, as unwelcome as a fart in an elevator, and I could only potter as I waited for it to clear. On Saturday, Ireland added a dramatic climatic twist. I was sitting on the couch drinking my morning tea and Lesley was just finishing a phone call to her mother. As she replaced the receiver and took one step away, there was a blue flash from the electrical socket and a puff of smoke from the telephone. She made a startled sound and turned towards me as I began to stand.

"What the–" My confused expletive was cut short by a colossal rolling boom, so loud it shook the windows.

Romany and Amber yelped in fright.

"Thunderstorm!" Lesley shouted, somewhat unhelpfully.

As if to confirm her supposition, a second thunderous roar followed, this time preceded by a flash of lightning. I flicked the light switch. Nothing. I flicked it again, as if that would make a difference.

"The power's out," I said, obligingly stating the obvious.

"I think we were hit by lightning," Lesley said.

"It probably hit the powerlines," I replied. "This is the last house on the line, so any surge would have nowhere else to go."

"We may need a new phone." Lesley pointed at the remaining wisp of smoke.

"If you were still holding it when that lightning hit, right now I'd be needing a new wife." I wasn't joking. She had been just two seconds away from electrocution.

The mobile signal was okay, so I called our electricity supplier. Ours wasn't the only incident, so it took a few hours before power was restored. They were apologetic, but adamant. Damage caused to electrical appliances by lightning strikes was not their responsibility. The insurance company took much the same view. We had to replace the telephone, the television, my desktop computer, and a burned out relay in our water pump. Our satellite receiver was also fried, but the supplier graciously replaced it with their latest model free of charge.

"We were lucky the lightning didn't hit the house," Lesley said, watching me tot up the bills.

"I don't feel very lucky," I growled. "Including the surge protectors I bought, that little incident cost almost two thousand euro."

"Should we get a lightning rod?"

"Only if we're going to stick it on someone else's house," I laughed. "The lightning hit the power lines about a mile away. There's no way to protect against that."

"Well, look on the bright side," Lesley smiled. "They say lightning never strikes twice."

"I hope you're right," I said. "I really do."

***

A week later I was at Shannon Airport to collect two gents on their first trip to Ireland. They were here to address a group of 20 golf professionals at a hotel in Ennis, in the hope of becoming new suppliers to our members throughout Ireland. The arrivals hall was quiet, so I had no difficulty spotting my charges. Tony, the sales director, was striding confidently ahead. He was smartly dressed for his presentation, wearing a beautifully-cut, and obviously expensive, Italian woollen suit. Stan was a factory worker, he was at the meeting because of his technical knowledge. He wore more casual clothes and was trudging along far behind his boss, loaded down with samples and leaflets. Immediately I sensed an air of tension between the two men.

After the usual handshakes and welcoming comments, I relieved Stan of half his load, and led the way towards my car. It was a lovely day, warm with a beautiful blue sky, although there were a few very tall and angry looking clouds around. I was just pointing out the distant Slieve Bearnagh mountains, which they had so recently flown over, when far to our right I heard a car alarm begin to bleat, followed by a second and a third.

Tony stopped dead and looked across the car park as a forth car alarm added to the commotion. "What the hell is going on over there?" he asked, squinting into the distance, where yet another car was now flashing and honking.

"Perhaps it's vandals – you know, kids or something," Stan said as we walked on.

"No, it isn't. There's something odd going on," Tony replied tersely.

I finally spotted my car in the distance and took a moment to look across to where another two alarms had just started honking. They sounded like geese preparing to migrate. Finally, I noticed the boiling blue clouds above us and what appeared to be hundreds of bouncing golf balls, marching across the car park in our direction, battering the cars and setting off the alarms along the way. Suddenly the penny dropped.

"That's hail – big hail," I shouted. "Quick, run to the car!"

We made the sixty-yard dash in record time. After a mad scramble for keys, Stan and I threw ourselves and his stock samples into the safety of the car. Just then, the full force of the storm hit with an explosion of lightning, water and ice. I started the car, turned the fan to full to try to clear the misted windows, and looked around to check on the welfare of my guests. It was only then I noticed we were one short.

"Stan, where's Tony?" I asked.

"I don't know. He was running along beside me and then he dropped his suitcase. Last I saw he was picking up his clothes," Stan replied, trying to keep the smirk on his face under control.

"Christ, he's going to get soaked," I said.

"Yes, and him in that lovely new suit as well," Stan chipped in brightly. "I suppose we'd better go and look for him."

"I can't see him anywhere," I said, peering over the roofs of a thousand rain-lashed cars. "Perhaps if I drove around a bit, we might spot him."

We unsuccessfully circled the car park for a couple of minutes, but it seemed like hours as the rain and hail intensified with each mighty crash of thunder.

"Maybe he went back into the terminal building," I proffered.

"If the weather is always like this, maybe he just went home."

Stan joked, and then pointed. "Ah! There he is – oh dear, that doesn't look good!"

"Oh dear indeed," I agreed as I spotted a bedraggled Tony, soaked through to the skin. He was standing pathetically alongside his broken suitcase and clutching an armful of muddy clothes.

We did our best to maintain our poker faces, as poor Tony told his tale.

"After my suitcase burst, I realised I was lost," he explained. "I didn't know which car you were in. I was still chasing my clothes around the car park when the full force of that storm hit."

Stan and I nodded.

"It was like standing in a carwash and being shot with golf balls," Tony whispered. "Is it always like this here?"

"Not at all," I replied. "We had a lovely summer. I think it was a Thursday."

Stan laughed, but Tony didn't. I tried to make light of the situation by pointing to the large 'Welcome to Ireland' sign at the exit of the airport. Tony refused to see the humour of the situation, particularly when it emerged that all of his clothes were soaked through. Because of his slightly rotund shape we were unable to lend any replacements. With only an hour to go before the meeting, and to avoid the prospect of the poor guy doing his sales presentation in a hotel bathrobe, I asked the hotel manager to arrange for Tony's suit and clothes to be dried as quickly as possible. However, to add another memorable moment to their trip, when his clothes were returned half an hour later, he discovered the laundry had tumble dried his beautiful woollen suit on maximum heat, leaving it looking like an undersized potato sack. The meeting was a roaring success and Tony cheered up considerably after securing several sales, despite his suit looking like it had been found in a skip outside a charity shop.

16. The bomb in the kitchen

The following weekend, lightning struck again. This time in the guise of a portly white Lhasa Apso.

As Lesley had volunteered to collect Joanne and Rebecca from the airport, I stayed behind and took the dogs for a long walk. On sunny mornings such as this, I was in the habit of walking across the beautiful gold and green moorland that sits to the west of our house. We followed a rough and rocky path that led from the road, winding through a field of car-sized boulders, before climbing up a hillside and along the clifftops opposite our home. Just as we reached the highest point of the path, around a mile from Glenmadrie, far below I spotted Lesley's car pulling into our driveway. She had returned from the airport.

I presume Romany either saw or heard the same thing, because as I looked over my shoulder to check her whereabouts, the little white dog was already a hundred yards away, bounding down the path towards the road that led back to our house and a cuddle from her mummy. When I shouted for Romany to stop, she ignored me, and when I bellowed and threatened, she only kicked up her heels and ran a little faster. We don't get much traffic up where we live, but when a car does come by, it will usually be travelling at speed, and the driver assumes any dogs in the road will get out of the way. Unlike an Irish dog, Romany was only ever taken on the road on a lead, and if she encountered a car whilst unshackled, she would probably stand in the middle of the road and stare defiantly until her swift and messy death. I quickly scooped Amber into my arms and then did my best to catch up with Romany, but it is not easy to run downhill, on rock lubricated with wet moss, whilst wearing rubber rain boots and juggling an excited puppy. As I reached the bottom of the hill, I heard a car speeding along the road. Still a hundred yards away, I could only close my eyes and wait for a screech of brakes, but the car passed on without slowing.

Luck was with us that day. Somehow Romany had negotiated the road unscathed. When I arrived back at the house, sweaty and panting, she was already there, woofing stubbornly at the front door.

"For a dog that won't even run after a ball, you can cover the ground rather well when you want to," I panted.

Ignoring my dagger-like stare, Romany looked at me with her liquid chocolate eyes and pleaded to be let indoors.

"I think we should change your name to Lightning," I said.

***

It was lovely to see Joanne again, as well as her flatmate, Rebecca. She was an old school friend of our daughter, who had been a regular guest in our house and even joined us on family holidays. The weekend was a whirlwind of sightseeing trips. Somehow we covered the Cliffs of Moher, the Burren and Limerick, all in one day. We also visited Galway, a first for Lesley and me. Although the city is surrounded by an ugly ring of motorways and retail parks, the interior is an enchanting complex of narrow, winding streets and antiquated shops. After being dragged around the clothes stores for half a day by our young companions, my wife and I got our revenge on the walk back to our car. We discovered a large second-hand book shop. It covered two floors of a disused grain store and boasted a fantastic selection of fiction, thrillers and biographies, all in paperback. They also had thousands of new hardbacks, in a remainders section on the first floor. A new life, a happy wife, and the company of my daughter, combined with as many second-hand books as I could carry. I felt like a lottery winner.

On the drive home, we stopped off to see the Kilmacduagh Round Tower and monastery, near to the village of Gort. There was a carpark, but little else. Rebecca laughed and pointed at a sign.

"Please bang on the door of number 23 behind you if you would like to purchase a visitor's guide," she read.

"That's pretty common around these parts. They're not big on advertising," I explained. "Apparently there are over 30,000 castles and monasteries in Ireland. Some are famous. Like Blarney castle in Cork, or Bunratty, where you're going tonight. But many of them are just ruins. Dots on the map that are free to explore, providing you're prepared to climb over a hedge and risk getting chased by a bull."

Rebecca shook her head in astonishment. "In England, they

would all have visitors' centres, a soft play area and an ice cream van."

The girls stared up at the tower.

"It looks like a medieval space rocket," Joanne joked. She was right.

I couldn't resist sharing one of my many useless facts. "At 112 feet high, this tower is the tallest pre-modern construction in Ireland." The girls groaned. "Or the shortest space rocket," I added.

"Oh look!" Lesley was pointing to one side of the carpark where several Japanese tourists had gathered to take pictures. We walked over to investigate. In the field, beyond the stone wall, was a new-born calf and its mother.

"How cute!" Joanne exclaimed.

The little calf, still wobbly on its impossibly gangly legs, was trying to feed. There was some confusion as the calf sucked first on the cow's shoulder then on its hip, but after a gentle push from its mother's snout, it soon found her teats and began sucking loudly. There was much oohing and aahing from the tourists, along with a volley of clicking cameras. The little calf broke contact and tried for another teat, but it couldn't reach. It turned away, becoming confused once again. Several people shouted directions, which the calf seemed to heed.

"It's remarkable how quickly these calves learn Japanese," I joked.

Circling around, the calf leaned under its mother's tail and grabbed a teat from behind. The crowd gave a triumphant cheer of encouragement.

"It's so sweet to see this caring side of nature," Joanne said.

As those words left her mouth, the cow promptly lifted her tail and dumped a colossal waterfall of liquid faeces along the back and head of her new child. The tourists groaned and turned away.

"And I guess that is one of life's little lessons," Rebecca added stoically.

That evening Lesley took Joanne and Rebecca to the medieval banquet at Bunratty Castle. Like a good husband, I remained at home with the dogs and went to bed early, leaving the girls free to make a proper night of it, which apparently they did. It was late morning when a bleary-eyed Lesley emerged to give me the edited version.

"We had a terrific time at the banquet. There was lots of singing and dancing and banging of mugs. The girls thought it was great craic. But when it was over, they didn't really want to come home. As luck would have it, we were driving back when Rebecca spotted a pub that was still open."

"I'm shocked," I joked. "That girl has a sharp eye."

Lesley tutted dramatically. "Anyway, she begged me to stop, which I did. I figured we'd just beat 'last orders', so there'd be enough time for one drink before we could come home."

"I'm guessing you were wrong?"

"Too right," she sighed. "The party was just getting started. There was a band, loads of people and even a couple of Guards drinking at the bar."

"In uniform?" I asked.

Lesley nodded. "Apparently, it's called a 'lock-in', where the barman locks everyone in. It's loosely classed as a private party."

"What time did you get back?"

"Around 4 am."

"Good grief," I exclaimed. "Had they forgotten they're flying back to England this afternoon?"

"I did mention it, several times." She glanced at the kitchen clock. "Goodness. I'd better go and wake them."

The girls were difficult to wake and considerably less convivial than a few hours earlier. With much coffee and cajoling, we managed to get them to the airport in time for their flight.

"They look like the last two zombies leaving the apocalypse," I remarked. "I'll bet even that calf yesterday feels better than they do just now."

"Fifty shades of green," Lesley observed dryly. "Just another of life's little lessons."

***

As the weather improved, the days seemed to blur into each other in a fog of cleaning, building, gardening, and seeing clients. The cleaning became an almost hourly chore, or so it seemed. We had two dogs that refused to wipe their feet, despite playing for hours in my pile of builder's sand. Inside the house, the rain of dust and soot from the ceilings was constant. It was particularly noticeable on windy days, and Ireland has lots of windy days. But not all the mess was caused by dust.

It was a warm spring morning and Lesley and I were upstairs. She was helping me repair the rotten floorboards in the front bedroom. Our quiet conversation was interrupted by what can only be described as a wet bang. This dull boom shook the floor I was kneeling on, as if someone had dropped a large over-ripe pumpkin from a height. We shared a startled look.

"What on earth was that?" Lesley asked.

"We'd better have a look."

As we started down the stairs, there was a second bang, every bit as wet sounding as the first. This time I could clearly hear the distinctive sound of flowing liquid.

Lesley looked confused.

"Sounds like a water leak," I suggested.

There was a leak, but it wasn't water. The kitchen floor was awash with sparkling liquid and the air was thick with the smell of apples.

"Oh no!" Lesley exclaimed. "It's that bloody cider. The bottles have exploded."

She was right. There were three bottles of Devil's Bite in the pantry. Two of them had burst like overinflated balloons, spraying sticky cider up the walls and across the floor.

"It's still fermenting," I explained. "The pressure inside the bottles must be tremendous."

As if to confirm my theory, the third bottle chose that precise moment to explode with a dull, wet thud.

"Oh no!" Lesley cried as we were both sprayed with cider.

It took several hours to clean up the mess. The floor had to be scrubbed twice and every jar, can, packet and shelf in the larder washed. On the upside, the alcohol in the fermenting cider did a magnificent job of removing some of the more stubborn stains from the kitchen floor. Suffice to say, I never bought that particular brand of cider again.

The renovations were progressing slowly, but every day brought some small signs of progress. I had installed the new roof on the wing, built the structure for the internal walls, extended the plumbing and added new lights and electrical sockets. Once the new windows were fitted, I would add the plasterboard walls and install the shower, toilet and sink. While we waited for the windows to be delivered, there was still plenty to do.

A 'proper builder' would simply have chucked all the scrap wood into a skip, or on a big bonfire, but to us this old wood was a valuable source of free heat. But recycling it was a torturously slow process. Before I could saw each length into pieces that would fit in the stove, we had to laboriously remove the old screws and rusty nails. Only then could it be stacked under cover, ready for the winter. It was a lot of additional graft and added considerably to how long each section of building work took, but we had plenty of time and probably saved thousands of euro on skips and firewood.

***

With our limited budget for the renovation, we had to get the best possible deal on every purchase, and keep our spending under control. Had we lived closer to the border, I would probably have made regular trips across to pay in sterling, but the time involved and travel costs from Clare would have made the benefit questionable. Although, whenever one of us visited family by taking a car on the ferry, rather than the much cheaper Ryanair option, we would return with the vehicle so laden with bargains as to be practically dragging the exhaust along the road.

Lesley has an eye for a good deal and during her trip to England she found a pet shop selling 20 kilogram bags of wild bird seed, for one third of the Irish price. We were getting through three sacks a month, so there was undoubtedly money to be saved. In her desire to capitalise on this windfall, my wife loaded her little Citroën estate to the limit. Although she arrived home safely, her trip was not without a little adventure.

"As I left the ferry at Dublin Port, the exhaust dragged on the ramp," she explained, sipping her coffee. "That little shower of sparks must have raised an eyebrow somewhere because a few yards later, I was stopped by a customs official."

"Oh dear," I said. "What did he want?"

"That's exactly what I asked *him*," she replied, shrugging. "He seemed a little taken aback by my tone. I guess I was a trifle irritated by having my journey interrupted. It's a long drive and I was keen to get home."

I grimaced and waited for her to continue.

"Well, even though he looked rather po-faced and officious, I smiled sweetly and apologised for snapping at him." Lesley rolled her eyes. "It didn't work though. He pointed out that the suspension looked rather low and asked what I was transporting."

"Ah!" I grimaced again. "And when you said 'Twenty-five sacks of wild bird seed' did he believe you?"

"No, he didn't," she growled. "He told me to unload the car."

"Really?" I exclaimed. "With your bad back, you had to unload all those sacks?"

"No." She shook her head. "As soon as I stood up, he realised I was in no fit state to do any lifting."

"So what happened?" I asked.

"Well, he was committed by then," she explained. Her blue eyes sparkled mischievously and she gave me an evil grin over her coffee cup. "So he had to do it himself."

"He unloaded all of them?" I laughed as she nodded.

"By the end, I actually felt sorry for him." Lesley shook her head and smiled. "The poor guy refused to believe anyone would willingly buy so much seed, just to feed some wild birds. But he unloaded every sack before realising I wasn't a drug mule, just an eccentric English lady."

Unfortunately, not every journey ended with a smile.

***

I recall it was a Wednesday in late spring when Lesley decided she would drive to Ennis. We needed groceries and she wanted to search out a garden centre she had heard about. I stayed at the house. There was work to do, but first I needed to check our email account and send a couple of messages. The computer desk was on the landing at the top of the stairs. Again the internet connection was painfully slow. I'd just slipped into that digital fugue state, clicking mindlessly on a couple of news stories, when I heard the front door slam shut.

"Nick!" Lesley shouted over the noise of barking dogs.

"You're back early," I shouted, starting down the stairs.

Silence. Lesley was in the kitchen, with her face in her hands, she was shaking visibly.

"What's the matter?" I asked.

"I've just wrecked the car," she sobbed, falling into my arms.

"What…? How…?" I stammered. "Are you okay?"

Lesley sighed.

"I'm fine, just a little stiff." She rolled her head and rubbed her neck. "I'm just annoyed."

"Sit down," I ordered, guiding her to a chair. "I'll make a drink."

"Thank you." I could see her hands were shaking.

"What happened?" I asked, passing her a cup of coffee.

After a couple of sips, she shut her eyes and shook her head, forcing herself to relive the moment.

"I had just passed the crossroads," she began, her voice faulting with emotion. "You know the bit where the road has been resurfaced?"

"The white farm with the little black dog?" I asked.

She nodded and wiped her eyes with a tissue.

"I was just driving along when this big red truck came flying around the corner. It was right in the middle of the road and the man driving was talking on his mobile phone."

I tutted in sympathy.

"I had to swerve and brake really hard, otherwise he would have hit me," she explained, her voice rising in anger. "The car skidded on the loose gravel and I spun around and hit the embankment."

I shook my head. "Are you sure you aren't hurt?"

"I'm fine," she replied. "I'm just shaken up. It all happened so quickly."

"How did you get back here?" I asked.

"This nice man stopped his car and gave me a lift back home." She started to sob.

I hugged her and waited for the emotion to pass. "Don't worry, love," I whispered into her hair. "It's just a car."

"Oh Christ!" she yelped, her eyes wide. "The car! We have to get the car."

"Don't worry. It can wait."

"But you don't understand," she replied, standing up. "It's right in the middle of the road. Come on!"

Lesley hadn't underestimated the significance of the crash. Our lovely Citroën was truly wrecked. On a bend in the road, it sat almost sideways to any approaching traffic. It was steaming gently and huddled as if in pain. The front was about a foot shorter than before, bent downward and twisted to the right. The lights, indicators and grill were just a tangle of unrecognisable bits. The bonnet was still attached, but pushed rearwards and riding up the windscreen. Underneath, there was a trickle of vital fluids making two puddles, one dark red and the other bright green.

"It looks like the radiator and power steering have leaked," I said. "I'd better try and move it. Where are the keys?"

"Still in the ignition," Lesley said, smiling tightly. "I don't think anyone is going to steal it."

"Can you wait over there?" I pointed to the far side of the corner. "Just in case another car comes, you can flag them down."

I waited until she was in place. The driver's door had popped out of its frame. I had to pull hard to open it. It finally complied, albeit with a tortuous creak. The trusty diesel engine started at the first turn of the key and the car moved okay, but it refused to turn. A quick investigation revealed the problem. The offside wheel arch was jammed against the tyre, and after a couple of mighty tugs, I managed to pull it free. With some semblance of control restored, I manoeuvred the car into a safe parking space.

I was clearing the debris from the road when a Garda patrol car pulled up. He wound his window down.

"I heard there was a crash. Anyone hurt?" he asked.

"She's a bit scared is all." I nodded towards Lesley. "Some idiot, driving too fast and chatting on a mobile phone, ran her off the road."

"It happens," he replied stoically. "Did she get a registration number?"

I shook my head.

"Do you need a tow truck?"

"No thanks. We're only up the road," I explained. "I'll manage."

"Okay. Good luck!" He sped away.

Lesley drove my car back to the house. I followed on behind in the Citroën, clanking, scraping and steaming. By the time we reached the house, several warning lights were glowing on the dashboard and the temperature gauge was bending against the high stop. As I parked in our driveway, our trusty Citroën wheezed and coughed once, before falling silent for the last time. A few days later, our insurance company had it towed away and scrapped.

Despite being apparently uninjured, by the weekend Lesley's back, neck, and right hip were so sore she could hardly walk. We made a trip to our local doctor. He was satisfied she had only suffered some bruising and recommended bed rest and painkillers. The accident was a terrifying incident, but the outcome could have been much worse, or so we thought.

17. A matter of death and life

Like a wasp in a jam jar held against my head, the gentle *purr-purr* of the phone ringing tickled my ear.

"*Please be there*," I prayed.

The distant ringing continued, unanswered. I stared glumly out of the car window.

"*I'll give it five more rings.*"

"Hello?" Lesley was panting.

"Oh, you've answered," I said.

"Of course I've answered," she replied.

"I didn't think you would."

"Then why did you phone?" she snapped.

"I meant I thought you would be in the garden," I explained. "I thought you wouldn't hear the phone."

"I didn't. I was hanging out the washing. But I heard Amber singing to the phone, so I knew someone was ringing."

"Oh yes, Amber." I pictured her standing on the couch howling at the phone. I laughed. "Silly dog."

"And?" Lesley elongated the word into a question.

"Sorry?"

"Why did you phone?" my wife asked somewhat more tolerantly than I deserved.

"What? Err…" Momentarily confused, I stumbled for a line of thought. "Oh yes. You need to come to town."

"Now?" she exclaimed, elongating the word again.

"Right now, please," I pleaded. "There's something you need to see. It's important."

"But I'm really busy. It's such a lovely day. I'm trying to get the washing done."

"Come on," I begged. "Take a break. It's important. I promise."

My wife must have sensed something in my voice, some air of desperation mixed with honesty. She agreed to meet me within the hour at the shopping centre where I was parked. While I waited, I visited the deli counter and filled my time and stomach with a cheese roll and a Danish whirl, all washed down with a cup of tea. I was just putting my rubbish in the bin when Lesley pulled up.

She was driving a hire car provided by the insurance company while we waited for our new (second-hand) car to be serviced and valeted. I smiled and waved for her to follow me. She nodded, but her face said *this had better be good.*

Minutes later, we parked outside a nondescript building at the far end of a dreary industrial park. As I helped my wife climb out of the car, she grunted and winced in pain. Her back and neck seemed to be getting worse, despite the painkillers. Casting her eyes over the grey frontage and barbed wire topped walls, she frowned.

"What is this place?" she asked. "It looks like a prison."

"Close," I replied. "It's the dog pound."

"Oh." Her face brightened and she seemed to stand a little taller. "I didn't know there was a dog pound here."

"Me neither." I pointed across the road. "I was looking for that plumbing merchants when I heard barking. So I went to investigate."

"You've been in?" she asked.

I nodded. "I'll warn you now, it's pretty grim. But I've found a lovely dog."

Lesley tutted, as if I were an impish but likeable child – which I guess I am.

I checked my watch, we were just in time. "It's the sweetest puppy, you must see it." I took her hand. "Come on."

The interior of the dog pound was hideously bleak. It was dark and damp, with industrial concrete walls, cement floors, iron cages, and everywhere the smell of fear, urine, and cleaning products. Our arrival triggered a cacophony of barking. A small bearded man in rough blue overalls, came around the corner, shouting for quiet. He saw me and raised a hand in acknowledgment.

"You're back then," he observed.

I introduced Lesley to Hank, the attendant.

"You'll be wanting to see that dog." He led the way to a cage at the far end. Inside there were two dogs, both puppies, both bitches. A black collie was curled in the corner watching warily but in the front a small brown and white dog was bouncing up and down, demanding our attention.

"Oh, how cute!" Lesley exclaimed. "Do you know what breed

it is?"

"I'd say it's a Foxhound, with perhaps a bit of Beagle," Hank suggested.

"That would account for the brown eyes and floppy ears," I said.

The little dog was licking Lesley's hand and desperately scrabbling for attention. She scooped it into her arms where it proceeded to lick her face. She giggled like a schoolgirl. Already it was a done deal.

"What's the procedure for adopting a dog here?" she asked.

When we rescued dogs in England, there was a good deal of form filling, followed by a home suitability visit and a not-insubstantial fee.

"You pays me 20 euros." Hank sniffed and spat on the floor. "But you'd better make up your minds, it's almost knocking off time."

"Oh, do you close early on a Friday?" I asked.

"We closes for the weekend," he explained. "Three o'clock on a Friday is when any dogs left over is knocked off."

There was a moment of stunned silence as we processed the significance of what Hank had just said. Even the dogs stopped barking. The casual nature with which he delivered this comment was chilling. Lesley and I stood, dumbstruck and open-mouthed.

"We got no staff you see," Hank explained, reaching out to give the puppy a tickle. Lesley involuntarily stepped back, drawing the little dog closer.

"All these dogs are going to be put down?" she whispered, her voice straining to contain her emotion.

"Except this one, I'm guessing," Hank smiled shyly.

"And that one." I pointed at the huddled form of the small black collie. It was a snap decision, but Lesley didn't contradict me.

"That one don't like men," he warned. "I expect she's been kicked around a bit."

I expect she has I thought.

"We're taking her!" Lesley insisted. And that was the end of that.

I felt sorry for Hank. He seemed like a nice man, struggling to do his best in difficult circumstances. It wasn't his fault a lack of funding was a death sentence for so many rescued animals.

The long walk out of that kennel block was one of the hardest things I have ever done. Passing 20 upturned faces, 20 sets of pleading eyes, 20 dogs about to die for the crime of being too old, too hungry, unloved, or just being lost, broke my heart. That we were saving two dogs from certain death, was of little comfort. By the time both dogs were safely curled asleep on the back seat of my car, Lesley and I were both openly crying.

"What a horrid place," Lesley sobbed, wiping her eyes. "I feel so guilty."

"Me too." I pulled her into a hug. "My head's in a spin. We wanted another dog and I thought adopting a rescue was a good idea. Now we have two, yet I feel shamefaced, leaving the others behind."

"We can only do so much." Lesley glared at the door of the dog pound. "Perhaps our 40 euro will go some way towards saving a few more."

We comforted each other with a shared hug. Our silent reverie was interrupted by a polite tapping on the side window of my car. The Foxhound was trying to attract our attention.

"Someone wants her dinner." I pointed and laughed. "Come on, let's go."

"We'd better stop at the pet shop on the way," Lesley suggested. "We need collars, leads, food bowls and puppy food."

"Don't forget dog beds."

"I suppose we should get a few dog toys as well," Lesley said. "Amber won't be happy if someone steals her Sucky Toy."

I looked at the Foxhound sitting on the rear seat, her intelligent brown eyes scrutinised me with a steady gaze. I brought my nose to the glass.

"We've owned you for less than 20 minutes and already you're costing a fortune!"

Clearly grateful, the little puppy licked the window, smearing my view with a thick trail of slob.

"Well, that's gratitude for you!" I laughed.

The drive home was uneventful, which is dog owner code for 'No one was car sick'. We drove in convoy and arrived at the house together. Whilst Lesley went indoors to settle Amber and Romany, I put our two new charges onto the lawn to give them time to settle and have a pee. The Foxhound was perky and inquisitive, but the Collie seemed shy and lethargic. Hank was right, she definitely didn't seem to trust men. Although she had seemed happy for Lesley to pick her up, whenever I approached she dropped to the ground and cowered in fear. I wondered what could have happened to make such a young dog so afraid of men. This moment of solitude and contemplation didn't last long, soon Romany and Amber came bounding around the corner.

I was prepared to intervene in the event of any fisticuffs, but I need not have worried. After a short period of cautious circling and some polite bum sniffing, our family of four dogs set off together to investigate my pile of sand. When compared to Amber, the new puppies were a lot bigger than I had first thought. Particularly the black Collie.

"That one's going to be big," I suggested. "Her paws are almost the size of my fist."

"She seems very gentle," Lesley said. "What shall we call them?"

"How about calling this one Lady?" I pointed at the Foxhound. "She's so demure."

"Okay, that fits," Lesley agreed. "But what about the Collie."

I tilted my head. "Blackie?"

"No."

"Inky?" I suggested.

"No."

"Sheba?"

"No."

"Tramp?"

"Don't be silly," Lesley chided. "That's a boy's name."

I grimaced and scratched my chin, lost in thought.

Lesley snapped her fingers. "Kia!" she shouted.

She must have been right, for Kia trotted over and sat at her feet as if to say, "You called?"

Bright and early the next morning, we took our new puppies to the vet for a thorough check-up and to begin their course of inoculations. Although everything went well, our initial optimism was short-lived, as I discovered a few days later.

Being an early riser, I am usually the first person downstairs in the morning. After putting the kettle on and two slices of bread into the toaster, I went to let the dogs out. But before I had even opened the conservatory door, the smell hit me. It was an acridly vile stomach-turning stink, reminiscent of the dog kennels, but exponentially more intense. The conservatory floor was liberally splattered with faeces, some solid and some runny, interspaced with a kind of blood-stained jelly. Holding my breath, I tiptoed a serpentine path through and threw open the doors.

Lesley came downstairs just as I was putting the mop and disinfectant away. Bleary-eyed and tousled-haired, she sniffed the air experimentally and wrinkled her nose in distaste.

"Did one of the dogs have an accident?" she asked.

"I'll say," I replied, spraying the air freshener for a second time. "I don't think Kia is very well."

"She probably just needs house training."

"I think this is a little more serious," I replied.

"It does smell pretty vile," she admitted.

"This is nothing, you should have smelt it earlier. The outside door's been open for 20 minutes."

Lesley looked at the kitchen clock. "It's a bit early yet, but I'll give the vet a phone in a while."

"Okay," I said. "In the meantime, I'll dish up some breakfast for the dogs that want to eat."

If we had any doubts about which dog was feeling poorly, they were soon dispelled once the food was ready. While the others cleared their dishes in a matter of seconds, Kia remained in her bed looking sad and miserable. Kneeling down I gently stroked her head, running my fingers through her silky, soft black fur. She felt hot to the touch. Two watery dark eyes watched me warily, but she made no effort to flinch away from my hand as she usually would. Her nose was dry and she seemed fragile and sleepy. As I returned to the kitchen, Lesley was just finishing her call to the vet.

"Katy said not to worry just now. Kia was fine when she saw her a few days ago, so she's probably just a bit upset by the change of scenery and the different food," Lesley explained. "She said to starve her for a couple of days and then try her on a little boiled rice and chicken."

I frowned. "She seems quite poorly."

"As long as she's drinking, there's nothing to worry about. It's probably just an upset stomach. I'm sure she'll be fine in a couple of days."

"Let's hope so."

We kept a close eye on Kia throughout the day. She was lethargic and sleepy, refusing to drink and only leaving her bed when forced by the frequent bouts of diarrhoea, which stank dreadfully. We spoke to the vet in the evening. She agreed Kia was definitely getting worse and asked us to bring her in first thing the following day. By that time the little dog was pathetically limp and unresponsive, her eyes dull and fearful. Katy finished her examination with a deep sigh.

"I was afraid of this," she said. "The smell is an indicator. It looks very much like she's got parvo."

"What's Parvo?" I asked.

"Canine parvovirus," she replied, putting her stethoscope aside. "It's the most infectious disease among dogs and the most deadly, particularly in puppies. The commonest form is enteritis, where the intestines are infected, hence the smell. That's what Kia has. The symptoms are fever, vomiting, diarrhoea, general lethargy and a loss of appetite. Parvo is a nasty disease. After invading and inflaming the small intestine, which stops the absorption of nutrients, the virus assaults the dog's weakened immune system, opening the road to secondary infections."

"It sounds dreadfully bad," Lesley whispered, as if she were trying to shield the little dog from the truth.

"I'm afraid it is," Katy was stroking Kia's head. "The mortality rate for dogs left untreated can be as high as 80 percent."

Lesley's hand covered her mouth, stifling an involuntary whimper.

"Can you cure it?" I asked.

Katy sighed and shook her head. "There is no cure, Kia has to beat it herself. But I can help."

"Oh please do!" Lesley sobbed.

"The most effective treatment is to keep her warm, well hydrated, and clear of secondary infections," Katy explained. "I'll need to keep her here, probably for some time. She'll need intravenous fluids and a high dose of antibiotics."

"Sure," I replied. "Do whatever she needs."

"Can we visit?" Lesley asked.

Katy grimaced. "Not really. It would be best if we keep her

quiet. You can phone though. I'll keep you informed."

"What are her chances?" I asked. Practical me.

Katy bit her lip and frowned. "I won't lie to you. She has a tough battle ahead, but she's fit and strong. If I can maintain her fluids and keep on top of the infection, she may pull through."

Every morning we phoned the vet for an update on Kia's health. Every morning the response was the same.

"I'm sorry, she's no better."

We dreaded that morning call, always anticipating the worst.

"Katie says Kia's still hanging in there," Lesley reported sadly. "She didn't sound very optimistic."

"I'm sure she's doing all she can." I hugged my wife close to my chest.

That Kia would have been euthanised had we not rescued her was of little comfort. We were emotionally invested in the little black puppy and desperate for her to pull through. For six days she hung in a fragile balance, somewhere between life and death. The outcome looked bleak.

Perhaps it was because she was such a gentle puppy, who looked so desperately helpless and frightened as the virus raged through her body, or perhaps it was because some vets have a kind heart and love dogs, but Katy refused to allow Kia to die. Later we heard that Katy had cared for Kia around the clock. For a week, she came in early, stayed late and visited in the night, administering fluids, heat blankets and huge doses of antibiotics. It was a herculean task of medical dedication.

One morning our phone rang. It was Katy.

"I think we've beaten it!" she reported, making no effort to keep the delight from her voice. "Kia has been eating and drinking without incident since yesterday. If she continues like this, you can collect her this afternoon."

"Oh how wonderful!" I said. Lesley was at my side clapping her hands and doing a little dance.

"Thank you, Katy!" she shouted into the receiver. "Thank you so much."

Once we had her home, Kia's appetite gradually improved and she started to put on a little weight, demonstrating remarkable resilience as she quickly returned to full health. It was delightful to see her joyously running along with the other dogs, joining in all of the games and adding her distinctive woof to the others in the pack. We will be forever grateful to Katy and the other vets in the village for another life saved.

18. The pillar palaver

It was an exciting day, at least for me. We were taking delivery of the car we had bought to replace Lesley's crumpled Citroën – may it rust in peace. I returned the loan vehicle and took possession of our new (second-hand) car from a local garage. Given how much trouble we'd encountered trying to buy the Ford, this purchase had been ridiculously easy. I'd spoken with the garage owner, told him what I was looking for and two days later I was taking a bright red Skoda estate for a test drive. Job done!

As soon as I arrived back at Glenmadrie, our new possession was surrounded by our dogs like fans mobbing a pop star, with considerably more sniffing. Lesley was rather more reserved, standing back with her arms folded but admiring the gleaming paintwork nonetheless.

"Come on, let's go for a drive," I suggested.

"I've work to do."

"So have I." I nudged her with my elbow. "Come on. It's a lovely day. We'll drive up to Lough Atorick."

"Shall we take the dogs?"

"Best not." I grinned. "I'd like to keep the car puke-free, at least for a couple of days."

Lesley laughed, reacting to my excitement. "Okay, let's go."

It was a bright, warm, sunny morning. The cloudless azure sky curved overhead from treeline to mountain top, broken only by the single white contrail of a commercial airliner heading west. The Skoda purred along happily as we plunged down the mountain road. I looked to the right and below, towards the hamlet of Caher sitting alongside the shoreline of beautiful Lough Graney, but all I could see was a sea of fog. Shining brilliant white in the dazzling sunshine, the impenetrable haze completely covered the lake.

"Oh, wow!" Lesley exclaimed. "How beautiful."

I nodded. "See how the treetops are sticking up around the edges of the lake. It looks like really deep snow."

Moments later we entered the fog bank. For a short while, visibility was no more than a few yards. I slowed the car to walking pace, but as we continued downhill the fog soon cleared.

"This isn't fog," I said. "It's low cloud."

Under the thick blanket, the world was grey, dank and miserable. We passed through Caher and turned off towards Lough Atorick. The little engine growled excitedly as we began the long climb up Knockbeha mountain and onwards to Lough Atorick. Again we entered the cloud, then moments later, like a whale breaching, we burst back into bright sunshine. The temperature rose appreciably, so I opened the windows.

"It's hard to believe the weather can be so different," Lesley remarked. "The people down there must think it's a miserable day."

"And yet at Glenmadrie the sun is shining," I replied. "The benefits of living up a mountain, I guess."

As the air cooled, my wife closed the windows and turned up the heater. Summer in Ireland.

"This is a nice little car," I said. "Low mileage and a good price."

"It's certainly clean in here," Lesley said, running her hand along the dashboard.

"I doubt it will stay like this for long. Tomorrow, it starts its new life as our builder's van."

"I thought everything was being delivered."

"A lot of it is. The cement, radiators, two kitchen units and a load of wood will come by lorry," I replied. "But I'll have to drive to Limerick to collect the doors and fixings."

"How many doors?"

"There's eight," I said. "Five internal and two for the front."

Lesley squinted and nodded as she considered my maths.

"Also, I have to collect the scaffolding from the hire company," I added. "That way we save on delivery."

"Will it fit in here?"

I nodded. "Apparently it comes to bits. It should fit just fine."

"Are you removing that pillar this weekend?" Lesley asked.

"As long as it stays like this." I squinted at the bright sunshine. "I wouldn't want to do it in the lashing rain."

"Are you sure it's safe to take out?"

"Definitely," I replied, with rather more confidence than I felt. "That pillar goes right to the roofline. It's purely cosmetic. It'll probably fall over with the first good shove."

I could see my wife thinking about the wall she pushed over in the cow shed.

"Shall I…?"

"No thanks!" I laughed. "Anyway, if you shove it over it will fall onto your vegetable plot."

It was getting much warmer inside the car as the bright sun shone through the windows. My eyes were getting sticky and I felt tired. I wished I could turn down the heat. Lesley and I always disagreed about the best temperature when driving. I preferred shirtsleeves and an open window, whereas she favoured two coats and the heater on full blast. The increasing warmth was accompanied by a peculiar aroma.

My wife sniffed and wrinkled her nose, eyeing me suspiciously. "Did you just…?"

"No!" I exclaimed, winding down the window. "It must be from outside."

But it wasn't. Each time we closed the windows the smell got worse. It occurred to me with the weather being dry and sunny, I had test driven the Skoda with the windows open. Now they were shut for the first time, the interior of the car held a very peculiar bouquet.

"What is that smell?" Lesley asked, twisting around in an attempt to identify the source.

"I have no idea," I pleaded. "But it's pretty rank."

"Perhaps the one careful owner was a goat," she joked.

"You could be right."

Later, I searched the car thoroughly and identified a sticky stain beneath the driver's seat that may once have been the contents of a yogurt pot. I gave it a good scrub with carpet cleaner and several proprietary chemicals usually reserved for embalming. Although the stain disappeared, the smell was still noticeable, particularly on sunny days. Fortunately, in Ireland, such events are a rarity.

***

Once the wing was finished and the pesky pillar removed, my next job would be to replace the Clearlite roof on a long, covered walkway enclosing our courtyard. Along with the new roof on the old milking parlour, we would then have some 500 square feet of covered workspace for storing supplies and cutting wood, as well as an ad hoc greenhouse.

The following morning I collected the scaffolding from the hire shop. It was just a large pile of aluminium poles and a platform, liberally splattered in paint and plaster. It fitted in the car as promised, leaving pink and blue marks on everything it touched. Arriving home just ahead of the lorry carrying our building materials, I was conveniently on hand to guide them in and help with the unloading. Once the lorry had gone, Lesley and I began the arduous task of moving everything from the driveway to the conservatory, which had become an impromptu staging area to keep things dry and safe. One unfortunate disadvantage of the quirky layout of Glenmadrie is the need to move building supplies several times before they are used. This is something Amber considers to be a jolly game.

Whenever we carry sacks of cement, garden peat, or some other unwieldy items to safe storage, Amber will dance around our feet, woofing for attention, *gr-rap gr-rap gr-rap*, until her ball is thrown. Lesley and I have become quite adept at kicking Amber's ball every eight paces, regardless of the weight we're carrying. Moving lengths of wood together requires a different technique and rather more co-ordination. After much practice and a couple of minor injuries, we established that only the person facing forwards was to kick the ball, using a gentle flick of the foot, so as not to lose step with the person walking backwards.

Like many terriers, Amber has quite short legs and a stiff, muscular torso. She loves to be placed on her back and given a tummy tickle, where she will squirm and giggle like a child. When she runs after her ball, she makes a *hup-hup-hup-hup* sound, like a Special Forces soldier abseiling down the side of a building. The combination of her barks and panting noises are quite distinctive, and potentially rather irritating, as I discovered later that afternoon.

As it was a dry day, I decided to clean out the guttering. At Glenmadrie, the air is pure and we are surrounded by tall pine trees. The combination of wind-blown pine needles and thick moss growing on the roof slates, fills the guttering with a gloopy, black peaty sludge. Left unattended, this rich compost will soon become a mini garden, blocking the guttering and sending rainwater cascading down the side of the house. The only solution is to don rubber gloves and laboriously scoop it into a bucket by hand. Although I now had some scaffolding to play with, unlike a ladder, it wasn't really a practical platform for clearing gutters. So I stuck with my tried and tested method.

I was halfway up, happily climbing the ladder for the sixth time when the darn thing suddenly snapped in the middle.

"Uh-oh!"

As the ladder hinged at the break, my legs shot forwards until my feet hit the wall. For an instant I was hanging horizontally in mid-air, desperately clutching the bucket to my chest and hoping for the power of levitation. As gravity took hold, I distinctly remember thinking *This is going to hurt*. With a clatter and an oof, I landed flat on my back in a flowerbed. My eyes watered with the force of the impact and I was temporarily winded, but otherwise unhurt.

As I lay staring at the sky and attempting to draw a breath, I waited for my wife to come rushing to my rescue. I pictured her concerned face hovering over me as she administered to my wounds with the first aid kit and a caring smile. In reality, Lesley was busy on the other side of the house and unaware of my fall. But I was not alone. The first sound I heard was the distinctive *hup-hup-hup-hup* of Amber approaching, followed by a demanding *gr-rap gr-rap gr-rap* as she motioned towards the ball she had just deposited at my side. Being a good slave, I grudgingly obeyed, throwing the ball twice before trying to extract myself from the remains of the ladder. Life is more interesting with the combined joys of dogs and DIY.

***

Although it was going to be a couple of weeks before the new window would arrive, I decided to get everything ready by removing the pillar, knocking off the old cement render, replacing the concrete sill and temporarily refitting the old windows. Mostly things went along swimmingly, except for that blasted centre pillar.

"This bloody thing's made of solid concrete," I exclaimed.
"Is that a problem?" Lesley asked.

"I'll say," I growled. "I've been at this for hours and I've hardly scratched it. If we hadn't already paid for the new window, I would just refit the old ones and be done with it."

"Maybe you aren't doing it right," Lesley suggested, somewhat unhelpfully. Perhaps she was hoping to empower me to superhuman strength with a burst of angry adrenalin. I took a deep, calming breath.

"It seems to be impervious to damage," I said, through clenched teeth. "The pickaxe just bounced off. Even my best masonry drill bit is ruined. I think this pillar's made of solid concrete, reinforced with steel rebar."

"Really?" Lesley exclaimed.

"It's ironic, given how everything else in this house is falling down. I'd call this a slight case of overkill. There's nothing for the pillar to support except for a lintel and the guttering above. It's just crazy."

My wife rolled her eyes supportively and left me to it. Secretly, I suspected she was tutting to herself at my apparent inability to complete a simple task. After all, hadn't she demolished an entire wall with a single shove of her slim shoulder?

After several hours using an electric chisel and a disc cutter, I managed to cut through the top of the pillar. In the process, I sprayed everything for 50 yards with dust and sparks, triggering several small fires. Luckily, before moving to Ireland, I had purchased two sets of purple motor racing overalls at a local market. They were on sale for the princely sum of just £10. Not only were they excellent value, but the bright colour would make it easier to spot my body in the rubble should I ever cock up the construction. More importantly, they were fireproof, which was a good thing, as I seemed to set myself on fire rather a lot.

It took almost another full day of hacking away before I had managed to cut a three-inch slot through the concrete at the bottom of the pillar, finally exposing the four pieces of steel rebar stubbornly holding it upright and in place.

"My plan is to cut through the two rebars on the inside of the pillar and then, by bending the two outer bars, lay the pillar onto the scaffolding," I explained.

"Well, mind you don't damage my garden," Lesley warned.

"Don't worry." I smiled reassuringly. "All I have to do is cut the remaining rebar and lay the pillar on top of the scaffolding. Then I can use a couple of stout planks to slide the pillar safely down. Easy-peasy."

My wife squinted at me as if I were a political candidate promising the earth in exchange for her vote. She tutted to herself. I was slightly disappointed by her lack of confidence in my abilities.

At first, my plan went swimmingly. I used my diamond-edged disc to cut the first two rebars and with a lot of pushing, bent the pillar outwards until it laid on the top platform of the scaffolding. The only thing holding this six-foot length of concrete in place was the final two sections of rebar, now bent almost double by the tremendous weight. I took a deep breath and began to cut.

Everything went as I had anticipated, until the last moment. As I dissected the second set of rebars, there was a sudden sound like a freight train driving through a lorry. I watched open-mouthed in horror as the scaffolding folded like a cheap lawn chair and disappeared in a cloud of dust and bent aluminium. Swearing like a Glaswegian squaddie on a stag do, I leaned forward to survey the damage. It wasn't a pretty sight. The scaffolding was folded in two and comprehensively wrecked. On the positive side, the window pillar was finally out, sitting undamaged in the crater it had carved in the centre of Lesley's prized vegetable garden.

My wife forgave me for flattening her squashes, but the damage to the scaffolding was another matter. I did my best to unbend and reconstruct the platform, but in the end I had to admit defeat. Sheepishly, I loaded the car and headed for the hire shop.

"Look, I'm ever so sorry," I explained as we examined the bent scaffolding remains. "It just collapsed. I did my best to fix it, but as you can see…"

The manager of the hire firm was biting his bottom lip and scratching his head.

I felt obliged to fill the dreadful silence.

"Of course I'll pay for the damage," I said.

The manager scratched his crotch thoughtfully.

"I'm really very sorry," I added.

The manager experimentally poked a mangled aluminium pole with his toe. Finally he sighed.

"Well, I guess you've been honest with me," he said. "It was obviously an accident."

"Oh, it was," I agreed.

"Okay." He nodded. "No charge."

I was delighted that things had worked out on the scaffolding front. Driving home, I calculated the money we had saved. My elation didn't last long. While I was out, we'd had another thunderstorm. Despite Lesley running around like a demented chicken unplugging every appliance at the first rumble of thunder, the telephone, satellite box and the water pump relay were once again fried. You win some and you lose some.

***

As a DIY builder, I have developed extensive experience of what can go wrong when doing any building work. Usually whatever can go wrong, will go wrong. In Ireland this is sometimes known as Murphy's Law. In the same spirit, I have developed my own set of rules for building cock-ups:

1. You almost only bang your head when not wearing a hard hat.

2. If you are wearing a hard hat, you will inevitably collide with a low beam, jarring your neck so, in your surprise, you drop the rock you were carrying.

3. A dropped rock will only land on your foot when you are wearing an old pair of trainers.

4. When wearing steel toe-capped boots, a dropped rock will always miss your foot, preferring to hit you on the knee, or shin, or both.

5. If you miss a nail when swinging hard with a hammer, you will always hit your thumb.

6. If you swing softly with a hammer, the nail will always shoot sideways and hit you in the eye.

7. Your last nail will always bend as you attempt to hammer it in.

8. A hammer, when accidentally dropped, will strike the least protected part of your body, usually your knee, shin or big toe, and sometimes all three.

9. A dropped hammer will only miss striking an unprotected part of your body if, as an alternative, it can hit your new ceramic

toilet.

10. Plumbing joints will only leak after they are concealed in a wall and the decorating is completed.

11. You only run out of something you desperately need just after the shops have shut.

12. An electrical wire will only be live if it is touched accidentally.

13. If you need 30 feet of something to complete a job, you will only have 29.

14. When you crawl to the deepest part of the loft and notice a huge, hairy spider inches from your nose, your torch will instantly cease to work.

15. You never need something just out of reach when someone is available to pass it to you.

16. The telephone will only ring when you reach the top of the ladder.

17. Your ladder will only slip when your wife is no longer holding it.

18. The most important information in the DIY manual is always on the page you didn't read.

19. The most helpful instructions are always provided for things any idiot could figure out unassisted.

20. The most expensive and fragile things always come without any instructions at all, or with directions so misleading you will accidentally cut two feet from the wrong end and must wait six weeks for another one to be delivered from China – rather than returning to the shop and admitting to the smug shop assistant you don't know what you are doing.

***

Finally the wing was finished, all gleaming and new and smelling of paint. It had a self-contained apartment, with a bedroom, sitting area, a bathroom, and a small kitchen. Perfect temporary accommodation for us while I got on with renovating the rest of the house.

"It looks lovely," Lesley said. "Well done."

"When shall we move in?" I asked.

"Ah…" Lesley grimaced.

"Ah…?"

"Do you remember the English couple we met at Limerick market the other day?" she asked.

"Sure. He was in IT or something," I said. "We got chatting because they were renovating their house as well."

"That's right. His wife was telling me they have been living in a caravan temporarily."

"I didn't hear that," I replied. "It sounds like a good idea."

Lesley skewered me with a steely gaze. "They've been living in that caravan, without a bathroom, for seven years!"

"Oh…" I mumbled. "That's not good."

"No it isn't!" My wife squared up and put her hands defiantly on her hips. "We are not living in temporary accommodation for seven years, or even one. We will live in the house while you renovate, until the job is done. Is that clear?"

"Well, there's going to be a lot of dust and…" I stammered.

"I said, is that clear?" she repeated, quite slowly and rather loud.

"Yes, dear," I said.

19. It's a dog's life

After surviving her early brush with death, Kia is now blessed with a robust constitution, apart from occasional sinus infections. Amber is almost indestructible, delighted to join in the rough and tumble of doggy life, able to endure more punishment than your average superhero and as willing to spar as a heavyweight boxer with gambling debts. Being the oldest dog, Romany is inclined to sleep a lot, rising only to eat or reluctantly trudge outside to do her business. Then there is the dog we named Lady. She is a short-legged Fox Hound, or an Old English Fox Hound, or perhaps just the result of a clandestine meeting between a lost and horny hunting dog, and a slightly bewildered Beagle. Whatever her parentage, I'm at a loss as to how someone would even contemplate giving up such an incredibly cute puppy.

For weeks, Lady has been stealthily watching me tapping away at the keyboard, all the time wondering why I would feel the need to write about anything other than her. As far as Lady is concerned, she is the centre of the known universe and everyone she meets has been specifically placed here to provide her with entertainment, or to be her slave, or both.

Within days of arriving, Lady had established herself as the Alpha Dog. This promotion from condemned prisoner to the dizzying heights of pack leader was achieved almost overnight and without any bloodshed. Rather than the traditional selection process of bribery, growling, posturing, and threats, Lady was elected leader through common consensus, combined with a singular lack of enthusiasm for responsibility from the other dogs. That's modern politics for you.

Aside from the mandated daily walks, a couple of times each day one of us will take our dogs up to the meadow for a good run around. If the mood takes her, Lady will chase a ball, but she is hopelessly inept at catching, particularly if there is some competition. Although she can get close to the ball in an all-out chase, she's inclined to panic and lunge at the last moment, missing the ball completely – or even worse – punting it with the end of her nose directly into Kia's waiting jaws. On the odd occasion she succeeds, she will immediately launch into her

Happy Dance, running around the field like a manic ragdoll, flapping her legs and ears in exquisite delight. Regardless of my threats and admonishments, she'll do her best to maintain possession of her prize and the resulting pleasure, even hiding it in the woods like a sack of stolen gold. If another dog has demonstrated their prowess by politely returning the ball, then, just like the teacher's pet showing off for the headmaster, Lady will obediently drop the ball at my feet every time.

Although chasing the ball can be fun for Lady, her favourite game by far is Tickle. When we are up on the field, Lady will trot over, bright-eyed and smiling, and lean against my thigh inviting me to begin the game. My task is simple: I am to tickle her ribs three times whilst saying, "Tickle, tickle, tickle!" After precisely three tickles, with the speed of a rocket-powered greyhound, Lady will explode away from my side and race around the garden like a demented roadrunner. Along the way, she will dive into bushes and clumps of long grass, where she will tear and pull at some roots for a few seconds, before bursting forwards into another circular dash around the lawn. All the while, her face will be positively beaming with delight and excitement. This enthusiastic demonstration of canine silliness can last for several minutes, with Lady repeatedly returning to my side for a top-up tickle, until she is breathless, shaking and unable to continue.

As the Alpha Dog, Lady's management style closely mirrors that which is common in many large corporations. In particular, the fondness for doing bloody pointless things, that really piss people off, just to prove you are still the boss. The bedtime merry-go-round at our house is an excellent example. Our dogs all sleep together in a large room that acts as a connecting corridor between the front door, the granny annex, the conservatory, and the main house. It is an excellent spot for the dogs to sleep overnight. Cool in the summer and warm in the winter, far enough away from us to avoid the dogs disturbing our sleep, but close enough for them to warn us of any intruders. Furthermore, it has an easy-to-mop tiled floor, in case of any overnight spills. At bedtime, all the dogs are kicked outside into the fresh air/snow/rain/slush to do their business before being tucked in for the night, and every night, all the dogs return within a few minutes, except for one. At a time of her choosing, Lady returns, ready to begin the bedtime merry-go-round.

By the time Lady returns from anointing the four corners of our land and howling at the moon, or woofing at her own echo from the cliffs across the moor, the other dogs have settled comfortably into bed. The length of the wait Lady imposes on us is directly proportionate to the amount of inconvenience it will cause. Sometimes, frustrated and tired, we will also have retired, only to be dragged out of bed, tired and frustrated, to trudge back downstairs and let the vexatious mutt back indoors.

At this point Lady will enter the house like a diva arriving on stage and approach the first occupied bed. There she will posture over the recumbent inhabitant until it reluctantly yields and vacates. While Lady prods and pokes at the bedding, circling in an effort to find the perfect spot for her slumber, the other dogs will all have to change places, clockwise by one bed in order of seniority. As soon as everyone is comfortably settled, Lady will decide that her bed is not at all satisfactory, and she will posture over the next bed in line. Once again, everyone will have to move, shuffling bleary-eyed to the next bed, while Lady pokes and prods at the blankets until she can be confident that this is also an unsatisfactory spot for sleep. After a few minutes, she will move to the next bed and the whole process will begin again, repeating the procedure until Lady ends up in the bed she always sleeps in – which was unoccupied in the first place. How she hasn't been ambushed by the other dogs and trussed up in the corner for the night is beyond me, but there you go.

Regardless of our admonishments, Lady applies the same system during the day to the dog beds we keep in the living room. These four-foot square, easy to wash, mini duvets were lovingly created by Lesley to ensure every dog could have its own bed. At least that was the plan. Lady will scrap and pull at each bed with quiet determination until they are arranged together in a small heap. She will push and massage this little linen mountain until it has achieved a satisfactory shape, before circling it three times and climbing to the top, where she will balance precariously and sleep the sleep of the justified. The other dogs are left to nap wherever they can, or they can wait and watch with envious eyes until we drag Lady aside and redistribute the beds.

Perhaps surprisingly, Lady is not particularly possessive of dog toys, probably because she sees such trivialities as being below her lofty status. Should another dog be getting some attention, that is a different matter. When Lesley is brushing the dogs, she will typically lock herself in the conservatory with each dog in turn, so she can work in peace. On such days, Lady will stand outside the door, positively bristling with the frustration of not being the centre of attention. If she happens to be outside looking through the window, her dagger-like stare is almost physical in its power and impossible to ignore.

***

Living in such a remote location we have few visitors, so it was a while before the new doggy collective had an opportunity to interact as a friendly, but overenthusiastic pack. The first time occurred while Lesley was away visiting her mother in England.

It was early evening and I was knocking off for the day. I had finished my list of chores, taken a shower and had just sat down to eat my supper and watch a little television. As I tucked into my feast, I was suddenly startled by the sight of a large, cream coloured cow looking at me through the front window. After coughing up a lungful of beer and bits of partly-masticated chips, I sprang into action. Still wearing my bedroom slippers and armed only with my fork and half an uneaten chip, I bravely ran outside to confront a dozen large cows happily grazing on my front lawn. In my blissful ignorance, I assumed our dogs would dredge up their natural herding instincts and calmly and quietly help me to guide the cattle back towards the open gate and freedom. What actually happened bore an alarming similarity to a stampede scene from one of those old cowboy movies.

First, the dogs chased the cattle in a clockwise circle around the lawn. As they became dizzy, they switched direction and ran anti-clockwise for a while longer. Next they split the cows into two smaller groups and encouraged them to comprehensively trample the seedlings in the vegetable garden. All the while the dogs were barking hysterically and ignoring my frantic calls to stop. Not to be outdone, the cows turned and chased the dogs until exhaustion set in. Finally, the excitement died down and the cows were content to watch impassively as I used a series of threats and bribes to persuade the pooches to return to the safety of the house. Once I was on my own and armed with a couple of bamboo rods from the remains of the vegetable garden, it was a fairly simple matter to guide the cattle out through the gate. Sadly, my slippers were ruined, the garden was a wreck, I needed another shower and the dogs had eaten my dinner. Since then, we have learned to manage our dogs' interactions with the outside world.

A couple of times a week we are graced with a delivery of post, but as our post box is outside the front gates, our postman can usually pull up in his van, lean out of the window to stuff the letters into the box and be gone before the dogs have even raised an ear. Delivery drivers are typically guided to our house via the telephone. We relate the complicated series of directions like an air traffic controller guiding a wounded bomber pilot to safety, still leaving plenty of time to corral the dogs before these strangers arrive.

Every two months, a delightful old gent comes to read our electricity meter. Each time, he dutifully opens the front gate and drives his small white van the 80 yards up the driveway to our house. There he rings the old brass ship's bell that hangs by our door and waits patiently while we attempt to calm the dogs. Sometimes they get to him before we can, but he seems unperturbed by the bouncing, yapping, slobbering hoard of excited mutts. He is always polite and chatty, usually talking up the weather, regardless of how wet it is.

Aside from friends and family, the only other visitors we see are those hardy groups of walkers who have chosen to ignore the signs offering the dire warning 'Danger! This walk is closed.' After they have fought their way through seven miles of mud and bramble, they will appear, wet, tired, and bleeding, trudging along the lane at the back of our property. At that point, they are usually too exhausted and demoralised to avoid our dogs and their muddy paws. All we can do is rush outside shouting, "Don't worry. They won't hurt you!"

As head of security, Lady does a magnificent job of ensuring we know when there are visitors around – whether friendly, or otherwise. Of course, not every passing walker appreciates the attention they may receive from our dogs. Although our little band of canine ninjas are fundamentally friendly and not at all aggressive, they see their job in life as protectors of the territory – a task they undertake with joyful enthusiasm.

In a government-sanctioned effort to encourage some couch potatoes to get out and see the countryside, a local rambling group arranged a bank holiday weekend walk in the area around Glenmadrie. To add to the fun, someone decided it would be interesting to take in the sights, by marching 50 or so unsuspecting individuals along the path at the front of my land. In an effort to keep them on track, somebody had helpfully put up a cardboard arrow with 'Walk this way' written on it. Knowing the enthusiasm with which our dogs would greet a group of 50 tired and bedraggled strangers, I had half a mind to add a second sign just opposite the house that said 'And now run!' The dogs stayed in the house for most of that weekend.

I wouldn't want to give the impression our dogs are running wild and free. That is not the case at all. In the winter they huddle around the fire all day, only venturing outside for their daily walks or a game of ball. During the summer months, they spend much of their time outside watching Lesley garden as they bask in the sunshine. That being said, people do pass by, even up here on the mountain. So the dogs must be prepared for all eventualities. Here are their rules:

1. Passing hikers and walkers must be woofed at and followed for several hundred yards, to ensure they have been seen off.
2. Walkers who demonstrate any signs of friendliness, or show little obvious fear of dogs, can be followed further, but with less woofing.
3. Should any walkers stop to converse with the servants of the dogs, all woofing will cease while stroking and playing takes place. Once the conversation is over, rule one applies again, even if the walkers came into the house for the afternoon and had tea and scones.
4. Cyclists must always be chased, but only until they fall off. Once they pick up their bikes again, they are classified as walkers and can be dealt with under rule one.
5. On warm days, all dogs shall be required to sleep in the

sun in the courtyard area, remaining motionless until passing hikers, exhausted from the muddy 800 foot climb from the river below, are level with the stone wall at the back of the house. At that point the hikers will pause and draw enough breath to say loudly, "What a lovely house," whereupon Lady will launch herself over the wall barking like a rabid hyena, and the other dogs will run into the lane via the greenhouse, in a flanking manoeuvre designed to confuse and trap the terrified enemy.
6. On quiet days, when no walkers or passing traffic is available, the dogs will, on a previously agreed rota system, take turns running outside and woofing wildly at nothing, thereby causing the dogs' servant to stop whatever it was they were trying to get done and go outside to investigate the non-existent intrusion.

***

Unfortunately, not all visitors to Glenmadrie are entirely welcome. On those rare occasions, it is good to know we have a few dogs around the place. I had always suspected any intruders would be roundly ignored by our so called ferocious guard dogs, as they lie like furry starfish by the fire. How wrong could I be?

It was a hot summer night when I was startled awake by the frenzied barking of the dogs. I sat up in bed, conscious the room was unusually bright. Lights and shadows were dancing along the wall opposite the window. Checking the bedside clock, I saw it was just after 2 am. I jumped out of bed, donned my dressing gown and slippers and peered out of the window. By the gate, at the entrance to our driveway, were three sets of headlights. At the front I could see the silhouette of a man trying to unshackle the gate and behind him half a dozen more. Intruders!

As I ran along the corridor, Lesley poked her head out of her room.

"What on earth's going on?" she asked, puffy-eyed and confused.

"There's a group of people down by the gate. They're up to no good." I handed her my mobile phone. "Lock your door and call the police."

"Don't be silly," she said. "They're probably just lost."

There was a crash and a cheer as our gates were thrown open. The dog barking intensified.

I put my hand on her shoulder. "Don't argue. Do as I ask."

Lesley closed the door. I waited until I heard the lock click. Glancing out of the window, I could see two white vans and a car. Perhaps they were lost. Just kids out looking for a party. Glenmadrie had a history for hosting such events. What to do? My options were limited. Even though I have a karate black belt, unarmed against a large group, I wouldn't last long. As I sprinted down the stairs, I had an illuminating idea. Sitting in its charger by the kitchen door was my latest toy, a super bright hand-held spotlight. Perhaps being unexpectedly lit up would discourage a potential home invasion.

I grabbed the torch, threw open the front door and hit the switch. Or I would have done, had I not been jostled aside by four dogs as they bravely charged forward to attack. After a brief fumble, I managed to turn on the spotlight at the second attempt. The timing couldn't have been better. The party-seekers (or ne'er-do-wells) were suddenly confronted by an unknown number of snarling, baying dogs, and hit by a blinding beam of light. There wasn't much debate, just some shouting and a few terrified screams. In seconds, they all piled into their vehicles and roared off towards Galway and the prospect of easier pickings.

The dogs stood in the road and woofed defiantly, until I called them in and closed the gate. It was bent and one hinge was broken, but with a good shove it swung back into place. Once inside, I locked the doors and called for Lesley.

"They've gone. We're safe now," I panted. My heart was pounding with the sudden surge of adrenalin. "Did you call the Guards?"

She nodded. "They said they'd try to get someone out here by lunchtime."

"Lunchtime!" I exclaimed. "What bloody good would that do?"

"It's what they said." She shrugged.

"If it was a home invasion, they'd be just in time to count the bodies."

"Well, it's a good job we have the dogs."

"For sure," I replied. "They were magnificent."

Lesley knelt down for a group fuss.

"Good girls," she whispered. "A special dog treat for every one of you, and then back to bed."

20. The magic potion

"The power was off again," Lesley groaned. "It's back on now, but we had a really big thunderstorm."

"Really?" I replied. I'd just arrived back from work. "It was roasting hot down at the golf club. I had to sit the kids under a tree for some shade."

"You were lucky. I didn't see the sun once today."

"You're exaggerating," I said, rolling my eyes. "I'm sure it wasn't that bad."

"How would you know?" Lesley snapped. "You're out every day teaching in the sun, and I'm stuck up here in the cloud. Look at you. You're all sunburned. The top of your head is bright red. It looks like a safety match."

"I suppose I did catch the sun a bit," I said, gently running my hand across my scalp. It felt hot and tender.

"Anyway, the water's off. I expect the thingy in the pump house got burned out again."

"Blast!" I hissed. "That's another 200 quid. I'd better phone the engineer."

"You'll have to use your mobile," Lesley grimaced. "The phone is burned out as well. And before you say anything else, yes I did turn off the power – thank you very much!"

I knew better than to attribute blame, especially when my wife was sending out such obvious warning signals.

"It's not your fault," I sighed. "Being the last house on the line, we're just vulnerable to lightning up here. I'll send him a text, then I'll have a shower while there's still some water in the tank."

"You'd better put some cream on your head." Lesley pointed. "And your nose. There's some aloe vera in the cabinet."

"Will do."

"Afterwards, there's a little job you can do."

Her matter-of-fact tone was concerning. It usually indicated some huge project she had been scheming, or a rocky path leading to the outlay of lots of money. In this case it was both.

"We need to buy a polytunnel," Lesley said, softening the blow with her sweetest smile.

"Oh." I groaned inwardly.

She was right of course. The site was levelled and ready and the weather was perfect. There was no excuse, other than the cost. I suspected a good quality 50-foot polytunnel was going to cost several thousand euro. I'd been subconsciously putting it off. But now Lesley was giving me her *you'd better get on with it* look, so I did.

After much shopping around and painfully slow internet research, we selected a 50-foot heavy-duty polytunnel from a firm in Cork. It was surprisingly decent value, given we needed something robust enough to cope with the high winds and violent rain that can frequent the area.

A few days later, we were the proud owners of a very large pile of steel tubes, some with curves and others with joints, a massive sheet of thick polythene, folded into something the size of a double bed, and a grubby sheet of A5 paper bearing words of wisdom to guide me through the construction process. The instructions seemed to have been written onto the back of an envelope, along with a few hand-drawn sketches, and photocopied onto some yellowed paper just prior to delivery. I imagined the research and development department had met with the only person in Ireland to successfully build a polytunnel and, during a conversation over a few pints on a wet Sunday afternoon, had copied down verbatim his description of how the mighty deed was achieved.

I stared in amused disbelief at instructions like: Around now you might be looking at a big pile of bits and be thinking 'Feck me! How am I going to manage?' But don't fret, it will all come right in the end.

And: Stick the stakes into the ground and bend them in a bit, like.

And finally: And fer Christ's sake, don't try and put the polythene over the frame on a breezy day. If the wind catches it you won't see it again before it reaches Birmingham.

I stopped laughing sufficiently to telephone the supplier, who was kind enough to explain the construction process in idiot-proof steps. It took a day to assemble and erect the frame, which was constructed from two-inch galvanised steel pipes that fitted together to create a series of interconnected loops, ten feet high in the centre and firmly anchored to the ground at each end. The tricky bit was getting the base pipes hammered into the ground at the correct angle and in an exact square. For the first time since I was at school, I was able to make use of the hypotenuse in calculating the sides of a right-angled triangle. This brought me halfway towards making my squares…well…square.

Everything went swimmingly and I soon had the framework acceptably in place. I had to secure it together with special bolts that drilled their own holes into the steel pipes. It was a tricky operation, balancing a ladder on soft mud and trying to attach the bolts. Whatever I tried, the ladder always seemed to be in the wrong place and it had a disconcerting habit of tipping sideways as it sank into the soil. To make matters worse, my 30-year-old Black & Decker electric drill was playing up.

"Argh!" I screamed in frustration.

"What's the matter now?" Lesley asked, looking up from her digging.

"It's this drill. The switch is sticking. Sometimes it won't start and sometimes it won't stop."

"You've been complaining about it for ages," Lesley sighed. "Why don't you just buy a new one?"

"This one's fine," I replied, thumping it with the heel of my hand until it burst into life. "There, that's better. It probably just needs some WD40 sprayed into the switch."

"Honestly, Nick," Lesley pleaded. "Just buy another. You're going to need a drill that works."

"This one's fine. It was my Dad's," I said, hoping to justify my reluctance. "Besides, this drill is much more powerful than those new battery-powered models."

"Well, it's up to you." Lesley sighed.

"Don't worry about it. Anyway, I'm nearly finished. This is the last bolt. If I can just reach up here…"

Inevitably the drill chose that exact moment to jam on full power.

"Owww!" I squealed. The bolt had stopped turning, but the drill continued going around, taking me with it. I watched in horror as my right wrist and forearm were rotated through some 400 degrees, before I was flicked off my ladder as if by an invisible judo instructor. Nothing was broken, but my wrist swelled up like a pregnant rat and continued to give me problems for some time.

We had to wait for over a week before the weather was calm

enough to fit the polythene, but at last we were able to drape it over the frame and secure it against even the highest winds by burying all the edges in a three-foot trench.

With the polytunnel completed, Lesley was finally able to launch into some serious planting, confident the weather would not wreck her plans by being too wet, dry, hot, cold or just too Irish. Although the polytunnel is pretty large, around one thousand square feet, it seemed to be bursting with plants no more than a few weeks after I had finished the construction. Apart from the usual range of beans, carrots, potatoes, squashes and cabbages, Lesley also planted peach trees, grapes and a range of companion plants to discourage unwanted bugs. I like cooking and I enjoy eating. Lesley loves gardening, she is an excellent cook and produces awesome jams, pickles and cakes. It seems we are well matched to each other.

***

A few days later, I was clutching my wrist again.

"What happened this time?" Lesley asked as I was putting the dog leads away.

"Someone tried to rip my arm off," I said, nodding towards Lady. Sitting there on the kitchen floor with her head tipped slightly to one side, watching us closely with her liquid chocolate eyes, Lady was innocence personified.

Lesley tutted. "What happened this time?"

"I took them down the lane and then cut through the woods and back up the main road," I explained. "Just as we got to the big field down here, Lady got on the scent of a fox and ran off."

"Of course the others followed," Lesley said.

"Absolutely. Lady was running around the field and yelping as if her tail was on fire. The other dogs were running behind."

"All of them?" Lesley asked.

"Well, Kia was," I admitted. "Romany ran a bit and then got out of breath, so she sat down. Of course Amber is too short to see over the long grass, but she was content to woof and run in circles. I guess that way she still feels like she contributed to the hunt."

Lesley laughed at the image. "Are you sure it was a fox?"

"Absolutely," I snorted. "It was sitting about ten yards behind me, watching the entertainment. After a bit, it calmly got up and walked away."

"So how did you hurt your wrist again?" Lesley asked.

"I was just coming to that. After a bit the dogs came back and we continued on with the walk. Lady looked very pleased with herself, but Kia's tail was covered in bramble. I had to wrap a handkerchief around my hand so I could clean it off."

"Is that how you hurt your wrist?"

"No, that was later," I explained. "On the way back home, I put the dogs on their leads so we could walk up along the road. Just as we got to the house, a pine marten walked out of the bushes and crossed the road. They're notoriously short sighted. It couldn't have been more than a couple of yards ahead."

"And is that when you hurt your wrist?"

"Absolutely!" I laughed. "I had three dog leads on one hand and Lady's lead on the other. She took off like a race horse, but the other dogs didn't. The pine marten decided to run downhill and Lady went to give chase. I tried to block her path, but somehow she dived between my legs. Obviously she was pulled up short by the lead, nearly ripping my arm off in the process."

"You poor thing!" Lesley said, laughing and wiping her eyes.

"It's not funny, you know," I complained. "I almost did a summersault!"

Lesley covered her mouth and turned away. I could see her shoulders shaking.

"Honestly!" I huffed. "What is our marriage coming to, if my wife only laughs when I hurt myself?"

"But you do it so well," Lesley sniggered.

I shook my head, feigning anger, but I wasn't cross. I love to see my wife laughing.

"Oh, I almost forgot," I exclaimed, waving my phone. "I got an email from the newspaper."

"Is this about you writing a golf instructional column?" Lesley raised an inquisitive eyebrow.

I nodded. "The email is from the editor-in-chief. He wants me to write a thousand words every week for their sports section."

"Every week?" Lesley squealed. "You said to me you might do a piece once a month. That's a lot of work. And you'll have to do photos as well. Will you have the time?"

"Don't worry, I'll manage," I said. "Anyway, it's good kudos that can only help my teaching business. In his email, the editor said I keep the rights, so I can put the content from the column into a book on golf instruction. Sort of two birds with one stone."

Lesley smiled. She was genuinely pleased, but with one reservation.

"Just make sure the renovations come first on your to-do list."

"Yes, dear," I replied, suitably warned.

***

We had a short interlude from the frenzy of summer work, renovations and gardening, when some old friends visited from England. Shortly after our daughter was born, Robert and Susan had moved in a few doors away and we soon became friends. They were around our age with similar interests and values. They are the sort of kind and generous people whose friendship we cherish. Moreover, they both have a cracking sense of humour. Even though we haven't been neighbours for more than a quarter of a century, we remain friends and get together for a meal and a good chat whenever we can.

As this was their first visit to Ireland, they had brought David and Andrew along, their rambunctious young boys. Robert's plan was to have a driving holiday, keeping the lads entertained by visiting the attractions along the west coast of Ireland. It was delightful to see our friends again. We had a cracking day chewing over old memories and discussing our plans for the house. Meanwhile, the boys kept out of any significant trouble by playing with the dogs on the land and climbing around in the quarry, just like two hyperactive kittens.

Robert is also somewhat of a home handyman, so he took particular interest in the progress of our renovations. After inspecting and approving my efforts in the wing, we moved our discussion to the kitchen.

"What are you going to do with this?" Robert asked, tapping the purple spiral staircase with his toe.

"It'll have to come out," I replied. "It's a real fire hazard having this in the kitchen."

"For sure. Any smoke would be drawn up like a chimney. I can feel the draught from here." Robert peered up. "Does it go all the way to the top?

"All the way to the roof. It's about 40 feet," I said glumly. "I think it may be holding everything together."

"That's possible. It's made of steel," he said. "How on earth are you going to get it out?"

"I guess I'll just have to start at the top and cut away small sections with my disc cutter until it's all gone."

Robert looked at me as if I had just declared a desire for juggling with hand grenades. We shared a knowing grimace.

"Come and look at the coverway," I said, pointing towards the courtyard. "It's almost finished.

As we took a quick tour, I pulled out my phone and shared a few photos I had taken during the renovations.

"This is when I had the digger…see where I removed the concrete…those are the new beams for the roofing–"

"What's that?" he asked, pointing at a picture that resembled animal footprints in the sand.

"Oh, that was here." I pointed at the wide path below our feet. "I'd spent all day mixing and laying concrete. It was dusk and I'd just finish getting it smooth and level. I swear, the moment I stood back and folded my arms to inspect my work, my dear wife opened that door and let the dogs out."

Robert's mouth fell open. "No!"

I nodded. "They always race each other to be the first out into the garden. Before I could take a breath, they'd run through 20 feet of my lovely smooth concrete!"

"It must have taken ages to put it right," he laughed.

"It did," I replied. "And Lesley had to wash four dogs."

"Did you mix it all yourself?" Robert asked, pointing at my cement mixer.

"Yep," I said proudly. "If you count the floor in the wing, I've done about 400 loads."

"Why didn't you just order a lorry load of ready-mixed?"

"Good question," I replied. "Come and have a cup of tea and some cake while Lesley tells you about Freddy."

When we were all comfortably settled around the table, Lesley told the story.

"Freddy is the husband of a lady I know, she's called Julie.

They're both English and renovating their place as well. Earlier this year, they decided to get a delivery of self-levelling concrete for their kitchen floor. The preparation work was finished. Freddy had already laid the damp-proof membrane, the insulation and the pipework for his under-floor heating. Everything was ready for his concrete.

"The delivery was promised and delayed several times. Inevitably it arrived on the wrong day. And it just so happened that Freddy was away in Limerick or somewhere. Poor Julie did her best in the circumstances, explaining to the driver he was there on the wrong day and trying to refuse the delivery. Apparently, the driver got rather foul-mouthed and belligerent. He even threatened to dump the load on the front lawn. Julie got quite upset, but she managed to contact Freddy on his mobile phone and he talked to the driver. They had no choice but to accept the delivery.

"Carefully following Freddy's instructions, Julie directed the driver to pour the self-levelling compound through the window and into the kitchen. Everything went well. Not a drop was spilled, but once the lorry had gone, it quickly became evident that there had been a horrible mix-up with the delivery. The self-levelling compound was actually quick-setting concrete!"

"Oh no!" Robert wailed, laughing. "The kitchen would be ruined."

"That's right," I said. "By the time Freddy had arrived back, the fully-set concrete covered half the kitchen. There was a big slope of concrete from the centre of the floor to the bottom of the window sill. The company refused to accept any responsibility, and it took poor Freddy several weeks to dig it out by hand."

"Ah! So that's why you mixed your concrete yourself?" Susan said.

"Yep!" I replied. "And I was happy to do it."

At the end of the week, our friends returned for a farewell visit before their flight home. I noticed that Andrew, the older of the two boys, had a big bandage on his thumb. Knowing his susceptibility for attracting accidents, I asked what had happened.

Robert casually explained that, despite numerous warnings to take care with the knife, Andrew had managed to slice a bit off the end of his thumb whilst doing some crafts. The injury was not a particular problem and would soon have clotted over, except that the young boy continued to lift the bandage to inspect the wound.

"It was just a flat spot missing from the tip of his thumb," Robert explained. "The cut was less than a centimetre square and unlikely to require stitches. It just needed some time to clot and heal."

"Of course, Andrew wouldn't leave it alone," Susan added. "He kept pulling off the plaster and fiddling with it, until the bleeding started over again."

"Did you have to go to the hospital?" Lesley asked.

"No," Susan replied. "Robert went to the local pharmacy to ask if they had something that would help clot the wound."

Robert pulled a small package from his pocket and handed it to me.

"It's brilliant stuff," he said. "You paint it on the wound and it stops the bleeding in seconds."

"And it resisted Andrew's repeated inspections," Susan added.

"That's great," I said.

"I love the health system over here," Robert said. "It's so uncomplicated."

I sensed there was a footnote heading our way.

"Read the label," Robert added.

Lesley and I almost bumped heads as we burst out laughing. The magic potion bore the words, "If symptoms persist, please consult your vet."

Susan and Robert are lovely people, good parents, excellent company and trusted friends with a great sense of humour.

Andrew seems none the worse for his visit to Ireland and the unusual medical care he received – apart from a tendency to chase passing cars and bark at the moon.

21. Lucky me

Lesley had an appointment to see a back specialist at Cork University Hospital. Although she had endured several rounds of injections, and begun to see some improvement, since her car crash, her neck and back had been more troublesome. Ireland's perpetually cool and damp climate undoubtedly wasn't helping either.

"Being realistic, it's probably a two-and-a-half-hour drive to Cork," I explained. "Your appointment is at half 11. I expect you'll be in there for a while, so we might as well make a day of it."

"Are you sure? It's only a consultation," Lesley replied. "I can easily drive myself."

"It's fine," I said, waving away her suggestion. "If I'm driving you can just lay back, take it easy, and enjoy the scenery. We've never been to Cork. It'll be an adventure."

On the day of Lesley's appointment, after taking the dogs for an extra-long walk, we bedded them down for the day, and set off around 8 am. It was miserable weather for a long drive, with a cold, grey sky, low clouds, and the sort of steady drizzle my windscreen wipers refused to clear without squeaking like nails on a blackboard. Never one to enjoy inclement weather, Lesley glowered silently at the passing hedgerows and the visible lower third of several hills. I did my best to lighten the mood by sharing a few fascinating facts I had prepared for the journey.

"The city of Cork dates back to around 900AD," I said.

"Hmph."

"The western end of the River Lee forks and splits the city into two islands. The river joins up again at the eastern end of the city by the quays and flows outwards towards Lough Mahon and the harbour."

Silence.

A dismissive snort.

"Cork Harbour is one of the largest natural harbours in the world," I added.

"Hm."

"We'll be passing quite close to Blarney Castle. It's one of the most famous visitor attractions in County Cork."

Lesley tipped her head and tutted.

"Most people would know it for the Blarney Stone, reputed to endow eloquence with a single kiss. However, the castle grounds have around 60 acres of beautiful gardens. From what I saw, they are similar to that place we visited in Cornwall. What was it called?"

Lesley squinted at me and frowned. "What? The Eden Project?"

"No. I mean the other place we went to. It was called Helly-something."

"Oh. You mean the Lost Gardens of Heligan."

"That's it!" I clicked my fingers. "Blarney Castle's like that. They've got ferns, a jungle, a Himalayan walk, a bog garden and loads more. I looked it up. They've even got a whole garden full of poisonous plants."

Suddenly, my wife looked interested. "What a shame we won't have time to stop by and get some samples."

I quickly changed the subject. "One of the most dramatic buildings in Cork is Saint Fin Barre's Cathedral."

"Oh yes?" Lesley mumbled.

"It's Gothic, with three spires," I added. "Very dramatic looking."

Lesley nodded silently. Lost in thought. Perhaps she was worrying about what the doctor would say. Her last trip to see the Butcher of Limerick, as she described the ham-fisted consultant who administered her recent round of injections, had not gone well.

"Of course, Cork is well known for its shopping," I continued. "And most famous for the English Market."

"I've heard of that," my wife commented. "It's a big indoor market."

"It was named *English* to distinguish it from the nearby *Irish* market," I said. "Although these days it is probably more of a *European* market."

"Pfft," she hissed. "We won't have time for that today."

"We probably won't have time to see anything but the hospital," I admitted. "But we can always make another trip."

"I guess," she said dully.

"Isn't it funny how they pronounce Cork?" I asked.

"Huh?"

"Andrew Rich says it with a quiet 'W' and an extended 'O'," I explained. "It's a subtle sound, like the call of a crow, C*woork*!"

Lesley smiled. "C*woork*," she whispered.

"The other day he told me he'd visited Lough Borgorough in England," I said.

"Lough Borgorough? I've never heard of it."

"Me neither," I laughed. "He was referring to the town of Loughborough." I pronounced it *Luff-burrah*, with an Essex twang.

"Lough Borgorough," Lesley giggled and shook her head.

We drove in silence for a while. My thoughts drifted to the local hamlet of Caher.

"Isn't it odd that Caher is either pronounced *K-A-her* or *Kay-her* or even *Cur-hur?*" I said. "But the more common village name of Cahir, which should be pronounced *Ka-her* is only ever pronounced *Care?*"

"Go figure!" Lesley snorted.

We were entering the village of Charleville. Lesley pointed. "This place looks pretty."

"Let's stop for a while," I suggested. "There's a café. We could stretch our legs and have a drink."

My wife squinted at the dashboard clock.

"Don't worry," I said. "We have plenty of time."

We only stopped for 30 minutes or so. Just enough time to work the kinks out of our backs, enjoy a good cup of tea and some cake.

Using a combination of imagery and visualisation, I had memorised our route to the hospital so perfectly that within ten minutes of reaching the outskirts of the city, we were completely lost. What's more, my erratic and unpredictable manoeuvres seemed to be acting as an irritant to the otherwise friendly and carefree citizens of Cork. Horns blared and fists waved as I changed lanes at the last moment, or circumnavigated a roundabout three times in search of the correct exit.

"It's most odd," I remarked. "When I was lost in Dublin, everyone was so polite and helpful."

"Perhaps we've caught them on a bad day," Lesley suggested.

"Why can't I find this hospital?" I growled. "Usually there are bloody great signposts."

"There's one!" Lesley shouted.

"Where?" I looked around, momentarily sliding out of my lane and receiving an angry toot of admonishment from a nearby taxi.

"Back there on that lamppost. There was a tiny red 'H'. I think it means hospital."

"Hang on!" I made a violent and dramatic U-turn. Strangely nobody complained.

When we finally found the hospital, there were no parking places.

"You go in," I said. "I'll keep driving around until I find somewhere to park. I've got a book. Call me when you come out."

"Okay." She gave me a peck on the cheek and hobbled away.

In under an hour, we were heading for home. Nobody tooted or waved a fist. Perhaps they were pleased to see the back of another crazy English motorist.

"That was a waste of time," Lesley said.

"What did they say?"

"Not a lot."

I waited.

"He looked at my scans and the reports," she continued. "Basically, my back is wrecked. Three bulging discs and some arthritis in my neck. He said the options are more injections, or an operation."

"A spine operation? Phew! That sounds rather serious."

"Don't worry," Lesley said. "It's not going to happen. He said the chances of surgery making my back better are slim to none. So I said no."

"Oh. I'm sorry." I put my hand on her knee. "I mean, I'm sorry for you. I know you were hoping they would be able to fix it, or at least manage your pain a bit better."

"It's okay," Lesley sighed. "It's what I thought they'd say."

"What happens next?"

"He's making an appointment for me to have some different injections. They're quite invasive," she said. "They'll give me some anaesthetic. I'll probably need to stay in hospital for a few days."

"So what now?"

"Now we wait for the appointment. In the meantime, I take painkillers."

"No," I laughed, "I meant do you want to do some sightseeing?"

She shook her head. "Let's get home. The poor dogs will think we've abandoned them!"

***

"The power's off again," I said.

Lesley had just arrived back from shopping. I came outside to help unload the bags from the car.

"Not another thunderstorm!"

"Not this time." I grimaced.

"What have you been up to?" She huffed and brushed at my dust-covered overalls. "This looks like pink dandruff."

"I was up on the coverway roof," I frowned and scratched at my chin. "Had a bit of an accident."

Lesley rolled her eyes. "Did you set yourself on fire again?"

"No!" I said. "That hardly ever happens."

"Did you fall? I've told you not to go climbing when you're on your own."

"I didn't fall. Well, not quite," I huffed. "According to my DIY manual, I needed to add some lead flashing to the coverway to prevent rainwater from running down the walls and onto the walkway below. I was using the disc cutter to slice a horizontal groove along the wall. It's a horrid job. Dust everywhere."

"On your own using that…" Lesley frowned as she tried to suppress her temper. "How irresponsible!"

She was right. My disc cutter is a metre long and has a powerful electric motor that spins the heavy diamond-tipped steel blade at an incredible speed. Because of the gyroscopic effect, the motor wants to turn around the blade, so this violent and noisy machine has to be handled rather carefully.

"What happened?" Lesley asked.

"Well, I was being cautious. After all, I didn't want to accidentally step in the wrong place and put my foot through the new roof, or inadvertently cut through my leg," I joked.

"Good thinking," Lesley said, somewhat sarcastically.

"Anyway, I was merrily working my way along the wall, making my neat little groove–"

"And spraying dust everywhere," Lesley added.

"Unavoidable." I shrugged. "I was just thinking how well I was getting on, when there was a sudden burst of yellow sparks, followed by a large blue flash and a loud bang. It blew me backwards fully six feet."

My wife put her hand over her mouth in shock.

"I found myself sitting precariously on the edge of the roof and clinging desperately to the disc cutter, which was jumping around like a wild stallion. When it finally stopped spinning, the cause of these violent gyrations was immediately obvious. Almost a third of the blade was missing."

"Had it snapped?" Lesley asked.

"No. It had melted into an ugly lump, and there was a large soot mark on the yellow paint where I had been cutting the wall."

"What on earth happened?"

"I'm not really sure," I admitted. "But the power is out. I think I must have cut through a cable."

"Up there?" Lesley frowned.

"I know it makes no sense. It's an outside wall of the house and I was cutting an inch-deep groove through the cement render. There are no electrics there, or at least there shouldn't be. But it's the only explanation. I called our electricity supplier. They're sending an engineer."

"That sounds expensive," Lesley said with a grimace.

The engineer arrived half an hour later. He took one look and shook his head. "I think you've cut through the mains cable. I'll have to call in a linesman."

"I can't have cut the cable," I pleaded. "The utility pole is over there, and the domestic fuse box is in the conservatory. Surely the cable wouldn't come this way?"

"I agree. But the evidence…" He tapped my disc cutter and its melted blade with his foot. "The evidence says different."

And he was right. An hour later the linesman arrived. He wouldn't touch anything until he had climbed the utility pole and disconnected the supply. After a brief inspection, he shook his head and delivered a diagnosis.

"Normally, the mains cable runs from the utility pole along the roofline, or along some other clearly visible route, until it enters the house behind the mains fuse board," he explained.

"But not here," I said, already guessing the answer.

He nodded.

"At some time in the past, the mains cable has been run diagonally along this side of the house." He pointed at my soot encrusted wall. "And then some idiot builder has painstakingly hidden the cable under a thick coat of cement render. It's criminal. They may as well have planted a couple of landmines."

"Not my fault then?" I asked hopefully.

"Of course not!" he exclaimed. "You're 20 feet away from the fuse box and there isn't a wire in sight."

"Not my fault." I smiled at Lesley. "Did you hear that?"

"You were dead lucky though, if you pardon the pun," the linesman said. "Because you cut through the cable between the utility pole and the fuse box, there was nothing to stop the flow of electricity. In fact, the business end of the cable was still live right up until I pulled the breaker."

"Oh dear," I said.

"Oh dear indeed." He nodded and drew a deep breath. "You are very, very lucky to be alive."

"That bad?" Lesley asked.

He patted me on the shoulder. "If I were you, matey, I'd go out and buy a lottery ticket."

A stout new cable now safely, and very obviously, brings electricity to Glenmadrie and the only expense for the entire incident was the cost of replacing the blade on my disc cutter and the two euro I wasted on a lottery ticket.

***

"Happy anniversary," I said, leaning forward to kiss my wife on the lips.

"Ooh, a card," she quipped. "How romantic."

"I know you usually detest such sloppy examples of compliance with retail hysteria, but this one's special. Go on, open it."

Lesley carefully opened the envelope, extracted the card and the contents.

"The ballet?" Lesley squealed. "We haven't been to the ballet since that night at the Royal Albert Hall. I've always wanted to see Swan Lake."

"I thought you'd enjoy a night of culture," I smiled. "It's been a while since we've been out."

"Ooh lovely," she said, squinting at the tickets. "It's tonight?"

"Yep. You can wear your posh frock."

"Thank you." My wife threw her arms around my neck and kissed me. "This is going to be great."

We arrived at the theatre more than half-an-hour early. Ample time to have a drink, enjoy the atmosphere, and find our seats. As we walked through the carpark, me in my black tuxedo and bowtie and Lesley looking resplendent in a long blue evening dress and simple pearl necklace, I felt like we deserved a red carpet. However, as we entered the foyer, something seemed amiss.

"You're the only person here wearing a tux," Lesley whispered in my ear.

I glanced around, standing on tiptoes to see over the mass of heads.

"That's not quite true," I whispered. "There's a chap over there by the bar."

"I think he's a waiter," she hissed. "None of the women are wearing evening dress. Everyone is staring. I feel like such an idiot."

"Don't be silly. They're only looking because you look so beautiful."

"Are you sure this is the correct night?" Lesley growled.

"Yes," I pointed to the poster behind us. "I expect they have a more casual dress code here for the ballet."

"Casual? You call this casual?" Lesley exclaimed. "There's someone over there in overalls, and that man is wearing Wellington boots. I don't mind, but I just feel so out of place."

"Let's go and find our seats," I suggested. "At least we'll be in the dark."

The ballet was excellent. Wonderful music and the dancing was sublime. There were lots of stunningly beautiful girls pirouetting on tiptoes and several muscular men flying through the air in very close-fitting tights.

At the interval we joined the queue at the bar. I was keen to calm Lesley's earlier concerns.

"See," I whispered. "There was nothing to worry about. Nobody is taking any notice of us."

Just then I felt a tap on my shoulder. A 20 euro note was thrust into my hand and a gruff voice spoke.

"Get me a pint of Guinness, two packets of crisps and a glass of the house white."

I'll bet James Bond was never mistaken for a waiter.

22. Bums and bombs

It was a Thursday in July. Roasting hot, even for Ireland. I was running a junior golf camp and the sun was so blistering I had to keep the pasty white, predominately ginger-haired kids in the shade for most of the morning. Nevertheless, we had a cracking morning of fun, instruction and competition.

Walking back to the clubhouse, I was on an emotional high. In four days, I'd taken a class of 22 children from raw beginners, to a point where they were grinding over their final putts like grizzled professionals fighting to win the Ryder Cup. Whereas I was delighted, the children were positively buzzing. All around, I could hear them reminiscing about the shots they had hit during the pivotal moments of the week. As we entered the carpark, many ran ahead to greet their parents. Their voices rose to excited shouts, a jumble of happy comments.

"Mum! You won't believe…"

"I was the best today…"

"I want to come next week…"

"We won! We won!"

I was bursting with happiness and pride. *This is why I teach*, I thought. But my delight was short-lived. Ahead I could see Anne, the manager of the golf club, and she was looking at me with a face like thunder.

Almost always innocent, but constantly wracked with guilt, I quickly scanned my memory for a possible infraction. What had I done wrong? Had my group of enthusiastic children been too rowdy? Did someone steal an errant golf ball? Had we somehow disturbed one of the other golfers – or worse, a member of the committee? Despite my best efforts, did one of the children complain of being left out, or bullied? I had no idea.

"We need to talk," Anne whispered.

"What's the matter?" I asked. "Did someone make a complaint?"

She frowned and shook her head. "Have you heard the news?"

"News? What news?"

"About the bombings?" she said.

My heart fell. The Troubles were over, consigned to history.

Weapons were given up, sins forgiven, and politics was the way forward. Ireland was now one of the safest countries in the world. A return to the old ways would be a disaster, especially if you were an English immigrant.

"The IRA?" I groaned.

Anne gently took my arm and guided me away from the crowd of parents and excited children.

"There's been a bombing in London," she explained. "They think it was Al-Qaeda."

"London?" My mouth fell open. "Where?"

"The news is still coming in," she said softly. "There was a bus blown up and bombs on the underground. One was near Liverpool Street. Lots of casualties."

Suddenly, my heart was pounding. My daughter worked in London. Every morning she took the tube from Liverpool Street.

"My daughter... What time?" I stuttered. "What time did this happen?"

"Er...I'm not sure...Just before nine I think."

"Oh God!" I grabbed for my phone, frantically trying to dial Joanne's number.

"If you need to go..." Anne said.

I nodded and, like a zombie, walked towards my car.

"Please answer, please answer," I whispered. But the phone continued to ring. I clicked off and dialled again. Same result. I called Lesley. Inevitably, she was out. Probably in the garden. What to do? My head was in a spin. I felt an overwhelming need to take some action, but I was 800 kilometres away and helpless to do anything. After sending text messages and leaving Joanne two voicemails, I packed my golf kit into my car and headed home.

The 40 minute drive was a blur. My head was spinning as I listened to the unfolding story on the radio and prayed for my daughter to be safe.

Back home, I marched past the dogs and turned on the TV news. Lesley came in a moment later. I was using the landline to try and call Joanne, again without success.

"You're back early," Lesley said.

I pointed to the TV. "Terrorist bombings. Right where Joanne would be." I held up the phone. "She's not answering."

"Oh God!" Lesley's hand covered her mouth. She stood at my

side watching the newsfeed.

The images were awful, just horrid. Blackened faces, slack and expressionless. A red bus peeled open by the force of an explosion. People lying in the street receiving first aid. Others crying, eyes wide in shock and confusion. A woman with a medic, covering her face with white gauze cut like a Halloween mask. More than 50 people dead, and many others injured in a senseless act of hatred. We stood watching, helpless and fearful. Even the dogs remained respectfully quiet, perhaps sensing the magnitude of the event.

Half an hour later, my phone chirped, telling me I had a text message.

"Oh thank goodness!" I exclaimed. "Joanne's okay."

Lesley closed her eyes and breathed a sigh of relief.

"Where is she?" Lesley asked.

"It doesn't say. Not in London though." I read the text. "*Just got your message. Am OK. Had a day off. Left phone in car. Will call later. xxx*"

"Phew!" Lesley sighed.

"That was too close for comfort." I pointed at the TV. "Those poor people."

"Sit down," Lesley ordered. "You look pale. Do you want a drink? I'll put the kettle on."

"Please," I replied. "I'm absolutely parched. It was so hot today. I had water, but I gave it to the kids. I haven't had a drop to drink all day."

Later, Joanne called. She'd been feeling a bit run down and on the spur of the moment had decided to use up a day of her holiday allowance. Meeting a friend for lunch in Chelmsford rather than travelling to London left her safe, but temporarily out of contact. In the circumstances, it seemed like a good trade.

The following morning, I had a problem of my own to deal with.

***

"That's odd," I said.

"Hmm?" Lesley grunted, looking at me over her glasses. Early morning and already she was knitting.

"I seem to be peeing blood."

"Oh." She glanced up again. "You should go to the doctor."

"There wasn't much."

"You should go to the doctor," she repeated.

"It was only twice," I said. "Last night, and again just now."

"You should go to the doctor," Lesley reiterated.

"I was probably just dehydrated after yesterday."

"You should go to the doctor," she sang.

"It was hot and I gave all my water to the kids."

"You should go to the doctor." Her voice was getting louder.

"It'll probably pass," I pleaded.

Lesley put her knitting down and glared at me. Her look was stern and uncompromising. "You should go to the doctor."

I nodded. "I should go to the doctor."

When we were living in England, even though it was a relatively small village, getting a doctor's appointment generally required careful negotiation with a dour and uncompromising receptionist, followed by a wait of several days. Since moving to Ireland, our medical visits had been mercifully infrequent, but sufficient to learn the local process: casually stroll into the surgery and ask to see the doctor.

"Hi, Nick," the receptionist said, giving me a bright smile. "What can I do for you?"

Even though we had only been in the area for a relatively short while, already everyone seemed to know our names. Perhaps my face was on a Wanted poster somewhere. I smiled and asked to see Doctor Mark.

"Take a seat, he'll see you as soon as he can," she said. "But I'm afraid there's a bit of a wait. It could be 20 minutes."

People in England would sell their firstborn child to get a doctor's appointment in 20 minutes.

"No problem." I smiled and took a seat.

In 22 minutes, I was describing my bloody urine to the doctor. He took some fluids and performed a thorough examination.

"There seems to be no pain, infection, or sign of further blood," he said. "I suspect the bleeding was probably due to dehydration, which dislodged a small kidney stone."

"That's what I thought," I replied.

"That being said, you're in the age range where prostate cancer is a statistical possibility, so I'd better do a prostate exam," he smiled disarmingly. "Hop up on the examination table and drop your trousers."

This delightful procedure involves having a gloved finger thrust up your bum, while your doctor asks you about your holiday plans and feels around for suspicious lumps. For some reason, doctors who perform this kind of examination all seem to have hands like a bunch of bananas and a desire to economise on the lubrication. I grunted and squeaked while he performed the examination. There was a snap as he removed the glove and dropped it in the bin.

"Right, that's grand," he said. "Hop down."

"Did you find anything?" I asked.

There was an ominous silence.

Our local doctor's surgery has three examination rooms and a reception area. At the end of his consultations, Doctor Mark has a somewhat disconcerting habit of simply walking out of the examination room without further comment and moving on to his next patient. It took a moment before I realised he had left and I was now talking to myself. Fearing another patient was about to walk in, I hurriedly dismounted the exam table. Or I would have done had I thought to rearrange my clothing first.

With my ankles effectively tied together by my trousers, my well-meaning attempt to step down turned into an undignified side-roll off the table and onto the floor. Although I was unhurt by this moment of stupidity, my glasses had fallen off and slid under the table. Momentarily stunned, I tried to recover them. It was at that moment, while I was kneeling with my naked bottom up in the air as I stretched for my glasses, that I heard the door open. I closed my eyes in horror and waited for the scream, but the only sound was the door quietly closing again. Praying my embarrassing predicament had been hidden by the partially pulled modesty curtain, I quickly dressed and went to see the receptionist.

"Oh, there you are. I thought I'd missed you," she said. "Doctor Mark wants you to pop over to A&E for some precautionary tests. Here's a letter."

Although the Irish health service is systemically flawed, dreadfully underfunded, and shot through with well-intentioned but disastrous anomalies, the medical staff are excellent and professional people. They all do an outstanding job, despite the conditions they have to work under. Nevertheless, I anticipated a long wait at the hospital and called my wife to let her know where I was.

"Well, you're in the right place," she said stoically.

"This is silly," I replied. "Nothing's wrong with me, I'm just wasting everyone's time. Perhaps I should just come home."

"You stay there until you get the all clear," Lesley warned.

I moved to a quiet corner. "Doctor Mark put his finger up my bum," I whispered.

"Oh don't be such a sissy," Lesley laughed. "I've had much worse. You should try having a baby."

She hung up.

An hour later, I was lying on a trolley when the curtain was pulled aside.

"Aye-oh," a voice boomed.

"I haven't heard that since I was in Lagos," I laughed.

"Oh! You been to Nigeria?" the doctor asked.

His accent was typically sing-song with rolling Rs and extended As. I said I had. We chatted for a moment about my disastrous but interesting visit to West Africa. The doctor was from Lagos, which is a hot and noisy city. As a recent immigrant to Ireland, he was finding the climate to be disagreeably cool, even though we were in the middle of a heatwave. He was a mountain of a man. Twice the size of the average lumberjack, but still looked too young to be out of secondary school, let alone a qualified doctor.

After grilling me about my symptoms, the gigantic doctor joyfully snapped a powdered glove onto a hand that was slightly larger than a coal shovel. He explained in broken English that he needed to examine my prostate. My eyes bulged as I watched him apply a pea-sized blob of KY Jelly to his cucumber-like middle finger.

"Is this strictly necessary?" I croaked. "My doctor has already examined me, he said my prostate was okay. It was all in the letter I brought."

His broad smile revealed perfect teeth, gleaming white against his jet black skin. "Yes, is good in letter, but I am the dokt-oor now and I must feel also. Is good?"

I pulled a face and assumed the position, resigned to my fate.

"Yes, is good," I said with a sigh.

He fiddled around behind me, as if hunting for a favourite watch that had accidentally fallen into the toilet. His tuneless humming was occasionally drowned out by my squeaks and grunts of pain. After what seemed like an eternity, he proudly announced that everything was "Goo-wed" but I should wait to see what the senior A&E doctor thought. So I continued reading my book and tried to relax while I waited.

About two hours later, a tall but slightly hunched Asian doctor peered around the curtain and enquired as to my wellbeing. Disappointingly, he was not the senior doctor I was hoping to see, just the regular A&E doctor in for the afternoon shift. I gave him a concise medical history while he flicked through my notes, squinting occasionally as he tried to decipher the squiggles the previous doctor had evidently made in response to my earlier answers.

"I wanted to be a doctor, but my handwriting was too good," I quipped.

He laughed and added a few of his own unintelligible squiggles before announcing he needed to examine my prostate.

I was starting to feel like the new boy in prison and defensively explained I had already been examined twice, my prostate was found to be absolutely fine, and it was recorded in the notes – twice.

He shrugged apologetically. "I must to check, you see. He must always to feel for himself," he said with a stiff but formal smile and a slight bow.

Resigned once again to the inevitable digital inspection, I lay on my side with my knees drawn up to my chest and tried to relax. A few yards away, a mop-wielding cleaner was squinting into my cubicle as if trying to read a distant road sign. I held up a middle finger to indicate what the doctor was about to do, but the cleaner may have misinterpreted this gesture. He responded in kind and turned away.

The doctor, obviously ignorant of the hospital's policy of cost saving, liberally slapped a litre of lubricant around my buttocks before expeditiously inserting a hot finger, and possibly half his arm, to facilitate his investigation. The examination ended abruptly, with an audible pop as he removed his hand with a speed worthy of someone avoiding a snapping dog. As my diligent doctor peeled off his glove, he reported proudly that all was well, but I should still wait to see the senior A&E doctor. He gave me a couple of sheets of stiff blue tissue paper, and left me to the impossible task of attempting to wipe the gelatinous lubricant from my derrière, before I accidentally slid off the trolley like a wet fish.

Some 45 minutes later, a flurry of activity from the nurses and junior doctors suggested that either the US President had suddenly been taken ill while on a secret visit to County Clare, or the elusive A&E senior doctor had finally arrived. Given the prospect of an even longer wait and the real possibility of the Secret Service conducting a cavity search, I hoped for the latter. Moments later the star of the show arrived at my bedside, accompanied by an entourage of nervous student doctors.

The softly spoken senior doctor had kind eyes and a pleasant smile. He looked rather like an elderly maths teacher from my school days. This short, portly man, in a dusty tweed suit with a pocket full of pens, was wearing a stethoscope and a brightly coloured tie that proudly displayed samples from his last twenty meals.

He took my hand and shook it formally, but then refused to let go. Addressing me as sir, he enquired empathetically about my health, as if he were a friend who had heard whispered rumours of some secret malaise. I squirmed uncomfortably as his large but disturbingly soft hands continued their embrace long after our initial handshake. I almost panicked when he started to softly stroke the back of my hand with his fingers. In the end I faked an itchy nose in an attempt to break his hold without further embarrassment, although I noticed several of the attending student doctors sharing a wry smile on my behalf. Undeterred by my well-used but futile objections, he insisted on examining my prostate as well.

Once he had his gloved finger inserted where the sun does not shine, he began a narration. In an extraordinarily loud voice, he explained every detail of the procedure for the benefit of his students, the hard of hearing, and possibly anyone sitting in the carpark as well. For obvious reasons, I was initially thankful for his soft hands, but the fervour with which he pressed and poked the gland caused me to squeak involuntarily as my eyes watered. I was appropriately grateful when the examination was finally over.

With a flourish worthy of a magician conjuring a dove from thin air, he removed his glove, and ignoring my existence, proceeded to address his findings to the students. All the while, I lay silently at his side, still bare bummed and slick with lubricant. It seemed to me that I was now as tiresome as the uneaten remains of a restaurant meal, waiting to be removed by the waitress. Perhaps I was lucky to overhear him report, "Nothing of interest was discovered during my examination. This patient can be discharged, once he has been seen by the urologist."

An hour and two chapters of my book later, the urologist arrived with a pocket full of surgical gloves and his own tube of lubricant. He was a tall and elderly Irish man, with the serious air of someone who cared passionately about his speciality, despite his colleagues' constantly repeated jokes about *taking the piss*. He listened attentively as I explained my initial medical history, then carefully read through my notes and test results, before conducting yet another prostate exam.

After what seemed like an eternity, he washed his hands, reread my notes and then said rather seriously, "Well, I can't see anything wrong with your test results, you seem to be in excellent health, but I am a little worried. Your prostate seems to be strangely swollen and tender."

Through gritted teeth I barely contained my temper as I pointed out that his prostate, too, would be strangely swollen and tender, if it had been examined so enthusiastically and frequently, in such a short time. In the end we agreed my medical needs would be best served if I was discharged immediately and treated at home with plenty of fluids and a nice hot bath.

23. Luv a duck

Joanne and I were on the train, travelling from Norwich to Chelmsford. We were on the return leg after meeting my mother for lunch. I sneezed again and dabbed at my nose with a tissue. Less than a week into my cold and already I felt as if I were rubbing my face with sandpaper. Taking another sip from my water bottle I coughed and winced.

My daughter looked up from her magazine and frowned. "Can you die quietly please? I'm trying to read."

"I don't mind the runny nose," I croaked. "But my throat is raw. It's so painful."

"Perhaps if you stopped talking, it would be better for everyone," Joanne quipped.

"Don't worry, I'll probably be dead soon," I joked. "It is man-flu after all."

Joanne tutted and continued to read. I looked out of the window and watched the Suffolk countryside whisking by.

"I thought my mum looked well," I said.

Joanne's eyes momentarily flicked up from her magazine, but she didn't comment.

"I didn't like that restaurant very much," I croaked, taking another sip of water.

My daughter ignored me, but the magazine lifted slightly.

"Big name chef and all that," I continued. "I thought it would be better."

"And I thought I would be able to read my magazine in peace," Joanne hissed. "Why don't you read for a bit."

"I'll get travel sick."

"Pfft."

I looked out of the window again. Autumn in England. The trees had begun to shed their leaves and many of the fields looked dull and lifeless in the weak grey sunlight. Day five of my trip to England and I ached to see the green fields of Ireland again. I could hardly wait for the morning and my flight home. Soon I would enjoy fresh air, sweet well water and the stillness of nature, far from the madding crowds. And the bliss of sleeping in my own bed once again. I closed my eyes and smiled. I must have dozed

225

for a while. An indecipherable tannoy announcement woke me. The train was slowing.

"Looks like we're coming into Ipswich." I took another sip from my water, finishing the bottle.

"I'm going to the buffet car." Joanne stood.

"Please do not flush the toilet while the train is standing in the station," I joked.

She glared at me. "Do you want anything?"

"Tea and more water please." I handed her some money.

The brakes squealed as the train shuddered to a halt. People got off and people got on. It was after six, the platform at Ipswich station was crowded with office workers heading home. Dull eyes, slumped shoulders and tired faces. Two years ago, that was me, burdened with debt, working too many hours, stressed and unhappy. Now we owned land in the beautiful countryside and didn't have to worry about paying the bills, or being made redundant. I closed my eyes. Life was good.

Doors slammed as the last passengers boarded. I could hear the sharp ting of metal cooling and smell the ozone tang of hot electrics. The train shuddered in response to the guard's whistle. I opened my eyes, coughed and winced.

A young man was sliding into the seat opposite. He was huge and muscular, like a rugby player, with short-cropped hair and a tight-fitting t-shirt. Dark, angry eyes glared at me from below a Neanderthal brow. Momentarily, we made eye contact. His threatening glare challenged me and his posture spoke of excessive testosterone and an undercurrent of violence. I looked away.

Joanne returned carrying our drinks. Two water bottles were sticking out of her handbag. "This train's packed." She slid in next to me, smiling at the lad opposite.

His cruel eyes softened slightly. Momentarily he shuddered and his face twisted, as if conflicted by emotions. His eyes quickly flicked back to me, hard and challenging, like a storm warning.

I looked away, twisting towards Joanne.

"I'll miss you, but I'm looking forward to getting home," I whispered.

"I won't miss your coughing," she laughed. "I hope Mummy's okay."

"She's fine," I said. "I spoke with her last night, she's finally got her hospital appointment."

"For her back injections?"

I nodded. "It's a routine procedure, but she'll have to stay in for a few days."

"When?"

"Mid-November."

There was a grunt opposite. Involuntarily, I looked over at the young man. He was shaking, as if he were fighting a seizure and his eyes were wet with tears. Sensing I was looking, he glared aggressively before turning away. His huge hands gripped and wrung at the plastic grocery bag he was holding. With a loud agonising groan his head turned to the left, like a slow-motion slap to the face. Alarm bells rang in my head and I felt on edge, waiting for the inevitable explosion of violence. Then something remarkable happened.

Joanne reached over and took his hand.

For a second, he froze in shock, his hard eyes flicking between his hand and my daughter's face. I tensed, ready to throw myself forward in her defence. Suddenly his shoulders slumped, his head fell forwards and he began to cry.

Still holding his hand, Joanne moved to his side and slipped her arm around his shoulder. Speaking softly, she pulled him close.

"What's the matter?" she whispered.

I couldn't hear his sobbed reply over the noise of the train.

"Oh, you poor thing!" Joanne said, patting his hand.

He mumbled some more. They exchanged whispers, their heads almost touching, like lovers sitting on a park bench.

She gave him my bottle of water and my packet of tissues. Now the big guy seemed much smaller, huddled in pain, but comforted by my daughter's empathy. As Joanne glanced at me, her eyes flicked left. The message was clear, *leave us alone*.

I nodded in reply and headed for the buffet car. When I returned, the train was just leaving Colchester station and the young man had left.

"What was all that about?" I asked.

"It's so sad," Joanne replied. "That poor boy–"

"Boy?" I exclaimed.

"I know he looked older, but Adam's just 15," she replied. "He was in Ipswich visiting with his girlfriend when the police phoned.

His mother has just been killed in a car crash. She was on business in France."

"How awful!" Horrified, I slumped into my seat.

"He only found out about an hour ago," Joanne said. "That poor boy is just mortified. Shocked. His dad died from cancer last year, so now he's an orphan. As soon as the police called, Adam came straight to the station so he could travel home. Once he sat down, the emotions just boiled over. I offered to drive him to his house, but someone was meeting him at Chelmsford station."

"I'm glad you were here for him." It was all I could think to say.

We sat in silence for the rest of the journey. Clearly, I had misjudged the situation. The wrath in Adam's eyes was actually discomfort. He wanted me to look away because he was too embarrassed to cry in front of another man. Joanne is a sensitive and caring woman. She had read the signals differently. What I had mistaken for anger and aggression, she had recognised as agony and distress. Not for the first time, I found myself wondering what part I had played in raising such a perceptive and caring daughter. After due consideration, I concluded this magical transformation was achieved despite my bumbling, but well-intentioned guidance. Whatever the cause, I could not have been prouder.

***

There is a real sense of satisfaction to be had from adding quality and value to our home. I tend to over-engineer things, so we could be fairly confident that my renovations were well insulated and wouldn't fall over. Although Lesley was keeping busy, creating and tending to the new garden and vegetable plot, she also helped with the building work whenever I asked, and sometimes when I didn't.

I arrived home from my trip to England, to discover she had taken it upon herself to put a cement render on the new wall of the wing. Neither of us have any experience of rendering, but despite the pain of her bad back, she had somehow managed to do a magnificent job. Her efforts blended perfectly with the existing lumpy render. I asked how she had done it.

"Well, I'm quite good at icing cakes, so I figured the technique would be much the same, only on a bigger scale."

I was delighted. Not only had she saved me several days' work if I had done the job myself, but more likely she had avoided us spending the thick end of a thousand euro in wages for a plasterer to do the job.

***

During the spring and summer our meadow became a sea of fragrant colour, alive with bees and butterflies. There were daisies, clover, poppies, tansy and hundreds of other flowers, including beautiful wild orchids. Entering autumn, with the moor on one side, the forest at the back and the grass on all of the other fields already cut for winter silage by the local farmers, our little meadow became an oasis for insects and wildlife. The grass and flowers can get up to waist height and are delightful to walk through, even when the dew makes my jeans as wet as if I had been standing in the pond.

I love to take long walks on the moor with the dogs, particularly on those early mornings when the sky is pale blue, the air is fresh and the valley below is still shrouded in thick mist. It was so peaceful and relaxing, until we disturbed a herd of feral goats.

The dogs were a short distance ahead of me on the long climb up the hill, so there was little I could do when the goats suddenly burst forth, other than add my breathless shouts to the clamour and kerfuffle. The herd had been hidden, feeding in the bushes high on the cliff tops when Lady bounded up. I fancy she was as surprised as the goats by this unexpected encounter. Everyone ran around in panicked circles for a short while, until consensus was reached about who would be chased by whom. Being a terrier, Amber is completely fearless and got stuck into the chasing with commendable alacrity.

After the initial adrenalin rush had subsided, a large buck quickly organised the herd and led them to the safety of the cliffs. I know these creatures are magnificent climbers, but I was truly impressed to see more than 20 goats perching effortlessly on a seemingly sheer rockface. Even the young kids seemed perfectly at home skipping along on mossy rocks, just one slip away from certain death. Their strangely slotted and alien yellow eyes stared up impassively at the dogs, who were cautiously peering over the cliff edge and woofing in frustration. Fortunately, the dogs soon lost interest and followed me on our walk.

Ten minutes later, I spotted the goat herd far in the distance, heading for a quieter feeding ground. Carefree and happy, with the cool breeze on my face and the sun on my back, I couldn't help but whistle the opening bars of 'High on a Hill was a Lonely Goatherd'. The dogs didn't get the joke.

Although the moorland may seem barren and lifeless, there is a good deal of wildlife to be seen. As well as the goats, there are hare, foxes, deer, and a plethora of birds. Because of the generally harsh conditions on the moor, every sheltered nook and cranny is a potential microclimate, becoming an island of colour on a beige ocean as these protected hollows are exploited by nature.

Even the seemingly consistent colour of the moorland is misleading. Throughout the seasons there are subtle changes. As the winter snows gradually clear, the dormant grasses make the moor appear dark brown, flecked with areas of black where the peat has been exposed by the goats, horses and cattle. In spring, the colour lightens as the grasses and heather sprout. Soon the gorse bushes bud, adding light greens and fragrant bright yellows to the palette. By the summer the bracken, ferns and bramble have made much of the moor a rich green, interspaced with heather, coloured soft violet and white. In the autumn, the fruits and berries add red and purple, and the wild cotton heads create a sea of waving white along the sheltered slopes. Without any doubt, the moor is a strangely attractive place. Seemingly desolate, isolated and unchanging, but at the same time alive with change and colour. Rural Ireland at its most beautiful.

To add to that morning's excitement, just as we were heading back down the hill, Lady killed a hare. When I say *killed a hare*, you may mistakenly be imagining a Fox Hound majestically bounding across the moor, before tackling her prey to the ground and administering a swift bite to the neck, thus bringing a merciful death. Lady spends a lot of time chasing hares, and anything else she can smell, but she's not very good at hunting. Typically, she will end up running in the wrong direction and yapping a lot, until she's breathless and bored. Lady had never before caught a hare, or even come close. This 'kill' was only achieved when she accidentally tripped over the hapless creature, thereby breaking its neck. The poor thing was safely concealed in some heather and only died because it had stuck its head up to find out what all the noise was about. In any event, when Lady proudly presented us with her kill, Romany took one horrified look at the corpse, did an about-turn, and headed for home.

This time I was close enough to keep up with the little dog as she trotted purposely towards the house. However, because I was carrying the dead hare, which I was using as a macabre incentive to ensure Lady's cooperation, Romany refused to come within ten yards. Ignoring my calls, she repeatedly glared at me over her shoulder, as if I were an axe murderer, ghoulishly brandishing my latest kill. Fortunately, we made it home safely, just in time for breakfast. Romany immediately relinquished her moral high ground to tuck into a bowl of her favourite tinned dog food (with rabbit) and Lady ate the hare.

As soon as we reached the house, our Fox Hound pulled her trophy from my hand and took it to a quiet corner of the garden. There she proceeded to consume it in a single sitting, bones, fur and everything. It was an incredible sight. The hare was considerably larger than our terrier, Amber, and must have weighed all of twelve pounds. Later that afternoon, it was a very proud, rotund and breathless dog that waddled back into the house. She collapsed prostrate on the floor, and there she remained, squeaking and rumbling as she noisily digested her catch. An hour later, Lesley wrinkled her nose and looked up from her knitting.

"Did you just...?"

I shook my head. "Did you?"

Lesley glared at me. Our eyes searched the room for the culprit, quickly settling on the quivering shaking mass at our feet.

"*Lady!*" we shouted. She ignored us.

***

I had just arrived back from work and was climbing out of the car, when I heard an almighty cacophony of squawks from the meadow. The chickens were being attacked. Although I was wearing new shoes and my best pair of trousers, I sprinted across the lawn and along the path to the meadow, but I was too late. The field was strewn with chicken feathers and the bloodied remains of one lone wing. Once I had rounded up the remainder of the terrified chickens, the count revealed we had lost four. I went indoors to relay the news.

"I'm so sorry, I didn't hear a thing," Lesley said apologetically.

"It's not your fault," I said. "Letting the chickens run free was always a risk."

"But they like foraging and scrapping," Lesley pleaded.

"They're not so keen on it now," I grimaced.

We decided we would need to keep the flock permanently penned. During the next few days I bought more chicken wire and angle iron posts and extended the pen considerably, more than doubling the surface area. The following weekend, I met with the Chicken Lady in the carpark in Gort and restocked our diminished flock.

Lesley had been out shopping that morning. On her return, she walked straight to the chicken pen, keen to inspect our new arrivals. She was in for a surprise.

"Those aren't chickens," she said perceptively, pointing to two snow-white, six-inch-tall, yellow beaked individuals quacking loudly at each other.

"Err, no," I admitted. "They're ducks."

My wife glared at me.

I shrugged. "I saw them and couldn't resist!"

"What type are they?"

"I think they are called Aylesbury ducks. They grow quite big," I explained. "They were going cheap – or quack," I quipped.

Lesley thumped me lovingly. "What do they do?" she asked.

"Well, the Chicken Lady had laying ducks and eating ducks. These are eating ducks, so I don't expect they will lay many eggs."

"Well I'm not going to feed these up and then eat them, if that's your plan," Lesley exclaimed.

"Of course not. I would never want that."

"So, what will we do with them?"

"Just keep them as pets I suppose. For the time being they can live in with the chickens," I suggested. "Perhaps later they'll live in the pond."

Lesley gave me a sideways look.

"Eventually," I added hopefully.

24. Oil and water

There was an unfamiliar car in the driveway when I arrived home from work. A huge blue SUV, an airport rental, parked in my usual spot up near the house. It was our friends, Robert and Susan.

"Surprise!" they shouted as I came into the kitchen.

"What are you guys doing here?" I asked, delighted to see them again.

"We had a few days of holiday to spare, and we found a cheap flight," Robert explained. "So, we thought we'd take a driving tour, but without the boys."

"We're B&B hopping," Susan said. "It's all very ad hoc and unplanned. Quite exciting."

"Goodness! How adventurous," I said. "I wish I'd known you were coming. I'd have come home sooner."

Robert waved my concerns away. "We weren't planning to call, but when we realised we were close by, we decided to pop in."

"It took ages to find your house," Susan added.

"We were coming to you from the north," Robert explained. "So the landmarks were unfamiliar, and the satnav was no bloody use whatsoever."

"Satnav? Up here? You'll be lucky!" I laughed. "Are you staying with us?"

"Thanks for the offer," Susan replied, "but we're booked into a B&B in Killaloe tonight. I wouldn't want to let them down."

"That's a shame," I said.

"You've always got a bed here," Lesley added.

Susan smiled and turned to Lesley. "Let's go and look at the garden. We can chat while these boys play."

Once they had gone, Robert grinned and rubbed his hands together. "Can I help you with anything? I fancy doing some demolition."

"And some heavy lifting?" I asked. "We could remove this spiral staircase."

"Absolutely!" Robert beamed like a kid with a new toy.

That steel monstrosity was the final obstacle before I could begin renovating the kitchen. Lesley and I would be turning an ugly, dark and cramped three-floor block into a homely kitchen with a master bedroom on the floor above. The steel spiral staircase had been built in situ. It was firmly connected to each floor, and the roof, with stout metal plates. Conceivably, it could have been the only thing stopping this end of the house from falling down. After much head scratching, Robert and I propped the floors up with a few bits of waste wood and, starting at the top, I bravely set about reducing the staircase into moveable sections with my disc cutter. Although I set myself on fire three times, within an hour we had reduced the staircase to a pile of steel bits, stacked neatly in the garden, ready for the scrap metal dealer to collect.

Robert made a passable fire warden, if you count pointing at the flames and laughing as a satisfactory method. He was delighted to get his hands dirty and I was grateful for his help. After we waved them on their way, I turned my mind to the task ahead, building the new floors.

"How are you going to do it?" Lesley asked.

"It's going to be a bit tricky," I replied, chewing on my lip. "Are you sure we couldn't just move into the wing for a bit?"

"I said no!" my wife glared threateningly.

"Only a thought," I grinned defensively.

"Why's it going to be so tricky?"

I pointed upwards. "All the water tanks and plumbing are up there. If we were living in the wing, I could just rip everything out, but as we're staying in the house, I'll have to work around the plumbing."

Lesley frowned. "I don't understand."

"The plumbing system is fed by gravity and the central heating is pumped. It's like this..." I used my hands to illustrate my point. "There are three floors. The cold water tank is at the very top. Below that is the hot tank, and below that the kitchen. We want to turn three floors into two, which will change all of the floor levels. If we were living in the wing, I could rip everything out, including the plumbing, fit the new floors at the correct level, then replace the tanks and pipes."

"But you can't do that if we're living in the house?" Lesley asked.

"Not unless you want to be without water and heating for about a month."

"We're not living in the wing," Lesley insisted.

"Agreed." I nodded. "So I'll have to add parts of the new floors and temporarily move the plumbing back and forth as I work."

Lesley frowned again. I tried a different tack.

"It'll be like that logic test. The one where you have to drive a thousand miles but your car can only travel two hundred without refuelling, so you have to shuttle back and forth with petrol cans until–"

Lésley was grinning. She lovingly patted me on the shoulder and shook her head.

"Don't worry, dear," she laughed. "Just get on with the kitchen. I'm sure you'll work it out."

And with that vote of confidence, I set to work.

***

Whereas Lesley is a free spirit, almost drifting through life like mist on a breeze, I cannot function without my lists and plans. After several hours of careful head scratching, I had produced a set of drawings, closely resembling a diagram of the London Underground overlaid with the wiring plan for the Large Hadron Collider. Along with the timeline and associated notes, I had everything I needed to guide me through the kitchen renovations. Like a child brandishing his first gold star from playschool, I presented my drawings to my dear wife. She squinted and frowned.

"Ack! What a waste of time," she groaned. "Can't you do anything without your little drawings?"

Romany was nearby, balancing on her bum and begging for my attention. I addressed my reply to her.

"Nobody in this house appreciates my talent," I joked. "It's such a waste."

Because of my detailed planning, the complicated movement of plumbing and floors went rather well. After a fortnight, the work was finished and I was ready to start on the last phase, demolishing the kitchen.

Almost a quarter of the original space was taken up by a walk-in larder, made up from rough bits of wood and some planking.

The larder was a shaky-looking affair, ready to fall down at the first shove and painted bright purple into the bargain. It needed to be removed. On closer inspection, I was horrified to discover the lovely oak flooring had been laid around the larder, rather than under it. It only took 20 minutes to carefully remove the purple monstrosity, but its absence revealed a gaping hole in the wooden floor which could not be patched. So, with no alternative left, I had to rip the floor up as well. Predictably, the wood had been nailed and glued so comprehensively I could only save a few pieces, which I used to patch some damage to the sitting room floor. The rest of the kitchen flooring ended its life as very expensive firewood.

There was protective plastic sheeting under the wooden floor. As soon as it was removed, the kitchen started to smell like an old oil tank. The fumes were so bad, we were afraid to turn the heating on. The culprit was the small oil leak underneath the Rayburn, which I had rectified on my first night in the house. Although my repair was sound, over the preceding years, many gallons of kerosene must have escaped, running underneath the plastic and soaking unnoticed into the concrete floor below. I'd hope the smell would dissipate, but I was wrong. After three days and nights, freezing our butts off without any heating, the fumes were only getting worse.

"This is hopeless," I wheezed. "I'll have to dig out the floor."

"Perhaps you should wait another day," Lesley suggested. Her eyes were red-rimmed and watering. "It might clear."

"I don't think so," I replied. "And even if it did, the kerosene will have degraded the concrete. I looked it up on the internet."

"Okay. Just get on with it," my wife coughed, waving me away with her hand. "I can't take this smell any longer."

It took several days of hard digging to remove the concrete floor by hand. During that time, the fumes were so appalling we had to keep all the doors and windows open. Even then, I flinched each time there was a spark from my pickaxe, imagining the misunderstanding should the gas combust like a bomb, scattering bits of Glenmadrie and Nick Albert all across this once Republican part of County Clare. Once the concrete floor was replaced and tiled, I was able to remove the old roof joists above the kitchen, by attacking them enthusiastically with my new petrol chainsaw.

What this method lacked in style, it made up for with noise and alacrity, as well as filling the house with exhaust fumes. After just an hour of cutting pulling and swearing, the old joists were out and we could finally see the new kitchen ceiling, which was almost three feet higher than before.

Although the stone walls throughout the house looked delightfully rustic, they were cold to the touch, gave easy passage to mice and draughts, and were so lumpy as to be completely impractical for hanging pictures and kitchen units. I decided to insulate and dry-line the kitchen walls.

To create a room that was the correct size to house the kitchen units we'd been storing since the previous winter, I had to build the walls perfectly square, vertical and exactly the right distance apart. As we had several heavy wall-mounted units to fit, I'd also added additional supports hidden behind the plasterboard. With the wooden framework completed and the wiring for sockets and lights in place, I was well into attaching the plasterboard slabs when I heard an innocent little voice beside me.

"Nick? I've been thinking," Lesley said sweetly.

A cold chill ran down my back. "Oh dear! Err, I mean, oh good! What were you thinking?" I asked with trepidation.

"Well, here's the thing. The Rayburn is nice to have, it looks lovely and it works fine for heating the house, but it's not very practical for cooking on – particularly if you just need to boil an egg."

"Okay... So what did you have in mind?" I asked with further trepidation, whilst trying to remember the last time we ate boiled eggs.

She gave me a bright smile. "I think we need to buy a gas cooker."

I gave a silent sigh of relief. "I agree, it would be an excellent idea. Unfortunately we're 20 miles from the nearest gas main."

"That's not a problem!" she told me triumphantly. "I've checked, and the cooker I like is available with bottled gas. We can have a tank just outside the window."

"Oh good," I said with a stiff smile. "I'll start redesigning the kitchen."

***

Amber had developed a stiff smile as well. She'd taken to sitting in the centre of the living room floor, grinning and panting.

"That's very odd behaviour," I said, pointing at our smallest dog.

"Hmm," Lesley looked up from her book. "What is?"

"Amber, grinning like an idiot," I replied. "It's almost as if she's in distress."

Lesley frowned. "She's probably just stressing. After all, she is a terrier. They're known to be rather highly strung."

"I'm not so sure. There," I pointed, "she's doing it again."

"Perhaps it's wind," Lesley suggested. "She does gulp her food."

"She's been doing it for a little while now. More frequently in the last few days. Whatever's going on, I think it's getting worse."

"Alright!" Lesley sighed and closed her book. "I'll phone Katy."

Amber went to the vet, and stayed. She needed an emergency operation to relieve an intestinal blockage. Everything went well. The following morning, when Lesley went to collect our beloved terrier, Katy showed her the cause of the problem.

"Oh," my wife said, nodding. "Stones."

"Yes, several stones," Katy said, poking the offending articles with her finger.

"No. I mean the game of stones," Lesley replied.

"Isn't that a book?"

Lesley explained. "Kia can be a little possessive when we play ball. After her illness, it took some time for her to learn how to play nicely. As Amber is a terrier, we had to be sure to protect her gaming rights as well, otherwise there could be a fight. During our walks, we play a clandestine version of Amber's favourite game, which is called *Stones*. Basically, we throw the ball for Kia and kick a stone for Amber. While the bigger dog is off chasing the ball and tackling Lady like a line-backer on steroids, Amber can pounce on the pebble like an excited kitten."

"Well, Amber had a tummy like a bag of marbles," Katy explained. "I suspect she was jealously guarding her prizes by swallowing them."

Lesley grimaced. "Game over, I think."

After much effort we have finally trained Kia and Amber to play in a way that avoids any possessive fighting. This new game involves throwing a tennis ball to Kia, who, at the command 'Give' will drop the ball so Amber can bring it back. It's complicated and tedious for the ball thrower, but good team building for the dogs, and avoids any further stone swallowing.

***

We named the ducks Jemima and Puddle, after the Beatrix Potter book. They grew at an alarming rate, almost doubling in size every few days. Soon they were the size of swans, and despite being *eating ducks* they both started laying large white eggs every day. Even for a duck, Jemima was cantankerous and argumentative, always quacking loudly and irritably and running away with her huge wings flapping whenever we went near her. Puddle was the complete opposite, incredibly friendly and welcoming. She would run over whenever she saw me, fluttering her wings in silent ecstasy, especially if I softly stroked her broad white back.

Contrary to popular belief, ducks do not need to swim in vast lakes to be happy. They only require a few inches of water to remain clean and contented. Nevertheless, as I had dug the pond, and it was regularly visited by some local wild ducks, I thought it would be nice to give our two Aylesburys the same privilege. One sunny morning, I let them out of the pen and led the way up to the pond. But this special treat didn't go quite as planned, as I explained to Lesley later that day.

"The 50 yard walk took about 15 minutes. They were so excited by their new environment, they kept stopping to inspect every flower and bug along the way. After a good bit of cajoling, encouragement and quite a bit of chasing, we finally arrived at the pond."

"Did they jump in?" Lesley asked.

"Not really," I replied. "Jemima and Puddle just stood there, staring at the water with suspicion."

"I expect it was all a bit new to them."

"That's what I thought. What with not being brought up by a mummy duck and being shown how to swim, I figured they needed some instruction in the art of being duck-like."

Lesley squinted at me with suspicion. "I hope you didn't throw them in?"

"Of course not," I exclaimed. "I would never do that!"

"You threw Joanne into the swimming pool when she was little."

"For the last time, she slipped," I growled. "Anyway, she was wearing water wings."

"If you say so," Lesley mumbled.

"Can I get on with my story?"

My wife nodded.

"I waded in until the water was almost lapping at the top of my wellies, and splashed gently with my hands. This did the trick. Both ducks waddled a few inches into the water and started to feed, sieving the rich mud with their beaks. They were having a great time."

"Is that it?"

"Not quite," I replied. "It was a lovely morning, so I sat on the embankment and watched. Everything went swimmingly for a while…"

Lesley winced at my clumsy pun. I continued with the story.

"Everything went well, until Jemima decided to take a shortcut to the other side of the pond. She happily walked out until she reached deeper water. As soon as she began to float, all hell broke loose."

"She couldn't swim!" Lesley laughed, guessing at what had happened.

I shrugged and smiled. "She didn't even try. I swear, I could almost imagine her shouting, *Holy crap! I can't touch the bottom!* Suddenly Jemima started to panic, flapping and quacking really loudly. Puddle joined in – and that was the end of that. Both ducks were out of the water and sprinting back to the chicken pen, quicker than I could run. They hid in the coop for the rest of the afternoon."

My wife laughed and shook her head. "Just our luck to get ducks that wouldn't float!"

After two further embarrassingly unsuccessful attempts to introduce our ducks to the pond, I relented and purchased a hefty child's sand box made of bright blue plastic. This held a few inches of water and was large enough for the ducks to bathe in comparative safety. That afternoon I set the makeshift pool into an indentation in the ground within the chicken pen and filled it with water from a hosepipe. Both ducks were already sitting in their new pool, even before I had finished filling it. Their playful dives and splashes were so exuberant that I had to top up the water twice within the first hour. It was a mild evening and at dusk, when I went to close up the animals for the night, both ducks were still paddling happily in their pond.

Disregarding my orders to go to bed, they were like a couple of school children playing with a new toy. As they looked at me with pleading eyes, I imagined them saying, "Please Dad, can we play a little longer? Ple-e-ease?"

25. Mouldy melamine

"Well, that's it," Lesley said. "All done."

We were standing in our newly-decorated kitchen. Really it was no more than an empty room, with a high ceiling, cream floor tiles, and walls painted in soft pastel green. The Rayburn, gleamingly clean and fully serviced, was still in its original place, and below the window our new gas cooker was installed and ready for use. All that was missing was the new kitchen units.

"You've done a lovely job on the decorating," I said. "It looks really nice."

Lesley smiled. "Compared to that dark old room, I can't get over how light is seems." She did a little twirl. "It feels so big."

"It'll seem a little smaller once the kitchen is fitted."

My wife glanced at me and grinned. "No time like the present!"

"I'll get started right away," I laughed, rolling my eyes.

"I can't wait to see it. And to have a proper kitchen. It's been almost two years since we moved in."

"You've been very patient," I smiled. "Mind you, we have done a lot. The polytunnel, the pumphouse, the wing, and all the landscaping. We should be proud of ourselves."

"Shut up and get on with your work," Lesley quipped, eager to see the kitchen taking shape.

"Yes, boss." I bowed slightly.

"Where are you going to assemble the units?"

"I think I'll move all the boxes into the conservatory, so I can figure out what's what. I can work from that plan the lady in the kitchen shop produced. Once I've made up each unit, I'll pull it through and slot it into the correct position."

"What about the doors?" Lesley asked.

"The book says to fit and level the carcasses first. The doors go on last."

"Can I help at all?"

"Don't worry. I'll shout when I need you." I smiled at her excitement. It was infectious.

The old music studio we used as a storage area was a large, low-ceilinged room, beneath the master bedroom at the south end

243

of our property. It was self-contained, with two entrances and a couple of small windows, and may once have been intended for use as a garage. One door was accessed from under the coverway through the courtyard, the other entrance was a large, yellow double shed door, made from rough timber. Soon after we moved in, I had screwed these doors to the frame and sealed them against the weather.

Our storage area was still tightly packed with suitcases and cardboard boxes filled with our belongings. Many of these boxes were still sealed from our previous house move, the list of contents long since faded and unreadable. Did they contain rare and valuable artefacts, a fortune in stocks and shares, or my dusty old trainset? Who knew? I resisted the urge to investigate, instead spending the first hour moving and restacking the boxes until I could reach the rear of the studio. There, stacked against the double doors, our kitchen had been safely stored for almost a year. Or so I thought.

As I moved the first of the flat-packed boxes, my heart sank. The cardboard was soaked through. I carefully slid the box from the stack and carried it through to the conservatory.

"I thought you'd fixed the leak in there," Lesley groaned.

"I had... I mean, I did. I think water has been getting through those flipping yellow doors."

"But you screwed the door–"

"I did," I snapped, "but obviously not well enough. The wind must have been blowing through. Over time the moisture has soaked into the boxes." I stripped away the wet cardboard. "Oh no! This kitchen's wrecked. It's all mouldy."

I swore loudly and stomped off to the studio to collect another box. Over the next hour, I moved the entire stack into the conservatory. The boxes nearer to the bottom were dripping with water and covered in a thick layer of fungus.

"Not only is this kitchen ruined, which has wasted thousands of euro, but we'll have to buy another one as well," I moaned. "It's bound to cost three times as much now the sales have finished, and we'll probably have to wait for weeks until it's delivered."

I pulled Lesley into a hug.

"Sorry, love," I sighed.

But my wife was unusually optimistic.

"Hang on a minute," she said. "Before you start building a bonfire, let's open all the boxes and see what can be saved."

Carefully keeping the contents of each box together, we stripped away the sodden cardboard.

"You know, ," I said, "the damage seems to be confined to the packaging. Apart from needing a good wash with some cleaning solution to remove the mildew, the units appear to be unmarked."

"Really?" Lesley smiled. "Do you think they'll be alright?"

I nodded. "I can't believe it. The boxes look so bad, I was sure the units would have been ruined. This melamine is fantastic stuff."

"Lucky us," my wife sighed.

"Very lucky. We've dodged a bullet here. If we'd been just slightly delayed doing the renovations…" I grimaced and shook my head. "Another winter with this lot stacked against that door…"

***

Provided you follow the directions and apply a little common sense, fitting a flat-pack kitchen yourself is not an especially difficult job, or so my DIY manual claimed. In this case, I would be working with square and true walls, which would make life a lot easier.

As the lack of water damage had shown, although it was inexpensive, our self-assembly kitchen was of a surprisingly decent quality. Unfortunately, the assembly instructions were of a different standard altogether. They bore little resemblance to the process required to successfully assemble the units, and were about as unhelpful as the worst telephone helpline. I suspect the person who lovingly crafted this exotic work of fiction had actually translated them correctly from the original Klingon, but accidently added the wrong pictures. With what I considered to be commendable persistence, I stuck to my task and figured out the correct procedure to turn the seemingly random pile of bits into something resembling a kitchen unit.

To add to the entertainment, a partially illiterate and completely innumerate drunk had obviously been recruited to count and bag the small accessories required for each package.

This poor person had obviously panicked under the strain of the new job and resorted to randomly stuffing great handfuls of irrelevant screws and hinges into the plastic bags.

Once I had completed the construction, even adding some extra screws for good measure, I still had almost a kilo of nails, hinges and screws leftover. There were also dozens of obscure little metal thingamajigs with a screw at one end, a lump of plastic at the other and a strange bump in the middle. They refused to fit anywhere in the kitchen, and may have originally been intended for the Large Hadron Collider. I put all of the leftover bits into an empty plastic ice cream carton, and hid it in my workshop.

Not to be outdone, the kitchen design expert in the DIY shop had somehow managed to miscalculate my order. I had twice as much base board as I had kitchen units, but only half as much pelmet. We took a trip to Limerick and tracked her down. While I went to the kitchen department, my wife headed towards the garden centre, smiling like a child entering Santa's grotto.

The kitchen lady was sitting at her desk.

"Hi. Remember me?" I asked, smiling brightly.

"Sorry." She shrugged.

I pulled out the receipt for the kitchen along with the plan she had prepared.

"My wife and I bought this kitchen from you," I said. "Unfortunately, there was a slight miscalculation."

"Oh dear," she said.

"Not to worry," I smiled. "You see, we seem to have too much base board, but nowhere near enough pelmet."

"Oh dear." She reached for the paperwork. "May I see?"

I handed her the papers. "You see, the quantities delivered were correct, it seems that your computer simply miscalculated what we needed."

"You seem to be correct," she nodded. "I'm terribly sorry for the mix-up."

I waved her concerns away. "I have the surplus baseboard in the car," I said. "If you could swap it for the pelmet, we'll be on our way."

"If only I could." The lady was tapping a perfectly painted fingernail on my order pages. "But this order was two years ago!"

"So?"

"Well, you can't possibly expect us to correct a mistake after so long?" she pleaded.

"Frankly, I do," I replied.

"But we can't!"

"Why not?" I asked. "It's obvious your computer has made a mistake. You still sell these kitchens, there's one behind you. I'm only asking you to swap one component for another. Easy-peasy." I smiled disarmingly, but apparently not disarmingly enough.

The nice lady shook her head firmly.

"Can't be done," she replied.

"Why not?"

"The computer won't let me," she explained. "After so long, I won't be able to book the parts back into stock."

"But it's the computer's mistake," I said. "Can't you just tell it that?"

"Sorry." Her face spoke of processes, procedures and bloody-minded bureaucracy.

My heart sank. I felt like a hostage with nothing to trade.

"At least can I buy some more pelmet?"

"Of course!" She smiled and began tapping on the computer. "It will take six to eight weeks to arrive."

"Six to eight…" I sighed and hung my head. "Can you deliver it?"

The nice lady squinted at my address, chewed on her lip and tapped on the computer. She quoted a figure only marginally less than what we had paid for the house, or so it felt."

"Good grief!" I exclaimed. "How much is it without delivery?"

"That is the delivery charge, the pelmet is extra." She quoted a separate but equally large figure.

"Phew!" I exclaimed. "Just call me when it's in. We'll come and collect it."

As Lesley and I loaded the car with dozens of plants and bags of compost, I shared my tale. She was unusually stoic.

"Can't be helped. Just forget it and move on."

I shrugged, knowing I was beaten. But I had one suggestion.

"Perhaps I can sell that box of surplus kitchen screws and unidentifiable widgets to pay for the missing parts."

When the kitchen was finally finished, we took a few moments out of our relentless schedule to admire a job well-done. The old kitchen was cramped, dark, cold and rather too well ventilated, with a low ceiling that rained dust and dead spiders onto the food below. Now, with an eight-foot high ceiling, well-insulated walls, unpretentious white melamine units, black marble worktops and cream floor tiles, the kitchen had become warm, bright and simplistically functional. With the addition of a large pine table and four chairs, it was now the welcoming heart of our home. Lesley was delighted with her new kitchen and I was quietly proud of my work.

***

Although Lady, the mighty hunter, has thus far failed to actually catch anything, apart from the sleeping hare she dispatched with an accidental kick to the head, she has managed to bring home some interesting finds. As a former goat farm, our land is littered with the buried remains of expired livestock. These either died of natural causes, or were slaughtered for meat after their milk yield fell to uneconomic levels. Lady will regularly bring me a leg bone, or part of a jaw, just to prove she can. She won't chew on the bones, they're just a cat-like gift, so it usually falls to me to dispose of the remains. Despite being just an average sized dog, our lovable Fox Hound returned from a solo foray through the forest with the neatly sectioned head and shoulders of a small muntjac deer. She was insistent she had killed this deer herself, but when I pointed out the bullet hole in its shoulder, Lady dropped her tail in shame and walked away.

With four dogs to care for, we became regular visitors to the vets: for Kia's illness, for puppy inoculations, Amber's bag of marbles and for Romany's frequently infected eyes and dickey tummy. However, the dogs are generally all in pretty good health, apart from the occasional mishaps.

When in full hunting mode, Lady is inclined to run into trees, graze herself on barbed wire fences, or cut a paw on a sharp rock. These wounds usually heal themselves without needing medical attention, except for on one cold rainy night.

"Oh my God, Lady's bleeding!" Lesley squealed.

After hunting excitedly for almost an hour, our Fox Hound had just trotted into the house, soaking wet, muddy and steadily dripping blood from somewhere. I rushed over to examine the poor dog, as she stood shivering by the fire.

"She's in shock," my wife groaned. "I think she's been run over."

"No. I don't think so," I replied, running my hands along her mud and blood-streaked flanks. "She seems fine."

"But she's shaking," Lesley said.

"It's excitement," I replied. "She's been chasing something in the forest."

"But the blood…"

I checked again. On closer inspection, the cause was obvious. There was a steady drip-drip of blood from a 2cm long cut on Lady's right ear.

"She must have caught it on a thorn or a bit of barbed wire," I explained. "Running around in the rain, the blood has splashed everywhere. That's why she looks so bad. I'll put some of that surgical tape on it for now, but it'll probably need a stitch or two in the morning."

"Oh thank goodness." Suddenly, Lesley held out a hand and shouted. "Lady! NO!"

But before we could react, Lady enthusiastically shook herself off, leaving the cream walls splattered with dirty water, mud and several suspicious looking splashes of blood. The cut only needed a couple of sutures, but the walls required a lot of cleaning before visitors stopped calling the Gardaí to report a possible murder.

Even if Lady is an appallingly bad hunter, particularly for a Fox Hound, there is something undeniably appealing about her ineptness. Perhaps it's my British sense of fair play, along with our overwhelming desire to always root for the little guy, but every time I see Lady tripping over her own paws in an effort to catch a distant herd of deer, or blindly running in the wrong direction after sniffing out a fox, I can't help but whisper proudly, "That's my girl!"

***

Power failures at Glenmadrie are quite common. It's a price worth paying for living in such a remote and beautiful location. We are the last house on the line and therefore instantly plunged into darkness by the slightest fault twenty miles away. For several months, a planned programme of line replacement has left us without power for eight hours every week. To add a little variety, the power will also cut out sporadically during periods of bad weather. At other times it will flicker and surge for a couple of hours, usually after some overexuberant driver has managed to damage a utility pole.

Most of these power outages are pre-planned and well-advertised, while for nature's interruptions there is usually a recorded message on the power company's emergency telephone line, accurately predicting when the flow of electricity will be restored. We try not to get too stressed about these power failures, being mindful that while we sit in front of the fire, trying to read a book by candlelight, some poor devil is out in the cold lashing rain, attempting to restore the electricity supply to our house.

Lesley and I hadn't experienced such a frequency of blackouts since the oil shortages in England during the 1970s, so there was a mild sense of excitement when the power first went off, but the novelty value was short-lived. Luckily we were well prepared to cope without electricity. With the wood stove we were able to heat the house, we could boil water and cook meals with the gas cooker, and I had acquired a small generator as a backup in the event of a long period without mains electricity. Furthermore, these situations were not without humour, as we discovered the night before Lesley was due to go into hospital.

"What time shall we leave tomorrow?" my wife asked.

"I figured 7 am. We've got to get across Limerick and I have no idea where the hospital is."

"Perhaps you need to buy one of those satnav thingies."

"Bah! Waste of money. I'm quite capable of reading a map."

Lesley shrugged, probably remembering our trip to Cork. "It's up to you."

"I may look out for a reconditioned one though. We'll see." I smiled at my wife. "Is your bag packed?"

She nodded. "Pyjamas, slippers, dressing gown, two books and toiletries."

"You'd have thought they'd have found a closer hospital," I remarked, muting the sound on the television. "It's almost a three-hour round trip."

"I don't expect you to visit every day," Lesley replied. "Anyway, I'll probably be home by Thursday."

"I hope it goes okay." I reached over and patted her hand.

"Ack. Don't worry. They're knocking me out, so this time the injections won't hurt. I'll be fine."

"Well, I hope your back gets better. That's the important–"

The lights flickered momentarily and we were plunged into darkness.

"Bugger!"

With a little assistance from the glow of the fire, I groped my way to the cupboard where we kept candles and matches. I pulled out two candelabra and three individual candle holders. They were the old-fashioned type, with a tray and a little carrying handle in the shape of a loop.

"I guess we'll just read for a while," Lesley said. "It's a bit early for bed."

Just as I was lighting the last of the candles, the power came back on.

"Ha!" I laughed. "Perfect timing."

I began blowing out the candles.

"Snuff them out properly, otherwise the smoke alarm will go off," Lesley said. "You know how it upsets Romany."

Even wetting my fingers, somehow I still managed to burn myself on the last candle.

"Blast!" I sucked on my thumb.

"I don't know how you manage it," Lesley laughed. "You're always getting burned."

"I only do it to keep your spirits up," I explained, putting the candles back in the cupboard. As soon as I sat down again, we were plunged into darkness once more.

"I don't believe it!" Lesley cried.

Grumbling to myself, I returned to the cupboard and retrieved the candles. As I bent over to light the first candle, the lights flickered on again, but as soon as I blew out the match, we were plunged into darkness once more. I waited.

"Just light the candles!" Lesley moaned.

I did.

"There. Happy now?" I sat on the couch and opened my book.

The lights came on again.

Lesley and I shared a look. She held up a hand. "Just wait." Ten minutes passed and the lights stayed on.

"I think it's safe to say, whatever the problem was, it's fixed now," Lesley said.

I began blowing out candles again. As soon as the last flame was extinguished, the lights went off.

"Are you sure the engineer isn't looking through the window and watching us?" I joked.

My wife laughed and began lighting the candles again.

"Surely, it can't happen again," she said. But it did.

As she reached the last candle, the power returned. We waited the requisite ten minutes before extinguishing the candles once more, but yet again, we were plunged into darkness as soon as the final flame was snuffed out.

"Surely someone's playing a joke on us. There must be a hidden camera somewhere."

Out came the matches, now diminished in number, and we set about relighting the candles. The process was repeated with exquisite comedic timing twice more. Eventually, we were both crying with laughter and decided to leave two candles burning until bed time. Inevitably, the power stayed on without so much as a flicker.

26. Doggy Ball Games

"How's Mum doing?" Joanne asked. There was a slight echo over the phone as the signal bounced off a satellite somewhere.

"She's not," I grumbled. "I saw her yesterday. They've put her operation off again."

"Operation? You mean procedure," my daughter corrected. "Why the delay?"

"Some bug they found," I said. "Because they're injecting into her spine, they did a skin swab. Apparently she tested positive for some sort of flesh-eating bacteria."

"Eww!" Joanne squealed. "Where did she catch that?"

"Your mum didn't catch it, it's just on her skin. She probably picked it up in the hospital," I grunted. "She hasn't tested positive before. Anyway, she has to shower with some special soap several times a day, until the swab is clear."

"Won't they let her come home?"

"Nope. It's something to do with waiting lists. If she's discharged she'll have to go back to the beginning of the queue. Her choices are to stay in hospital, or wait for a couple of years for another appointment."

"I'll bet she's loving this," Joanne quipped.

"Like a migraine on a sunny day," I replied. "You can't even call her, there's no phone reception over there. She really is like a bear with a sore head."

"And a sore back."

"Hmm," I agreed. "Sitting around all day, or lying in bed reading, isn't helping. She's been getting dreadful muscle spasms."

"Oh the poor thing," Joanne sighed. "Give her my love when you see her."

"Will do," I replied. "I'm heading over there now. I'll tell her you called. It'll cheer her up."

***

My wife was sitting up in bed, looking surprisingly chipper. She had good news.

"The doctor has just been doing his rounds," she smiled. "The last two swabs were clear."

"That's great news," I exclaimed. "So they can go ahead with your procedure?"

She nodded. "I'm first on the list tomorrow morning. If everything goes well, you can take me home on Friday."

"Oh no!" I jested. "I'd better clean up and wash the dishes."

"Probably!" Lesley grinned. It was nice to see my wife looking happy.

"I've made you something." I took an envelope from my jacket pocket and handed it to Lesley.

She opened it carefully and extracted the contents. In the boredom of the long lonely evenings, I had filled a little time by photoshopping a collage of dog photos onto a card.

"Dear Mummy, we're sorry to hear you are as sick as a dog," she read. "Get well soon. Woofs and kisses from Romany, Amber, Lady, Kia and Nick."

Lesley wiped a tear away and pulled me over for a kiss.

"Thank you," she sobbed. "That's so sweet."

I nodded and smiled tightly, slightly shocked to see how emotional my wife was. The frustration of living with such pain and immobility had taken a bigger toll on her than I had realised. I reacted in the only way I knew, with hugs and humour.

"There's something else," I said, pulling another sheet of paper from my pocket. "Over the last few days, I've spent quite a bit of time up on the meadow playing ball with the dogs."

"Oh yes?" she frowned.

"Well, you know how we've been struggling to get them to play nicely?"

"Yes." Lesley was squinting suspiciously at the sheet of paper I was holding.

"I think I've figured it out." I smiled, offering Lesley my sheet of paper. She waved it away.

"You read it." She closed her eyes and smiled. "Please."

"Okay. This is entitled 'Doggy Ball Games'."

Lesley squinted at me through half-lidded eyes. "You've been busy writing."

"Kia helped," I joked.

"Carry on."

I read from my sheet of paper. "Managing a game of ball is a tricky business, particularly with four dogs of vastly different shapes and with egos in inverse proportion to their sizes. Fortunately the Queen's Rules of doggy-ball games (second edition) is a useful guide. Here are some extracts:

1. In the spirit of fair play, the chase for a ball/stick and/or other items (hereafter known as the ball) shall be won by a fair pursuit, demonstrating fitness and enthusiasm.
2. The 'thrower' of said ball is required to provide this service whenever the dog(s) deem it necessary.
3. The dog(s) shall only be required to chase said ball when:
    A. It suits them to do so.
    B. They haven't already found something interesting to sniff.
    C. The thrower wants to go home.
    D. The ball has accidently rolled into a muddy puddle and there is no towel in the car.
4. Under no circumstances shall the thrower use sleight of hand, or other devious methods, to mislead the dog(s) into believing the ball has been thrown in a particular direction, when in fact it has not.
5. The dog that has won the chase shall be required to coat said ball with liberal amounts of saliva, and/or mud, before returning it to the thrower.
6. All dogs shall wait patiently until the ball has been thrown, and its trajectory is clear, before any retrieval activity shall begin. Under no circumstances shall the chase to retrieve the ball commence before the thrower has thrown the ball."

"Except for Amber," Lesley added, laughing "She always goes running off before the ball is thrown."

"I guess it's a small dog thing," I said.

"So, have you taught the dogs to play nicely?" Lesley asked.

"Almost." I grimaced. "Romany is too old to join in, but now we've banned the game of Stones, Kia and Amber are getting quite good at playing ball."

"What about Lady?"

"Ah," I sighed. "Lady considers such games to be beneath her lofty skills and prefers to augment her walks by sniffing out squirrels and foxes."

"Oh dear," Lesley said. "What a shame."

"I guess her attitude is unsurprising, given that Kia, in her determination to get to the ball first, has recently been body-checking like a line-backer on steroids."

"Isn't that a breach of these rules?" Lesley laughed.

"I think Kia considers herself exempt," I smiled. "Yesterday, we were on the logging road, up in the forest. After one particularly violent body-check left Lady upside-down in a gorse bush, I imagined I could hear her mumbling, *Bloody Kia...taking it a bit seriously...only a game after all*, as she limped away."

My wife was laughing. I waited for her to dry her eyes.

"Are you feeling a bit better?" I asked.

"Yes." She nodded. "Thank you for cheering me up."

I guess laughter really is the best medicine.

***

For a dog that had such a rough start in life, Kia is extraordinarily confident, although she still retains an inbuilt fear of men and is likely to pee on the floor if I even attempt to pick her up. Then again, perhaps this is just a cunning plan to avoid having a bath.

Whenever she strolls over with her favourite toy, we both know she will repeatedly offer it to me and then pull it away from my outstretched hand, for as long as I will cooperate. I play along, resisting the unseemly urge to snatch the toy from her mouth, because each time I reach and miss, there is a delightfully devilish twinkle in her eye as if to say *Oh, I'm way too clever for you!*

Like all of our dogs, Kia likes her luxuries, particularly at midday. Our dogs all get a chew for good dental health, a marrowbone roll to wash it down, and a biscuit because...well, because I'm standing there by the biscuits. Usually, a quiet whisper of the magic word 'biscuit' will have the dogs pounding chaotically out to the utility room, where we keep the chews, dog biscuits, dog food, and other essential supplies. But not Kia. Recently, she seems to have taken a more laidback attitude to these canine delicacies.

By midday, she will have found herself a prime spot on one of the dog beds in the conservatory, where the sunshine and temperature is just right. There she will remain, stubbornly entrenched, regardless of the treats on offer. Lesley's attitude to such blatant laziness is *if she can't be bothered to get off her fat arse, then she can do without.* Whereas I am a well-trained slave, who puts the welfare of my masters above all else. If the mountain will not come to… then I must take the biscuit to Kia. But will she gratefully spring to her feet and reward my obedience with tail wags and some dog slob? No.

Kia stubbornly remains in her bed, opening a weary eye and reviewing my offering like Caligula being presented with a bunch of grapes by a serving wench. Finally, with a gentle sigh she leans forward to accept the biscuit. By now the impish disobedient in me is taking over. I hold the biscuit an inch away from her nose, and encourage her to reach for it. As she does, I gradually move the biscuit away, maintaining the one-inch gap. The only purpose of this gentle teasing is to satisfy my curiosity. Now that she can see and smell the treat, will Kia actually leave her bed to complete the transaction? She leans forwards slightly, and I respond by gently easing the biscuit away. She sits up and reaches again, each time I maintain that tantalizing inch of separation. By mutual consent, we continue this gentle dance, until Kia is balanced precariously with her front paws on the edge of the bed, still refusing to give up her domain. Although she will stretch forwards to the extreme edge of her stability, with her tongue trying to hook the biscuit from my fingers, she has never stepped out of the bed. Perhaps she knows that whatever happens, I will always reward this little act of defiance with a biscuit.

***

The hospital called at lunchtime. The procedure had gone well. I breathed a sigh of relief. The nurse said Lesley was still sleeping off the anaesthetic, but I could visit later if I wished. I told the dogs. They seemed pleased, as was Joanne.

That night I braved the cold rain and icy-slick roads to visit my wife. But the three hour round trip was of little benefit. She was fast asleep, her tray of food uneaten by her bedside. I sat in a chair and read for a while before kissing her softly and heading for home.

***

Now the kitchen was completed, it was time to begin work on the room above. My idea was to make the space into one large bedroom, with a high ceiling, fitted wardrobes and lots of natural light, courtesy of three large windows. Because of the design of the plumbing, the room would also need to house the hot water tank in a traditional airing cupboard, called a hot press in Ireland, as well as the cold water tank, which I planned to hide in a false loft.

The house is similar to a Dutch barn. It is a long narrow building, a single room deep, with windows on both sides. In the original upstairs layout, the rooms above the kitchen and sitting room were connected with doors in the centre of the house, exactly the same as the rooms below. We were quite happy with the design of the downstairs rooms, but we wanted to modify the upstairs to add a connecting corridor, to provide privacy for each bedroom and to act as an escape route in the event of a fire. The corridor upstairs would run along the entire length of the northwest side of the house, connecting the two bedrooms at either end, a new centre guest room, the bathroom and the staircase.

It was a nice idea, but to connect the new corridor with the bedroom above the kitchen, the original door into that room needed to be blocked up and a new doorway created in the corner. That sounds easy enough, but the connecting wall where the door had to go was made of stone, over four feet thick and 12 feet tall, stretching up almost all the way to the roof. I needed to remove several tonnes of stone, all by hand.

The construction method in these old houses is much the same as that used by the Romans, thousands of years ago. The walls are actually two parallel lines of stone, built close together. The gap between is filled with sand, mortar, small stones and the occasional dead mouse. The filling acts as a binding agent. At the top are placed the largest and longest stones, spreading the load and keeping the entire wall stable.

Carting so much stone and associated dust through the entire length of the house, down the stairs and out through our new kitchen, was not an acceptable option. I had seen long chutes used on building sites as a method of channelling waste into rubbish skips, so I decided to try something similar. At the north end of the house there was a tall narrow window with a conveniently placed opening at the bottom, about a metre square. By nailing together some old joists and a bit of left over chipboard, I managed to construct a fairly decent slide. The window was only fifteen feet from the wall I was demolishing. All I had to do to remove each stone was carry or slide it across to the window and let gravity help it down the chute to the driveway below.

Taking the wall down was a dirty and somewhat dangerous process. For protection, I wore goggles and a dust mask, a hard hat, steel toe-capped boots and thick leather gloves. As each stone was pried out, it was accompanied by a shower of dust and sand. Sometimes there was a small avalanche of larger rocks. I had escaped most of these landslides with nothing worse than a face full of dirt. Everything seemed to be going well.

Perhaps I was rushing, keen to complete the job before Lesley came out of hospital, or perhaps I was cocky and careless. Just as I was pulling another large rock loose, there was a small avalanche. Instinctively, I turned my face away, but forgot to move my hands. Suddenly there was a crash and I felt a searing pain in my right hand. As the dust cleared, I could see a huge rock had fallen from above, landing squarely on my hand.

I groaned and tried to pull free, but the slightest movement caused an agonising pain to jolt up my arm. Completely trapped, I looked around for a solution. Then I spotted the prybar. Of course! I could use it to lever the rock upwards so I could slip my hand free. Inevitably, it was just out of reach. My right hand was firmly trapped and the prybar was leaning against the wall on my right side. Despite the excruciating pain, I twisted and turned as far as I could and stretched out with my left hand, but I just couldn't reach. An attempt to hook it with my foot just made matters worse. At the first touch of my toe, the prybar fell over, clattering to the floor completely out of reach. My last hope was to lift the rock with my left hand, or at least move it a little, but I just couldn't do it. My right hand was pinned palm-down at chest height and the rock was just too heavy to move one-handed at such a difficult angle. I was trapped.

At first I laughed, but then I realised my situation was

potentially quite serious. Lesley wasn't expecting me to pick her up from the hospital until the following day. Soon the dogs would need feeding, and eventually, so would I. My hand was trapped and beginning to go numb, the circulation cut off. It wouldn't take long before the lack of blood flow permanently damaged nerves and muscle. Also, I needed to pee. How long could I hold it? Probably not for long.

For almost an hour, I stood waiting. Nobody was coming to my aid. My legs ached and my bladder was bursting. My hand was numb. Wait! My hand was numb. I had no feeling. No *pain*. There was a chance I could drag my hand out. It may do some damage, but there was no pain to stop me. Wedging my knee against the wall, I pushed with my left hand against the rock and pulled with my right as hard as I could. It was heavy, but I had one thing in my favour (apart from an overwhelming desire to pee): I was wearing a glove. I heaved again, rocking from side to side and abruptly I broke loose. The glove remained trapped, but my hand had slipped out. The release was so sudden I stumbled and fell over, landing flat on the floor. Winded, but free, I dashed to the bathroom. Sweet relief.

My right hand was pasty white, like a frozen pork chop. I washed it and carefully checked for damage. Apart from a large split along the side of my pinkie finger, everything seemed intact. As the circulation returned, so did the feeling. For five minutes I grimaced and hissed as I endured the worst case of pins and needles I have ever experienced. My hand coloured up nicely, but the split bled copiously, only stopping with the help of a few drops of super glue and a strip of surgical tape. I didn't mind. It could have been worse.

***

It was late afternoon when the hospital finally released Lesley into my care. Her short stay had stretched to 14 days. She was delighted to be heading home. I tossed her suitcase into the boot of the car before helping her slide into her seat. The doctor had prescribed an exotic cocktail of painkillers and anti-inflammatory tablets, along with strict instructions for bedrest. Lesley had received several injections directly into her spine and was understandably tender. I tried my best to make the journey home as smooth as possible, but somehow I seemed to hit every pothole in the road. The largest, most teeth jarring impacts were all on Lesley's side of the car. My poor wife winced and moaned all the way home. I was mortified, apologising profusely for every bump.

"Don't worry," she hissed. "It's not your fault. It's not like you're doing it on purpose." When we hit a particularly large pothole, she added. "Although I am beginning to wonder."

"I'm sorry, love," I said.

Lesley waved my apology away. "Not your fault." She spoke through gritted teeth.

"We'll be home soon."

"What happened to your hand?" she asked.

"Nothing really," I replied casually. "I cut my finger on a rock."

27. A close call

Perhaps five or six times a year, during the summer months, a wild bird will find its way into the house. Typically they enter through an open door or window and end up crashing around in the conservatory. The resulting scramble to rescue the poor creature before it's devoured by one of the dogs, necessitates nimble feet, a tea towel and a good bit of shouting. The aftermath only requires the righting of some disturbed furniture, sweeping up a few feathers and mopping up any spilled beverages. With the doors and windows tightly closed against the cold, such invasions are unheard of during the winter. Except once.

"NICK!" Lesley bellowed. It was the morning after she'd been released from hospital. Already she was fighting me on the whole bedrest thing.

I sprinted down the stairs, concerned for her wellbeing. I need not have worried. "What?" I panted, staggering into the kitchen.

"There's a funny noise coming from the Rayburn."

I squinted at our cooking range and frowned. "It's not even switched on."

"I know it isn't on," Lesley sighed. "I was just reaching for the switch, but there was this funny noise."

I cocked an ear. "I can't hear anything. Perhaps it was the wind."

"It wasn't the wind. It was a scratching sound."

I moved closer and listened again, but all I could hear was my tinnitus.

"There's definitely something there," Lesley insisted.

I gave the black enamelled-steel chimney an experimental tap with my knuckle. Immediately there was a tinny scrabbling noise.

"Something's trapped in this chimney," I said.

"Can you get it out?"

"Not without ripping the walls out." I pointed upwards. "The top of this flue is hidden behind the new plasterboard. Removing it would make a hell of a mess."

The scrabbling sound repeated.

"It's probably a bird, fallen down the chimney," I suggested.

"What's going to happen to it?"

"I'm afraid its prospects are a bit grim," I grimaced. "It won't be able to fly back up the chimney. By now it's probably terrified and covered in oil soot."

"The poor thing."

I had an idea. "If I can lift off this hotplate, I may be able to reach into the chimney and snag the bird. It may not work, but it's worth a try."

"Oh please do!"

The hot plate is a two-foot long slab of thick cast-iron. I'd seen the boiler engineer removing it with the aid of two hooked handles. As these were not a common toolbox accessory, I repurposed a couple of wire coat hangers to make some lifting hooks.

"Be careful the bird doesn't escape," Lesley warned. "I don't want it flying around in here and messing up my lovely new paintwork."

"Don't worry," I replied. "It's probably dead by now, or too encrusted with soot to stand."

Inevitably, I was wrong. The instant I lifted the hot plate from the cooking range, the soot-covered bird burst into the light and made a desperate break for freedom.

"Grab it!" I shouted.

With a shriek, Lesley dashed forward with a tea towel, unsuccessfully endeavouring to snare the wretched feathered chimney sweep.

Amber, who had been roused from her afternoon nap by the commotion, was now running in circles around the kitchen, panting *hup-hup-hup* and wishing she could fly. Lady and Kia quickly joined in, woofing excitedly and running back and forth. After flying three circuits, the bird landed atop a kitchen unit and eyed us suspiciously. Romany leaned over in her bed to peer through the kitchen door, but seeing the other dogs had the situation in hand, she farted, closed her eyes and went back to sleep.

"Can you please take these dogs out of the kitchen?" I asked. "I'm going to trip over and break my neck in a minute."

Lesley bribed them into compliance with a dog treat, which worked well for Lady and Kia, but Amber was too engaged with the chase and needed to be physically extracted. Once the field of play was cleared of obstructions, I was able to get on with the pursuit. Armed with a child's pink-handled fishing net and a white tea towel, I quickly proved I was considerably less nimble than my prey. Fortunately, the bird soon became tired of the game and settled on a window sill, allowing itself to be caught and thoroughly cleaned before being released back into the wild. All we had to show for this episode was a little environmental hubris, a ruined tea towel, and several bird shaped motifs in oily soot on our new walls and kitchen units.

***

"I'm going to bed," Lesley groaned. "I've got such a headache."

Whereas I like to share my medical misery with as wide an audience as possible, my wife prefers to hide under the covers and sleep until her malaise has passed.

"Would you like a hot milk or something?" I asked.

She shook her head and winced. "It's just a bug. Probably the 'flu. I'll be alright in the morning."

"You do look a little pale." I kissed her cheek. "Shout if you need anything."

In the morning, I rose early. After quietly taking a shower, eating breakfast and walking the dogs, I looked in on Lesley again. She was still asleep. An hour later, nothing had changed. As it was now after ten and past time for her cocktail of painkillers and anti-inflammatory tablets, I decided to bring her a cup of coffee. My wife is a deep sleeper, more so when she is unwell, but her lack of response to my vigorous shaking of her shoulder was rather alarming. I drew the curtains and tried again. Slowly she opened her eyes and squinted at me.

"Good morning," I whispered. "I've brought you a coffee."

She mumbled something unintelligible and closed her eyes.

"Come on, Lesley." I shook her again. "Wake up."

"Leave me abroad," she groaned.

I shook her again. "Lesley. Come on, open your eyes."

She pushed at my hand weakly, trying to roll over. "I'm tired. Elephant feeling very well."

"Lesley!" I spoke louder and rubbed my knuckles on her sternum. "Lesley! Wake up."

"Sausage my head…" she mumbled.

I pulled the covers back. "Come on. You're going to the doctor."

My wife resisted weakly, but with commendable determination, as I pulled her upright. Once she'd had a few sips of coffee, she seemed a little more cognisant and rather less belligerent, but as I helped her to dress it was obvious something was wrong. Her back and chest were liberally peppered with small circular bruise-like marks and her skin had a decidedly yellow tinge.

Although several people were waiting, the receptionist at the doctor's surgery took one look at Lesley and pointed to the exam room. When Doctor Mark came in just five minutes later, Lesley was asleep in the chair. She woke with a start. His examination was swift and his diagnosis blunt and uncompromising.

"Well, my dear," he said, holding her hand. "You look like shit. You're to go directly to A&E."

"Right now?" I asked. "Is she that bad."

Doctor Mark looked at me and nodded towards the door. "It will be quicker than waiting for an ambulance. I'll give you a letter to speed things along when you get there."

I made the trip to Limerick in record time. With letter in hand I guided Lesley into the A&E department. The combination of her buttery pallor and Doctor Mark's terse instructions did the trick. In under five minutes we were talking to a doctor. Within a couple of hours Lesley had been thoroughly poked, prodded, examined and assessed. When the doctor entered the cubicle, my wife was fast asleep, curled up on a trolley, twitching and shaking like a puppy chasing a rabbit in its dreams. The doctor was a short, brunette lady, probably younger than my daughter. She looked like someone who had recently seen too little sunlight, too many patients and not enough sleep.

"Are you Nick?" she whispered. Her South African accent made it sound like *Neek*.

I nodded.

"I'm Doctor Wilson. Call me Suzanne." We shook hands. "And I presume this is Lesley?"

When she looked towards my slumbering wife, Suzanne's eyes caressed the trolley with an envious glint, as if she also longed to curl up and rest for a while. I imagined, had she given in to the urge, this poor girl was so exhausted she would have instantly fallen asleep. Doctor Wilson flicked through the notes, blinking several times to focus her eyes.

"I'm afraid your wife is rather unwell." She bit her lip as she flicked the pages. "It's her liver function." She quoted some numbers. They meant nothing to me, but I guessed the significance.

"Is that bad?"

Suzanne nodded sombrely. When she quoted the healthy liver value, it was a long way from the first number.

"Right now her liver function is almost non-existent. That's why she's so poorly."

"Oh. She was okay yesterday, apart from a tummy bug." I couldn't think of anything else to say.

"Vomiting and a headache?" Suzanne asked.

I nodded.

"Fatigue?"

I nodded again. "She thought it was the 'flu."

"When did the rash appear?"

"I only noticed it this morning."

"Then perhaps we've caught it early." Lesley's tablets were lined up on the table. Suzanne leaned forward and tapped a box with her pen. "This is the culprit. In rare cases it can cause toxic hepatitis. Liver failure."

"And that's what Lesley has?"

Suzanne nodded.

My head was reeling. "W-what's the t-treatment?" I stumbled over the words.

"We remove the toxin, in this case the tablets, and wait for the liver to heal itself. Your wife will be staying with us for a while. She'll need to have intravenous fluids to help flush her system. We'll need to monitor her closely and scan the liver to assess the damage."

"Is she going to get better?" It was the one question I was afraid to ask.

Suzanne's mouth tightened involuntarily. "I won't lie to you. Right now, she's very poorly. We can only watch and wait."

"And if she doesn't improve?" I glanced at Lesley's huddled

sleeping form. How could she have been chasing a bird around the kitchen yesterday and be so ill today?

The doctor reached over and squeezed my hand. Her fingers felt hot and bony, as dry as parchment.

"One thing at a time," she smiled. "We've caught this early. Give her time to fight it."

I nodded, too numb to speak.

"Does she have a bag?"

"A bag? No. Sorry…I didn't think to…"

Suzanne squeezed my hand again. "Not to worry. She'll be going up to the ward in a bit. Your wife is going to be very sleepy for a while. Perhaps you can bring one by later?"

"Sure," I mumbled.

"Pack some toiletries, underwear, pyjamas, a dressing gown, slippers, and suchlike."

"Books," I added. "But I can't remember which book she was reading."

"I'm sure whatever you bring will be fine," Suzanne smiled. "I don't think she'll do much reading for a while."

I nodded. Suzanne patted my hand.

"Go on home. We'll look after your wife."

I kissed Lesley and whispered goodbye, but she didn't stir.

The traffic was mercifully light for my journey home. With my head swirling and my heart thumping, I made it out of the city without incident, but once I reached the countryside, I pulled over at the first opportunity. As the car stopped, the bottled-up emotions overwhelmed me. After that, it was a blur. I know I cried and I remember screaming in anger and frustration and pounding the seat with my fist. Why was this happening to Lesley? What had she possibly done to deserve this? Of course I was sad and upset, but my personal pain was insubstantial in comparison to the fear and agony I felt for my wife. Where women hug, console and empathise, men try to fix things. But this wasn't something I could repair. I had never before felt so wretched and utterly helpless.

Lesley wanted to start a new life, far away from the stress and strain of the city. She wanted to live somewhere where the air was pure and there was space to live. Moving to Ireland was our shared dream. Everything had been going so well and suddenly now it wasn't. How had this tragedy unfolded? Was it a celestial conspiracy or just dumb luck? It all came back to that car crash.

Had a moment of carelessness by some random stranger really changed our lives? One man, driving his big, shiny, tank-like 4x4 and feeling invulnerable. He was driving too fast and chatting on his mobile phone. As I gazed listlessly out of the window, watching a blackbird digging for worms at the roadside, I wondered what was so important about that call. Was it a life and death conversation, or just a mate calling to chat? That moment of inattention put his vehicle out of position on the bend and caused Lesley to swerve. She skidded on some loose gravel and collided with a wall. By then, the 4x4 had gone. The driver was probably still chatting on the phone, oblivious to the sequence of events he had just started. From phone call, to car crash, to back pain, to injections, and ending many months later with the single tablet which poisoned my wife and stopped her liver. Dumb luck.

I couldn't fix this. That task fell to the extraordinary staff of the Irish health service. All I could do was look after our dogs, chickens and ducks, talk to every medical expert I knew, hope for the best, and visit my wife every day. With new determination, I dried my eyes, started the car and headed home. Later, I called my mother, sisters and Lesley's mother, Muriel, but made light of the situation. There was no need to worry them unduly. If I had, Lesley would have been upset. Joanne sensed the seriousness of the situation from my voice.

"I'll come over," she said.

"Not now," I replied. "There's nothing you can do. Your mum just needs to rest. Someone holding a bedside vigil will only disturb her."

"But I want to help."

"I know," I sighed, searching for optimistic thoughts. "She's going to get better. When she's home, perhaps you can visit then. I'll pay for your flight."

"Sure," Joanne said. "Just tell me when."

"I'll tell you what," I suggested. "We'll keep it a secret. Make it a surprise. Mummy will love it."

"No she won't! Mummy hates surprises." I could hear a smile in her voice. I felt better too. Planning ahead made things seem more positive.

Christmas and New Year slipped by almost unnoticed. Lesley

seemed to be making no progress. She was listless, tired and dreadfully depressed. Her skin was yellow and bruised, her urine black as Barry's Irish Tea, and her blood tests showed her liver was barely functioning. The doctors were hard to contact, their assessments vague.

Every morning, I called the hospital. Every afternoon, I visited. Every night, I telephoned Joanne. There was nothing new to report.

"She's not getting any better," I groaned.

"She's not getting any worse," Joanne replied. "I called the hospital this morning and spoke with the ward sister. She was very nice."

"What did she say?"

"She said Mummy is hanging in there. Not getting any worse is a good thing."

"Let's hope so, in case not." It was Lesley's favourite saying.

Secretly, I despised making my daily visits. Although this hospital was closer than the one before, the two-hour round trip on icy, unlit roads was treacherous and depressing. Driving out, I felt positive. Looking forward to seeing Lesley, sharing the news of the day, or showing her the latest Get Well Soon card I had made. But seeing my darling wife huddled in the bed, sullen and lethargic, made me feel so helpless and guilty, I had to fight the urge to spin on my heel and leave.

She slept a lot. It's nature's way of healing. Frequently, she would nod off while I was talking, even during the interesting bits. We would chat about current affairs. I'd tell her about the dogs and my progress building the new bedroom over the kitchen. I brought her books, magazines and the latest craze, Sudoku. But, with the distractions on the ward and the toxins in her blood addling her brain, she found it almost impossible to concentrate.

Lesley was in a semi-private room, shared with two other women. One was an elderly Irish lady, suffering from end-stage dementia, the other was a painfully-thin young girl with an eating disorder. Hardly an environment conducive to encouraging thoughts and a swift recovery. I did my best to remain positive and upbeat during my visits, but on those lonely drives back home, my eyes filled with tears and my mind fixated on the implications of a negative outcome.

Finally, on the 13th day, there was a glimmer of light.

"Her bloods are a little better today," the nurse said.

"She's improving?" I asked, desperate for some good news.

"It's early days," she cautioned. "But it's an encouraging step forward."

The following morning, her bloods were a tiny bit better again, and by day 15, the trend was positive and undeniable. Lesley's liver function was gradually returning to something resembling normality. She was sitting up in bed, more alert and with an improved appetite.

"The scan shows some residual scarring," her doctor informed me. "But that's to be expected. She'll heal in time."

"She's going to get better?" I asked.

He nodded. "She's been very lucky. It was hit and miss there for a while. We were worried."

"Phew!" I sighed. "When can I take her home?"

"Probably next week," he replied, smiling. "I'd like to keep an eye on her for a bit longer, just to be sure."

By the time I drove her home, Lesley had spent 21 days in hospital. The dogs were overwhelmed to see her; it was all I could do to stop them from knocking her over. It wouldn't do to be heading back to hospital with a broken hip. The house was as spotless as I could manage, given the presence of four dogs and the constant snowfall of woodworm dust from the unrenovated rooms. I made up a daybed on the couch and lit the fire.

"Thank you for trying," she said, closing her eyes. "But I wouldn't have cared if the sink was full of dishes and the floors were unwashed. I'm just so glad to be home."

"And we're all delighted to see you." I leaned over to give her a kiss, but my wife was already asleep.

28. A new beginning

Shannon airport arrivals hall is a vast, cavernous, warehouse-like structure, with bright lights, high ceilings, red walls and shiny cream and grey marble floors. I crossed my arms and leaned against a pillar while I watched the world go by, all six of them. Shannon is a wonderfully quiet airport. A man leaned on the other side of my pillar. We briefly made eye contact.

"How're-ya?" he grunted.

"Grand-so," I replied with a cursory nod.

My phone vibrated in my pocket. A text message from Joanne. *Just waiting for my bag xxx.*

I typed a quick reply, *I'm here.*

The sliding doors marking the terminator between 'airside' security and the freedom of County Clare, remained firmly shut. Only one plane had arrived, the 9 am Ryanair flight from London Stansted. Any moment now, the first fleet-footed passengers would come through. I looked around at the empty concourse and pondered how the airport ever stayed in business. Perhaps its position as the first available landing ground on the western European coastline gave it some unique status.

There was an elaborate nativity scene against the wall between the waste bins and the toilets. I idly watched the jerky animatronics, wondering why they were still operating in February. The first passengers came through the doors, a dozen men and three women. Heads down, with carry-on bags in hand, they strode purposely towards the carpark. After this initial flurry of activity, there was a momentary lull before the first luggage trolleys came through. The man next to me stepped forward and greeted a pretty redhead. They brushed lips and he took her bag. As they passed, he nodded to me.

"See-ya."

"Mind how you go," I replied. Very Irish.

Joanne came through next, pushing a trolley. Her suitcase was the size of our cooking range.

"Good grief!" I laughed. "Are you moving in?"

We hugged, long and hard. Suddenly I was fighting tears.

"It's great to see you," I croaked. "Thanks for coming."

"I'm so pleased to be here," Joanne replied. "Does Mummy suspect anything?"

I shook my head. "I told her I had to come out to collect a broken golf club, I said it was an urgent repair for an important client."

"Do you think she believed you?"

"For sure," I replied. "She was giving out about me making a long trip for a ten euro club repair."

"You're beginning to sound quite Irish," Joanne sniggered.

"We call it becoming acclimatised," I quipped.

It was only a short walk to the car. Once we were underway, our conversation turned towards the inevitable.

"How is she?" Joanne asked.

"Marginally better than she was."

"That doesn't sound good."

"She was very ill, but she's getting better," I said. "It's a slow process."

My daughter said nothing.

"She cries a lot," I added.

"Oh dear," Joanne groaned.

"It's okay." I reached over and patted her hand. "She's depressed because of the illness, most likely chemically as well as emotionally. The liver problem has probably messed with her brain chemistry, but also she's just fed up with feeling so useless."

"Can't the doctor give her something?"

"Best not," I grimaced. "The fewer pills she takes just now, the better. Given what happened, she may never take another pill again."

"I can understand that," Joanne said. "I'm sure you're doing your best to keep her spirits up."

"Not always successfully," I admitted. "I cooked her a steak a few nights ago. She was having a job cutting it up. Frankly it was more to do with my cooking than her ongoing muscle weakness. Anyway, I helped her to cut the meat, but I made some silly joke to lighten the mood 'Shall Daddy help you?' or something… Suddenly she's howling her eyes out. God, I was mortified."

My daughter squeezed my hand. "I'm sure she knew you didn't mean any harm."

"Thanks," I smiled.

"Is she going to get better?" Joanne asked. "Back to her old self?"

"I hope so, or something close to it," I nodded. "The human body is a phenomenal machine and able to repair any manner of damage, given enough time, fuel and space. Your mum is still rather yellow, very weak and immensely tired, but at least she's getting better. The hospital stay was tough on her. Now she's home she can eat properly, rest as much as she needs and, most importantly, sleep without being disturbed."

"Except for the dogs barking," Joanne said. "I can't wait to see the new ones."

"Perhaps tomorrow you and I can take them to the lake?"

"That would be nice."

When we reached the house, Joanne hid in the car until I had gone in and settled the dogs.

"How did your meeting go?" Lesley asked. She was laid on the couch, wrapped in a bright pink blanket. It highlighted the stubborn yellow tinge in her skin.

"I didn't see that bloke," I admitted.

"Well that was a waste of petrol," she huffed.

"Not exactly." I grinned and wiggled my eyebrows. "I made a slight detour and brought you a special gift."

Joanne walk into the room.

"Oh!" Lesley's hand covered her mouth.

Joanne rushed forward. "Mummy, I was so worried!"

Mother and daughter hugged, bursting into floods of tears. It was an exquisite moment which cheered everyone up immensely. Joanne could only stay for the weekend as she was busy at work, but my girls had a lovely time lounging around the house, playing board games and enjoying each other's company. That evening, I sat quietly watching my wife and daughter chatting happily together. As I contemplated how dreadfully different things could have been, my eyes wet and my chest painfully constricted. It really had been a close call.

Early on Sunday morning, Joanne and I decided to take the dogs for a long walk at Silver Sands, the beautiful beach at the head of Lough Graney. It was Joanne's first visit to this lough.

"Oh, it's so beautiful," she gushed as we walked across the long sandy beach. "But where are all the boats and people?"

"This is about as busy as it gets," I replied.

"Two rowboats and one fisherman?" Joanne gasped. "On a lake this big?"

"Well, it is February," I quipped. "There's another rowboat which usually comes out if it's sunny."

Despite the biting cold wind, we were thoroughly enjoying this quiet time walking together. Lady and Kia were having a fantastic time looping about in the shallow water, unsuccessfully chasing after the waterfowl and running like feral children through the woods. This was new territory for the two puppies, so they were careful to keep Joanne and I within sight.

"I think your mum looks better for your visit," I remarked. "Happier at least. Thank you for coming."

"Thanks for having me," Joanne replied. "And for booking my flight."

I pulled her into a hug. "I'll send you the invoice."

My daughter ignored my joke. "I love the new kitchen, and the wing," she said. "I can't believe it's the same building."

"It's coming along," I smiled. "I'll have that bedroom finished soon."

"What will you do next?"

"As soon as it's warm enough, I'll start renovating the middle of the house."

"Why warm enough?" Joanne asked.

"Well, as the rafters are rotten with woodworm, I need to rip out the upstairs rooms and all the floors. If I wait until it's a bit warmer, I can disconnect the plumbing and heating in that part of the house. It will make the task much easier."

"Mummy said you're going to raise the ceiling height."

"About six inches," I nodded. "It'll make the lounge seen much roomier. It was her idea."

"What about that lovely old staircase?" Joanne asked. "Surely you'll keep it."

"Absolutely. It's a couple of hundred years old. Apparently, the previous owner saved it from a derelict building in the village," I explained. "But I'll have to take it down to refit it to the new floor level."

"How will you do that?"

"No idea!" I shrugged. "I guess I'll have to figure it out."

Joanne laughed. "It's not in your DIY book then?"

I grimaced and shook my head.

My daughter frowned. "I've just thought. With the floors out, how are you going to go to bed?"

I smiled and held up a finger. "Ladders!"

We crossed the beach and picked up a path leading through the forest to a second beach, where the river joined the lake. As usual Romany plodded along behind and Amber ran frantically back and forth, chasing sticks and woofing crossly if we didn't throw quickly enough. Sometimes Lady and Kia would decide to join in the stick chasing, causing things to get a little too boisterous, so I took to throwing the sticks further out into the water, in an effort to calm them down a bit. It worked perfectly. Lady and Kia happily crashed into the water with a mighty splash and paddled out to recover the stick, while Amber was left behind, able to chase a second stick without risking any further unpleasantness.

"You seem to be settling in very well," Joanne observed.

"It's a wonderful country," I replied. "It was all a bit confusing at first, but we're gradually learning the nuances of the culture and language."

"You're learning Irish?" my daughter asked.

"No!" I laughed. "Very few people use Irish in day-to-day conversation, I meant we're getting used to a different way of speaking English."

"Oh. A bit like American English?"

"Yes, but every bit as different," I replied.

"For example?" Joanne asked.

I frowned. "It's hard to be specific. The first word I noticed was *Robbed*. Where we would say someone stole my car, over here they say someone *robbed* my car."

"How odd."

"I read somewhere it harks back to how verbs and adjectives are used in the Irish language."

"That makes sense," Joanne nodded. "A bit like French or German."

"Perhaps," I replied. "But I read somewhere else that when the British forced the English language on to the population here, the Irish deliberately changed some words so as to piss off their oppressors."

"That seems more likely!" Joanne laughed.

"That's what I thought too." I smiled. "They have some great slang though: *gas* is funny, *jacks* is the toilet, a *stook* is an idiot or fool, *langered* means drunk, as does *on the lash*. They seem to have a lot of words for drunk. My favourite slang so far is *bolloxology*, which means time wasting, or messing around."

"It sounds to me as if you are loving life here," she said.

"Oh we are."

"No regrets?"

"None. Apart from missing you." I pulled Joanne into a hug.

We walked on for a while, casually repeating the stick throwing exercise several times, until the dogs were tired and we were both getting cold and hungry.

As we turned back towards the car, I threw one final stick for the always energetic Amber. But this time she swam in the wrong direction, towards a small branch that was sticking out of the water about 15 metres out. The branch was bobbing up and down with the waves, rather like a fishing float, and was an irresistible challenge to the tiny dog. Joanne and I laughed as Amber paddled determinedly against the waves, pausing occasionally to check her bearings, before paddling on reinvigorated as she neared her target.

After nearly a minute of tenacious swimming, Amber grasped the stick in her tiny mouth and turned for home, cheered on by our shouts of encouragement from the shore. Unfortunately, despite her best efforts, Amber could only swim in little circles. The stick she had captured was attached to a submerged tree, washed downstream in the swollen river.

Initially we giggled helplessly as she gamely paddled in circles, clearly confused by her inability to progress towards the shore. But terriers are tenacious and Amber was unable to admit defeat. Undaunted, she continued paddling.

"Let go, you stupid dog!" I shouted.

"Let go!" Joanne yelled.

"Amber, leave!" I tried.

Our shouts made no difference.

"It's no good, Dad," Joanne laughed. "You'll just have to go in and rescue her."

"I will not," I snorted. "That water's freezing! Anyway, she's bound to let go in a minute. No dog can be that stupid."

"I'm not so sure," my daughter replied. "I think Amber is in danger of sinking. That stick is the only thing keeping her afloat."

"You might be right," I grimaced.

I could see Amber was in real distress. The cold water and exertion were taking a toll. Desperately clinging to the stick with her mouth half-open, she was panting audibly. Just then a wave splashed some water into Amber's face and she choked.

"Quick, Dad!" Joanne shouted. "She's sinking!"

"Damn it," I growled.

I threw off my coat and waded in to rescue her. The icy water came to chest height. It was so devastatingly cold, it took my breath away and shrivelled my man bits in an instant. I reached Amber just as she went under for the third time. She threw herself into my arms, coughing and shivering uncontrollably. Back on shore, Joanne took charge of the pathetic bundle, wrapping Amber inside her coat for warmth. The hero of the day received somewhat less attention.

Joanne laughed at my predicament, while I poured water out of my wellies and debated whether to undress, or just drive home in my wet clothes.

"I-I g-g-guess I'll have to s-s-stay like t-this," I moaned through chattering teeth.

"It's probably best," Joanne replied, failing to hide a smirk.

"I'm a h-hero you know!" I snapped.

"Pfft."

We trudged along the forest path back towards the car, Amber keeping warm inside Joanne's coat. Romany plodded behind, refusing any invitation to walk faster. Squelching along and shivering uncontrollably, I was looking forward to a roaring fire, a hot cup of tea and the prospect of getting myself dry and warm. Lady and Kia were paralleling our path somewhere in the trees. Suddenly the air was filled with horrifically desperate yelping and squealing, supplemented at odd intervals by Kia's frantic barking. The sound was so awful and unexpected, one could easily have imagined our terrified dogs were caught in a deer trap.

"Oh my God!" Joanne exclaimed. "What's happening?"

My shoulders slumped. "That," I sighed. "Is the sound of a Fox Hound hunting. Lady has probably disturbed some deer."

"She's not hurt?" Joanne's eyes searched my face for

confirmation. Amber was squirming in her arms, keen to get down and join in the fun.

I rolled my eyes. "She's fine, but I'm not. I'm cold and I want to go home. If Lady is true to form, we won't see her again for about half an hour."

"No problem. I'll soon get her back." My daughter put two fingers in her mouth and blew a shrill whistle.

"I've never been able to do that." I winced. My ears were ringing.

Joanne's piercing whistle didn't work, nor did anything else we tried. Gradually the barks and howls faded into the distance. After 70 minutes of pointless calling, I gave up all hope of recovering the dogs.

"It's no good," I said. "We'll have to head home."

"We can't just leave them," Joanne pleaded.

"They're probably somewhere deep in the forest. You couldn't find them with a helicopter," I explained. "As soon as I get into some dry clothes, I'll come right back and wait for them to show."

"Promise?" Joanne asked.

"I promise."

With that settled, we headed back. When we reached the car, our delinquent duo were laid in the sunshine, patiently waiting. As we approached, they jumped up, all waggy tails and smiles, as if to say *ah – there you are. We were getting worried.*

Seething, shivering, swearing, but secretly rather relieved, I drove home sitting on an old plastic shopping bag I found in the boot.

"You were a long time," Lesley said.

"We had an incident," I replied, sloshing towards the fire.

"Amber nearly drowned," Joanne said.

"Oh, the poor thing." Lesley jumped up and scooped the little dog into her arms. "Nick! Move away from the fire."

"But I'm all wet," I complained. "And cold."

"Wet?" My wife noticed my damp attire for the first time.

"Eww!" You're putting water all over the floor." She pushed me with a finger. "Get out!"

"But I'm a hero," I pleaded.

"Of course you are," Lesley snorted, waving me away.

"He was very courageous," Joanne conceded.

Ultimately, Lesley was unimpressed with the tale of my bravery in valiantly rescuing the little dog from the raging river, but she laughed enthusiastically as Joanne described how I waded into the freezing lake to recover our stupid mutt. So I received neither a medal nor any sympathy for my heroics.

Amber is a short dog with an equally short memory. She was none the worse for her adventure, but delighted in the additional attention of a rubdown with a fluffy towel and a bowl of warm milk. I was pleased to remove my cold, wet clothes and stand in a hot shower until the feeling returned to my frozen feet, and some bit of the river smell had gone.

On Monday morning, I drove Joanne to Shannon airport for the early flight. Lesley came too, even though we had to be there at 5.30 am. The girls chatted like long lost sisters, Lesley turned the heater up full, and I drove in silence, concentrating on staying awake.

"I love the way the house is shaping up," Joanne said.

"It's coming along nicely," Lesley replied.

"I love the chickens, and the ducks. They're so cute!"

"They are sweet," my wife agreed.

"The garden will be nice, especially the polytunnel."

"Oh yes," Lesley said, unusually peppy for so early in the morning. "I think it will be a good year. Did you know I'm growing peaches?"

"Peaches!" Joanne exclaimed. "In Ireland?"

"And grapes!" Lesley smiled.

Perhaps it was good timing and part of the natural recovery process, but Lesley's eyes were suddenly alive with excitement. It was as if Joanne's surprise visit was just the medicine she required to kick-start her recovery. After such a near thing with her dreadful illness, my wife had seemed so dull and lifeless. Now the old sparkle and enthusiasm was written large across her face. I looked on with glee. Everything was good and our dream life was back on track. It was like a new beginning.

"What are you grinning at?" Lesley asked.

"Nothing really," I replied, casually wiping a tear. "I'm just happy."

29. Epilogue

Like a hibernating bear, Lesley arose from her daybed with the first spring sunshine and cautiously began some gentle gardening. Recently, she announced a desire to begin baking cakes, so she can sell them at the local market. She's still fragile and easily exhausted, but I'm confident the worst is now over.

Fortunately, our story goes on. There is much more to tell.

The renovations are likely to take several more years. By then, we may need to go back to the beginning and do it all again. I hope the project will be finished before our money runs out.

Every day we learn more about our adopted country, but there is so much we have yet to see. We've pledged to take some time away from our schedule to visit some of Ireland's fine gardens, castles and museums. As yet we haven't even visited Killarney National Park, Dublin, Waterford or Connemara. Some people would consider such an oversight to be almost criminal.

We plan to expand our flock. Lesley wants to buy a cockerel so we can breed the chickens and begin selling eggs. Perhaps I'll get some more ducks as well.

And what of the dogs? I am sure we will soon have more, but for now…

Romany becomes more myopic and cantankerous every day. I hope she lives for many more years.

Amber shows no ill effects from her near-drowning and continues to defend our home with her usual enthusiasm. Yesterday evening, she joined me in the garden for a little stargazing and chased off the International Space Station as it passed over. She is particularly proud of that achievement.

Lady has not improved much as a hunter, except in volume and duration. Most days she will spend a happy hour charging up and down the forest, or bounding across the moor, woofing and howling like a banshee. These jaunts are always without harm or success. In truth, her best hunting is done while she sleeps, twitching and farting in front of the fire.

And finally there is Kia. The dog who should have died.

More recently, Kia has taken to sitting outside in our courtyard, where she can watch the comings and goings around our bird table. She is looking for a mouse. Not any mouse, but a particular mouse. It once had the good fortune to escape from her grasping teeth and slavering jaws. The lucky rodent escaped from death and then ran to ground beneath one of the rocks that adorn the base of the bird table. On that day, Kia remained on guard, excitedly waiting for the mouse to reappear, until we dragged her indoors so she could eat her supper. Now, like a jilted bride, still wearing her faded dress and standing alone outside the church, Kia waits forlornly for the love that will never return.

With a demonstration of diligence that goes beyond commendable, Kia waits. For several hours each day, as still as a statue and regardless of the meteorological conditions, she sits and watches the bird table in the hope her mouse will reappear. Perhaps that mouse was her muse and she feels lost without it. Kia has now become such a feature in the courtyard the local wildlife has come to accept her presence as if she were a somewhat elaborate, but peculiarly furry, garden ornament. Furthermore, even the juiciest and most cautious of our local rat population, and a few mice that do not fit the description of the escaped prisoner, seem to have negotiated a ceasefire from the usual hostilities, so Kia can continue with her vigil.

She usually lays in a spot directly below the bird feeders hanging from the rafters of the coverway. Perhaps through the confidence of habit or because of some previously agreed peace treaty, the birds seem entirely happy to peck at the seed that has fallen around this dog. Any day now, I expect to see a robin sitting on Kia's head.

By now, the mouse in question is either long dead, or the oldest and wisest mouse in Ireland. Nevertheless, for Kia, that eternal optimist, the wait goes on. She's out there right now, undaunted, sitting on the cold concrete and wearing a light dusting of snow and birdseed, while she waits for the mouse that will never come.

THE END

Acknowledgments

Writing a book is very much a team effort and there are many people whom I would like to thank:

First of all, to Victoria Twead and the staff at Ant Press, thank you for your vision and belief.

Many, many thanks to Zoë Marr, for your keen eye, honest opinion and exceptional editing.

Lesley, my beautiful, intelligent and supportive wife, who gave me the time and space to finish this book, thank you for accompanying me on this search for a better life – and for all the cakes.

Joanne, our daughter, who gave her unflinching support to each of our nutty ideas. She politely pointed out my mistakes and gave me the motivation to continue writing.

Richard Clarke, you are a great friend and an inspiration.

Thanks to our dogs, cats, chickens and ducks, past and present, you make our lives richer and more interesting.

Finally, thanks to the good people of Ireland, who have made us feel welcome and at home in a foreign land.

About the Author

Nick Albert was born and raised in England. After a hectic career as a training consultant and sports coach, Nick and his wife, Lesley, decided it was time to leave the stress of city life behind. In 2004, they made the sudden decision to begin a new life in rural Ireland, a country they had never visited. There they bought a dilapidated farmhouse and, with the aid of a second-hand do-it-yourself manual, began renovations on their new home. When the refurbishments were complete, Nick began writing full-time.

Contact the Author

Facebook https://www.facebook.com/author.nick.albert
Email: nickalbert@outlook.com
Chat with the author and other memoir readers at We Love Memoirs https://www.facebook.com/groups/welovememoirs/

Ant Press Books

If you enjoyed this book, you may also enjoy these Ant Press titles:

MEMOIRS
Chickens, Mules and Two Old Fools by Victoria Twead (Wall Street Journal Top 10 bestseller)
Two Old Fools ~ Olé! by Victoria Twead
Two Old Fools on a Camel by Victoria Twead (thrice New York Times bestseller)
Two Old Fools in Spain Again by Victoria Twead
Two Old Fools in Turmoil by Victoria Twead
One Young Fool in Dorset (The Prequel) by Victoria Twead
One Young Fool in South Africa (The Prequel) by Joe and Victoria Twead
Midwife - A Calling by Peggy Vincent
Midwife - A Journey by Peggy Vincent
Into Africa with 3 Kids, 13 Crates and a Husband by Ann Patras
More Into Africa with 3 Kids, some Dogs and a Husband by Ann Patras
Fat Dogs and French Estates ~ Part I by Beth Haslam
Fat Dogs and French Estates ~ Part II by Beth Haslam
Fat Dogs and French Estates ~ Part III by Beth Haslam
Simon Ships Out: How One Brave, Stray Cat Became a Worldwide Hero by Jacky Donovan
Smoky: How a Tiny Yorkshire Terrier Became a World War II American Army Hero, Therapy Dog and Hollywood Star by Jacky Donovan
Smart as a Whip: A Madcap Journey of Laughter, Love, Disasters and Triumphs by Jacky Donovan
Heartprints of Africa: A Family's Story of Faith, Love, Adventure, and Turmoil by Cinda Adams Brooks
How not to be a Soldier: My Antics in the British Army by Lorna McCann
Moment of Surrender: My Journey Through Prescription Drug Addiction to Hope and Renewal by Pj Laube
Serving is a Pilgrimage by John Basham
One of its Legs are Both the Same by Mike Cavanagh
Horizon Fever by A E Filby
Cane Confessions: The Lighter Side to Mobility by Amy L. Bovaird
Completely Cats - Stories with Cattitude by Beth Haslam and Zoe Marr
From Moulin Rouge to Gaudi's City by EJ Bauer

Fresh Eggs and Dog Beds: Living the Dream in Rural Ireland by Nick Albert
Don't Do It Like This: How NOT to move to Spain by Joe Cawley, Victoria Twead and Alan Parks

* * *

FICTION
Parched by Andrew C Branham
A is for Abigail by Victoria Twead (Sixpenny Cross 1)
B is for Bella by Victoria Twead (Sixpenny Cross 2)
C is for the Captain by Victoria Twead (Sixpenny Cross 3)
* * *

NON FICTION
How to Write a Bestselling Memoir by Victoria Twead
* * *

CHILDREN'S BOOKS
Seacat Simon: The Little Cat Who Became a Big Hero by Jacky Donovan
The Rise of Agnil by Susan Navas (Agnil's Worlds 1)
Agnil and the Wizard's Orb by Susan Navas (Agnil's Worlds 2)
Agnil and the Tree Spirits by Susan Navas (Agnil's Worlds 3)
Agnil and the Centaur's Secret by Susan Navas (Agnil's Worlds 4)
Morgan and the Martians by Victoria Twead
* * *

Chat with the author, other memoir authors, and readers at **We Love Memoirs**:
https://www.facebook.com/groups/welovememoirs/

Printed in Great Britain
by Amazon